Opening the Nursery Door is a fascinating collection of essays inspired by the chance discovery of the nursery library of Jane Johnson (1706–59), wife of a Buckinghamshire vicar. The discovery of this tiny archive – which contained her poems and stories for children – captured the scholarly interest of social anthropologists, historians, literary scholars, educationalists and archivists and opened up a range of questions about the nature of childhood within English cultural life over three centuries.

The contributors to this book focus on the cultural and social history of children's literature and literacy development from several different perspectives. It reconsiders the central importance of literacy practices in childhood in its examination of the process by which children came to read and write. At the centre is the work of Jane Johnson and the many ways in which her archive has prompted us to raise important questions about women, children and literacy.

Mary Hilton, **Morag Styles** and **Victor Watson** are all based at Homerton College, Cambridge. Mary Hilton is the author of *Potent Fictions* which considered the effect popular culture has on children's literacy. Morag Styles and Victor Watson have co-edited four books on children's literature: *Talking Pictures* (1996), and, with Eve Bearne, *After Alice* (1992), *The Prose and the Passion* (1994), and *Voices Off* (1996). Morag Styles' history of poetry written for children, *From the Garden to the Street*, will be published in 1997. Victor Watson is editor of the forthcoming *Cambridge Guide to Children's Books*.

OPENING THE NURSERY DOOR

Reading, writing and childhood 1600–1900

Edited by Mary Hilton, Morag Styles and Victor Watson

London and New York

First published 1997
by Routledge
11 New Fetter Lane, London EC4P 4EE

Transferred to Digital Printing 2004

Simultaneously published in the USA and Canada
by Routledge
29 West 35th Street, New York, NY 10001

© 1997 selection and editorial matter
Mary Hilton, Morag Styles and Victor Watson
individual chapters © their contributors

Phototypeset in Times by Intype London Ltd

British Library Cataloguing in Publication Data
A catalogue record for this book is available from the British Library

Library of Congress Cataloging in Publication Data
Opening the nursery door: reading, writing, and childhood, 1600–1900/edited by
Mary Hilton, Morag Styles, and Victor Watson.
p. cm.
Includes bibliographical references and index.
1. Children's literature, English—History and criticism. 2. English literature—
Early modern, 1500–1700—History and criticism. 3. English literature—18th
century—History and criticism. 4. English literature—19th century—History
and criticism. 5. Children—England—Books and reading—History. I. Hilton,
Mary, 1946– . II. Styles, Morag. III. Watson, Victor.
PR990.064 1997
820.9'9282—dc20 96–27224
CIP
ISBN 0–415–14898–7(hbk)
0–415–14899–5(pbk)

CONTENTS

CONTENTS

FIGURES

CONTRIBUTORS

Janet Bottoms is Senior Lecturer in English at Homerton College, Cambridge. Among her published work are several articles on approaches to Shakespeare in education, including a chapter in *Voices Off: Texts, Contexts and Readers* (1996). She is currently working on a history of prose adaptations of the plays for children.

Shirley Brice Heath is Professor of English and Linguistics at Stanford University. She is the author (with Shelby Wolf) of *The Braid of Literature: Children's Worlds of Reading* (1992), *Ways with Words: Language, Life and Work in Communities and Classrooms* (1983) and numerous writings on the everyday life of children.

Norma Clarke is a literary historian and children's novelist. Her most recent children's books are *Theo's Time* (1994), *The Doctor's Daughter* (1996) and the forthcoming *Oscar and Anna*. She is author of *Ambitious Heights: Writing, Friendship, Love: The Jewsbury Sisters, Felicia Hemans, and Jane Welsh Carlyle* (1990).

Heather Glen is Fellow and Director of Studies in English at New Hall, Cambridge. She is author of *Vision and Disenchantment: Blake's Songs and Wordsworth's Lyrical Ballads* (1983). She has also edited Emily Brontë, *Wuthering Heights* (Routledge English Texts, 1988) and Charlotte Brontë, *The Professor* (Penguin, 1989). She is currently completing a critical study of Charlotte Brontë's writings.

Mary Hilton is Senior Lecturer in Primary Language and Literature at Homerton College, Cambridge. She has worked on community literacy practices and has published chapters on the development of children's historical thinking, on boys' reading in the nineteenth century and on children's popular culture. She has recently edited *Potent Fictions: Children's Literacy and the Challenge of Popular Culture* (1996).

Jan Mark is a distinguished novelist for children and is the editor of the *Oxford Book of Children's Stories*. Some of her best known novels include *Thunder and Lightnings* (1976), *Trouble Halfway* (1989), and *Hairs in the Palm of the Hand* (1989). An expert on the history of children's literature,

Jan Mark also reviews and writes for journals such as *Signal* and the *Times Educational Supplement.*

Hilary Minns is a lecturer in English Studies in the Institute of Education at Warwick University. She is the author of key texts on children and reading, such as *Read It To Me Now!* (1990, 1997), *Language, Literacy and Gender* (1991) and *Primary Language: Extending the Curriculum with Computers* (1991). She has recently completed her Ph.D. on the move into childhood experience that was made by migrant Irish working children who came to live in Derby, in the English Midlands, in the mid-nineteenth century.

Margaret Spufford is Professor of Social and Local History at Roehampton Institute, London. She is author of *Contrasting Communities: English Villagers in the Sixteenth and Seventeenth Centuries* (1974), *Small Books and Pleasant Histories* (1981), *The Great Reclothing of Rural England* (1984) and editor of *The World of Rural Dissenters, 1520–1725* (1995). She has worked extensively on people below the level of the gentry in the sixteenth and seventeenth centuries and has a particular interest in ideas circulated through education and cheap print.

Morag Styles is Language Co-ordinator at Homerton College, Cambridge. She is the editor (with Victor Watson and Eve Bearne) of a trilogy on children's literature, *After Alice: Exploring Children's Literature* (1992), *The Prose and the Passion: Children and their Reading* (1994), and *Voices Off: Texts, Contexts and Readers* (1996). She is the author of numerous publications relating to children and poetry. *From the Garden to the Street: An Introduction to Three Hundred Years of Poetry for Children* will be published in 1997.

Julia Swindells is Senior Lecturer in English at Homerton College, Cambridge. She is author of *Victorian Writing and Working Women: The Other Side of Silence* (1985), and co-author with Lisa Jardine of *What's Left? Women in Culture and the Labour Movement* (1990). She has recently edited *The Uses of Autobiography* (1995).

John Rowe Townsend was Children's Book Editor for the *Guardian* until 1978. He has written more than twenty books for children, including the ground-breaking *Gumble's Yard* (1961). He is the author of the well known guide to the history of children's literature, *Written for Children* (sixth edition 1995) and recently edited a collection of writings on a critical biography of John Newbery, the famous children's publisher of the eighteenth century, *Trade and Plumb-Cake for Ever, Huzza!* (1994).

Nicholas Tucker is a distinguished Lecturer in Psychology at the University of Sussex. He is well known as a critic, broadcaster and lecturer.

Publications include his highly regarded *The Child and the Book: a Psychological and Literary Exploration* (1981).

David Vincent is Professor of Social History at Keele University. His publications include *The Autobiography of the Working Class* (1984, 1987, 1989), *Bread Knowledge and Freedom* (1981), *Poor Citizens* (1991), *Literacy and Popular Culture: England, 1750–1914* and the forthcoming *The Culture of Secrecy in Britain* (1997).

Victor Watson is Senior Lecturer in English at Homerton College, Cambridge. He is the editor (with Morag Styles) of *Talking Pictures: Pictorial Texts and Young Readers* (1996) and (with Morag Styles and Eve Bearne) of *After Alice: Exploring Children's Literature* (1992), *The Prose and the Passion: Children and their Reading* (1994) and *Voices Off: Texts, Contexts and Readers* (1996). He is editing the forthcoming *Cambridge Guide to Children's Books*.

David Whitley is Senior Lecturer in English at Homerton College, Cambridge, where his main areas of teaching are in early modern literature and media education. He has written on children's experience of television, and on various aspects of the tradition of the Aesop fable in *Voices Off: Texts, Contexts and Readers* (1996), *Potent Fictions* (1996) and *Greater Expectations* (1995).

INTRODUCTION

Mary Hilton

HANDMADE WORLDS

This book opens with scholarly appreciation and exposition of the recently discovered work of a remarkable woman. Jane Johnson, 1706–59, wife of a Buckinghamshire vicar, inadvertently left to posterity an archive of tiny objects, her handmade nursery library, contained in a shoebox which was discovered in a dusty cupboard in the USA two hundred and forty years after her death. The contents of this box soon became a spark that lit a veritable bonfire of academic interest and speculation as historians, literary scholars, collectors, archivists, anthropologists and educationalists discovered overlapping and complementary fields of enquiry about the nature of childhood within British cultural life over three centuries: the debates that have surrounded the texts written and read to children; the multifarious ways childish consciousness has been considered, shaped and schooled; the emotional and moral investment that has been placed in children by adults; and, most centrally, the hitherto neglected role of woman educators in early childhood.

When Shirley Brice Heath first showed slides of the exquisite handmade items of ephemera from Jane Johnson's shoebox – card sets, crib mobiles and tiny books – to a fascinated audience in Cambridge, there was instant general recognition that enormous questions of cultural history were being set out in these dainty and entrancing material objects. Jane Johnson had clearly been lovingly engaged in teaching her young children to read and had spent many hours of handwork in adapting and creating literacy artefacts for this purpose. But she had been doing far more than presenting them with predictable, graded and utilitarian exercises; rather she had been deeply involving them in a vital project of mutual, loving and moral interpretation of the social and physical world around them. She was, possibly like many other women educators in the private sphere, engaging the young in a dialogic and imaginative construction of their social possibilities. As Shirley Brice Heath shows in her opening chapter, Jane Johnson's materials are fascinatingly open-ended, multifaceted,

1

strangely empowering, yet modestly home-made – cut with tiny scissors, written by hand, glued with paste. Brice Heath goes on to investigate the typologies of this eighteenth-century upper-middle-class world, its observations of daily life and social roles, its possibilities for social critique and the complicated semantic and grammatical criteria with which this mother grouped words and relationships between things. As Brice Heath points out, Jane Johnson rarely simplified the complexities of life or literacy for her children but clearly invited them into an intellectual and discursive relationship with the world through carefully constructed games, puzzles, intertextual references, riddles and jokes. Only the moral and religious aspects of the artefacts seem didactic and to lack the playful ambiguity that characterizes the collection. Otherwise the objects openly encourage childish curiosity and activity.

This delightful archive led to many wider questions. From where did Jane Johnson's religious morality and confident child-centredness spring? How widespread were her particular habits of domestic literacy and her devotion to the education of her young children? What were the texts that formed and sustained her own literacy? What published materials for children would have been available for her to use and discard at will? In 1744 she wrote a long story for her children which has also been recently discovered along with her commonplace book of quotations and other ephemera. In the story, as Victor Watson shows, several of her own literary sources can be sensed and assembled, shedding light not only on her own originality and liveliness as a writer, but helping to round out a picture of the cultural milieu in which she was writing. Through fascinating literary detective work he suggests that she draws on images and ideas from Bunyan, *The Spectator*, the translated fairytales of the Comtesse d'Aulnoy and possibly the fairytales in translation of Perrault. Jane Johnson's commonplace book of extracts 'shows a woman who was familiar with the classics and also read a wide range of popular fiction'. She quoted from *The Arabian Nights*, *The Tatler*, Milton, the Bible, Juvenal and Pope's *Homer*.

Jane Johnson was writing in the period between two highly significant dates for historians of children's literature: 1693 when John Locke published *Some Thoughts Concerning Education* and 1744 when John Newbery published what came to be thought of as the first children's book, *A Little Pretty Pocket-Book*. Locke's ideas about using books for children that yielded pleasure and were suited to the more limited capacity of the child were eventually turned into a rationale for published texts by Newbery fifty years later. But, as Victor Watson points out, what happened in these intervening fifty years to general ideas about childhood and the functions that books had for the moral and intellectual growth of the child, remains to be discovered and considered. It is here that the Jane Johnson archive begins to fill this historical gap, both in the texts

2

and ideas upon which she drew and in her sophisticated sense of playfulness which respected and encouraged the child learner.

Another pressing historical question opened up by the archive is one of the prevalence of this domestic literacy education throughout the seventeenth and eighteenth centuries. Was reading enjoyed and taught only by the upper and middle classes? Did the poor read and were they too taught at home? Margaret Spufford addresses these important questions by first dispensing with an old myth that education for the poor began with the Charity school movement. Evidence from local studies in Cambridgeshire, Leicestershire and Kent shows clearly that in these counties (and probably across Britain) schooling for the poor was not a new phenomenon in the eighteenth century, but was widespread and available much earlier, usually within walking distance. What is equally fascinating is that evidence exists to show that many children of the poor could read at an early age and were often taught at home by mother or grandmother. A survey in an Eccleshall manor in the 1690s showed labourers' wives busily at work teaching very young children to read. An enormous volume of hornbooks and ABCs was produced by a single publisher in the late seventeenth century: indeed 'England was saturated with the basic equipment for learning to read'. From the few autobiographies of humble people available, Margaret Spufford shows that learning to read in the domestic sphere again involved an intricate theory of method, involving, often as not, a process of developing handmade materials and pleasurable texts from cheap ephemera at hand. Thus the opening up of new worlds of imaginative possiblity through early literacy was happening across all classes, and considerably earlier than has been previously thought.

'SOME EASY PLEASANT BOOK'

The evidence for widespread literacy by the end of the seventeenth century in England continues to be collected.[1] Clearly chapbooks and other simple reading material were produced and peddled across the country throughout the seventeenth century. Added to that volume of cheap story material in broadsheet and chapbook was a large amount of religious tracts and biblical material which already existed for people of all classes. And as the urban middle classes continued to expand in the eighteenth century there was a steadily increasing number of courtesy and conduct books written to describe and regulate patterns of behaviour in an evermore complex social world. In addition the multifarious blossoming of new technologies and trades within rapidly industrializing Europe was also being captured and explained in print. It is not surprising therefore that the business of rearing children became part of this instructed, explained and moralized literate universe. Parents of all classes had increasing access to books and materials which told them how best to rear their children, how to regulate their children's conduct and to educate them for the future. As the eighteenth century progressed, however, a significant change appeared in books about and then for children. John Locke's more liberal idea with regard to the growing child was increasingly emphasized. This central idea was that *texts that yield pleasure* are of better value; that through *respecting playfulness in the young* adults could bring a more lasting educative influence to bear on them.

David Whitley shows how Samuel Richardson's *Aesop*, published in 1740, marked a watershed in published texts for children. By giving the Aesopic project a new, complex and multilevelled narrative structure which opened up a space for the childish, Richardson anticipated the tradition of a pleasurable literature for children which was about to emerge. Through the form he inherited and reshaped, Richardson developed a particularly clear vision of the role a children's literature within a Lockeian tradition should take. In 1744 John Newbery turned the philosopher's ideas into a successful publishing venture with his first of many books for children: *A Little Pretty Pocket-Book*. John Rowe Townsend shows that Newbery brought two streams of popular books together to achieve a pleasurable, educative result for children to read for themselves. He combined narrative material from the chapbook tradition with moral advice from the conduct-books for children from a variety of adult and religious sources into a new entertaining yet improving genre. Like Jane Johnson's nursery materials, the *Pocket-Book* is for both instruction and amusement, combining games and riddles with morals, engaged in making learning both painless and useful. Eventually Newbery produced books, principally the famous *Tom Telescope*, which, in the tradition of the trade manuals that disseminated the new technologies, helped to explicate and delineate central scientific ideas of the Enlightenment such as Newtonian philosophy. Although clearly written for young minds, entertainingly shaped with fictional characters engaged in lively debate, indeed – 'a brilliant book for adolescent children' – it was also a considerable contribution to education in the days before public provision.

WOMEN WRITING FOR CHILDREN

By the late eighteenth century a huge yet differentiated middle class was constructing its moral and practical behaviour within three powerful ideological discourses: the scientific ideas of the Enlightenment, the rapidly expanding challenge of commerce and the evangelical revival. Each individual's and family's public and private practice had to be worked out according to overarching moral principles that were by definition rational, enlightened, commercially viable, yet concerned with individual salvation won through active struggle. As Leonore Davidoff and Catherine Hall point out, one of the strongest strands binding all members of the middle class was 'the commitment to an imperative moral code and the reworking of the domestic world into a proper setting for its practice'.[2] By the late eighteenth century, books and stories for children had come to occupy a highly contested area within an increasingly literate, moral and politicized middle class. Literature itself and the major literary figures of the day embodied and focused the intellectual and ideological attention of a variety of readers. Within the new complexities of a now rapidly industrializing society, relationships could be explicated, explored, tried and tested within new genres. A society used to tract, pamphlet, broadsheet, manual and conduct book now embraced the novel where a variety of roles and moralities could be presented within the framework of narrative realism. Novels for and about children were increasingly written to both describe and define their proper roles, upbringing and conduct.

During this time of social change, intricately reflected in novel and story, there was an intense shaping and reforming of individual identity, particularly roles and positions associated with gender. Rapid financial growth had given rise to a feeling of cultural crisis. In particular 'the sexual freedom of educated women, and the prominence accorded female writers and artists, gave rise to an increasingly tense debate as scholarly argument combined with sensational journalism to investigate the changing roles of the sexes'.[3] It is not surprising therefore that during the late eighteenth century when gender roles were being explored, contested and redefined considerable ideological debate took place around the nature of suitable stories for children, particularly in terms of the conduct of the different gendered identities within them. Sexual roles were clearly organized through a complex system of social relations and during this time of cultural change writers of both genders cared much about the early formation and conduct of those relations. They also argued fiercely for their conception of the proper regulation of the domestic world in which the stories were placed. A typical tract was *Female Government* by William Alexander published in 1779, where the author recommended that men should see women only at night and that male children should be removed from their mother's presence as soon as they are weaned from the breast, so that a masculine and proper education could take place away from that dangerous female parent. Such attacks on female influence and competence were commonplace. According to Paul Langford: 'The torrent of sermons and addresses which descended on wives and daughters in the 1760s and 1770s was meant to extinguish any flickers of feminism.'[4]

Norma Clarke shows that in this period many admired and influential women writers had emerged, writing books which stemmed from teacherly roles primarily for other women working in the domestic space of families and schools. From this central anxiety about the nature and regulation of the proper private world they created and maintained a powerful moral discourse of female rationality, one which challenged the growing orthodoxy that assumed that public roles should be reserved for men. By writing publically about these highly affective concerns they moralized daily living in such a way that sought to oppose the whole basis of the masculine ideology that was simultaneously working in society to enclose women's competence in the private and domestic sphere. Clarke describes the denigration the women writers of didactic tales for children received from powerful members of the male literati such as Wordsworth and Lamb. By the end of the eighteenth century the 'useful knowledge' of such important, lively and widely read women as Anna Barbauld, Mary Wollstonecraft and Sarah Trimmer was successfully caricatured by many leading literary figures as dry, inhuman and dreary. The promotion of female rationality in these women's polemical stories, their declared object of producing mature and reasonable adults, particularly women, who would have a measure of control over their lives was, according to Clarke, effectively spurned by society in favour of a cult of childhood, a celebration of prodigy. This cult was in opposition to the Lockeian view of a developmentally organized rationality in the growing child for which the adult has an intense didactic responsibility. Within the new culture of sensibility children were increasingly categorized with the natural world, innocent yet wise, like members of a primeval species. Child actors became the fashion and children were encouraged to show off extraordinary talents, to learn to carry out unusual feats of memory or performance for adult praise. And as the eighteenth century drew to a close there was, according to Clarke, a resultant weakening in cultural proscription of the authoritative female. The male poets had successfully propagated a Romantic myth of the child, essentially positing a boy child 'from which the adult male self struggles to emerge'. By the early nineteenth century this myth helped to eclipse a whole generation of women writers by alienating their literary tradition of the rational and didactic.

Nicholas Tucker, in taking a sympathetic look at the early nineteenth-century female opponents of fairy tales, also offers a reappraisal of the moral and literary positioning of such women as Sarah Trimmer. Her sustained public attack in her paper *The Guardian of Education* on the morally debasing nature of fairy tales does not seem so dry and unimaginative as such major literary figures as Wordsworth and Coleridge claimed in castigating her views, when her rationality and responsibility towards the young are recontextualized. A major figure in her own times, she saw herself, as did many of her educated female contemporaries, as protecting children from being terrified and, in a Lockeian spirit, from having their impressionable minds distorted by superstition and ignorance played out in fictions of limiting and disempowering social circumstances. Nicholas Tucker points to the incipient conservatism and the feudal nature of many fairy tales to which enlightened women with radical and reforming instincts naturally objected. He suggests that it is the very narrowness of social circumstances and limited possibilities (particularly for females) within the fairy tales which has been the chief source of appeal to many arch-conservatives who have believed that the values enshrined in them, rather than being ideologically organized at different points in history, are instead immutable and eternal.

Adding to this central theme of the book, that women's writings for children have been overlooked and devalued by a powerful male literati, presumably with a subconscious drive to foreground their own version of childhood with a Romantic and essentially masculine identity, Janet Bottoms reappraises a novel which achieved a shower of rich praise when it was first produced in 1808, but since then seems to have been almost systematically overlooked: *Mrs Leicester's School* by Mary Lamb. At the time it 'was both a critical and popular success'. Although it was written within the tradition of stories designed to make the children who read them wiser and better, Janet Bottoms shows how radically different it was in spirit and construction from the accepted genre of improving and moralistic school stories. Set in a girls' school where a group of girls have newly arrived, homesick and lonely, it is an artful collection of their life stories. By treating the supposed children's narratives as valuable in themselves, the teacher encourages each girl to reflect upon her own life, but without, as was common literary practice in the genre, pointing out a moral in each tale. As Bottoms suggests there is a finely wrought sensibility that permeates the novel, allowing it to speak on several levels: a primary level of childish innocence, a level of experience as the voice of each girl reflects on her own younger self, and also the level of 'the adult author, whose subtly ironic perspective on the social world within which the children struggle to make sense of their lives informs the whole'. Janet Bottoms demonstrates that in this complex novel, Mary Lamb showed an unusual capacity for empathizing with the young, an ability to view the world from their perspective, providing an oblique but telling commentary on the relations between adults and children. Like other contemporary women writers Lamb found ways to comment on the world through the eyes of the child, particularly the female child.

Within this tradition of women writing for children lies a spectrum of female work from the heavily rational and didactic story to subtle ironies and layered sensibilities allowable within the novel. Women continued to write for children in a tradition of didactic realism throughout the nineteenth century, their work contrasting, as Jan Mark suggests, with the great male fantasists such as MacDonald, Carroll, Kingsley, Stockton and Baum. Jan Mark explores the work of women writing for children and finds there a central imaginative challenge: that good families which provide the serene and stable environment where parents and elders can function as exemplars were 'soon found wanting as a form of entertainment'. It was, as she points out, the *bad* family about which it was far more stimulating to read and write. In a variety of novels for children written by women in the nineteenth century, the good and bad families were first set in contrast to each other and then progessively internalized into the moral possibilities of one family, such as the Bastables of Edith Nesbit's *The Wouldbegoods*. In a literary survey of nineteenth-century novels written by women Jan Mark suggests that for a variety of social reasons, not least their own lives, women continued to write for children about domestic discord and unhappiness, often foregrounding female competence against a background of death and hardship, thus honing an essentially female tradition of close-worked didactic realism within children's literature.

Springing from this idea, that women occupied a space which was physically closest to children and were therefore less likely to romanticize childhood, but to view it with immediacy and tenderness, Morag Styles shows that another whole genre has been largely forgotten in our literary history. She explores the sensual, apparently 'simple' verse that women wrote for young children sometimes, as in the case of Dorothy Wordsworth or Jane Johnson, in the private sphere without thought of publication. Even when this verse was published, its value as poetry has not always been recognized. The exception is Christina Rossetti whose 'nursery rhyme book', *Sing Song* came out to good reviews in 1872, but has since been neglected. Other women writing in this genre such as Jane and Anne Taylor, Sara Coleridge and Mary Howitt fared worse and their work is all but lost to view. Influential nineteenth-century anthologists such as Coventry Patmore and Andrew Lang selected poems only from the adult canon to produce collections for the young, thus marginalizing poets who had written directly for children. This naturally disadvantaged the women poets who had succeeded in getting published as writers for children. Starting with the work of Christina Rossetti (1830–94) Morag Styles traces back to Jane Johnson a whole 'secret history' of tuneful, sometimes nonsensical rhymes, lullabies and other nursery verse expressing love and physical closeness between women and children.

LEARNING TO READ IN SCHOOL

So a central theme emerges in this book which points to a subtle and complex pattern of learning for children of all classes over three centuries, carried out within a private domestic setting, surrounded by primary carers, usually women, who move in a world of other concerns, with literacy practices delicately woven into a developing tissue of understandings that embrace the social and physical world of the family in all its complexity. Linda Pollock has shown that childhood, far from being 'invented' at any stage of history, has continuously been addressed, and that children have been cared for throughout this whole period and probably before.[5] It is reasonable to suppose that the nursery library of Jane Johnson stands at the tip of an otherwise invisible mass of reading materials – verse, stories for the young, their own scribblings, games and word lists, chapbooks, hornbooks, spelling and reading primers. David Vincent, in setting out on an exploration of the domestic curriculum of the nineteenth-century working-class child, shows there is evidence of a huge diffusion of literacy in the form of 'various heaps' of cheap elementary textbooks in circulation in the early decades of the century. He points to the rather conservative search for evidence that has characterized most history of education. An exclusive preoccupation with official and published sources, he argues, has meant a continuation of a top-down, middle-class perspective on the literacy habits of the poor. When other evidence such as printed textbooks and simplified reading materials is considered, as well as oral and biographical evidence from the poor themselves, a whole new arena of the domestic curriculum of the working-class child comes into view. Vincent reminds us that 'two thirds of grooms could write their names before the state spent a farthing on education'.

Ignoring the domestic curriculum of the poor child meant the early nineteenth-century state put in place a system of learning to read that was based on the ancient technique of breaking words into lists of syllables and 'unmeaning combinations'. Carving up words had been workable in a small domestic and interactive setting but was too mechanical and strange to be successful in a huge classroom for children who had naturally mastered spoken language in infancy through individual and active exchanges of meaning. By the mid-nineteenth century, a whole-word teaching of reading words called 'look and say' had been introduced in elementary schools. Educators, under pressure to raise reading standards, had been forced through expediency to listen to and use *the oral vocabulary the children already possessed* in the development of literacy. So, painfully, and never completely, state educators began to appreciate that, within the busy environment of home, important skills, information, imagination and morality were already being dispensed to all children: 'however harsh and brief childhood was always a time of learning'.

Vincent points out that although literacy was gradually increasing the range of technical and scientific information for the labouring poor, important craft skills, morality, and a sense of the past were still learned by children from the people around them. It was in the sphere of the imagination where in childhood there was the greatest appetite for the printed word, and it was here that reading in school yielded some hope of pleasure and fulfilment, so eventually literary anthologies were allowed in an effort to attract the attendance and attention of pupils. Finally it was in the revised Code of 1862 that the state officially acknowledged the wishes of parents: for their children to be literate and numerate, rather than morally instructed, and legislated in an effort to bring the curriculum of school closer to the real world of the pupils and their parents. It was, as Vincent argues, within the subtle interrelationship of the domestic and the school curricula that the learning of literacy both happened and where it can be properly studied.

It was the Newcastle Commission of 1861, enquiring into The State of Popular Education, that first formally articulated the new relationship between written words in textbooks and primers and the world of meaning of the child. Hilary Minns investigates some of the texts that were used to teach pauper children in workhouse schools in Derby in the 1840s and 1850s. Entering the workhouse set these children into a regimented, institutionalized existence where learning to read was part of a consistent moral and intellectual regulation of their lives. Considering the textbooks, particularly the Irish *Lesson Books* used by these institutions, she explores the different ways these textbooks opened up new learning possibilities. She demonstrates that within natural history the somewhat heavy and moralizing tone of the widely used Irish *Lesson Books* was diminished and a different and inviting voice, enlisting the curiosity of the child, became evident. The *Fifth Lesson Book* was criticized by the Commission in 1861, particularly its presentation of science in a 'form too technical for the purpose'; with what David Vincent has shown to be its new insight about children and learning, the Commission recommended translating it into 'familiar language'. However, as Minns demonstrates, the *Second Book of Lessons* and its sequel had already achieved a remarkable bond between author and reader in the area of natural history, using a voice and prose style which compares favourably with modern non-fiction texts for children.

In the history of nineteenth-century working-class schooling, close observation of the children themselves, and the ways they were presented with and made meaning from the written word, is still lacking in the historical account. Julia Swindells turns to textuality to show how working-class children were represented in the period and how both genders of children within the poorest classes were constructed differently in relation to schooling. Using the investigative record of Henry Mayhew on children in Ragged Schools in the period 1770 to 1840, alongside the fictional representation of children by his contemporary Charles Dickens, Swindells suggests that boys' and girls' consciousnesses were interpreted differently for ideological purposes. Swindells suggests that the testimony of working-class boys represented by both Mayhew and Dickens was held up as evidence that the schools were seedbeds of essentially male criminality or at least masculine collective identity. But that girls' testimony is not generally taken as evidence and only certain individual girls are chosen by these writers to represent a virtuous, literate but isolated and ineffectual commentary on the failings and inadequacies of the schools. A huge moral load is therefore embodied in the 'natural' and moral working-class female, one which is resistant to the processes of education and which indeed questions whether such girls should be educated at all. In these representations Swindells points to schooling as a powerful organizing agency of class and gender relations.

'CONFIGURING A WORLD'

In the final chapter of *Opening the Nursery Door* the child herself moves into centre stage as Heather Glen considers the childhood writings created within the constraints of tradition and convention of a famous nineteenth-century literary family: the imaginative juvenilia of Charlotte Brontë. Here the power and pleasure of the written word for children is displayed in breathtaking richness as the four remaining children in that motherless household created an imaginary world 'which continued to allure and preoccupy each of the four well into adulthood ... elaborated in writing – in dozens of microscopically printed poems, stories and journals, produced over a period of nearly twenty years'. As Heather Glen points out, like the Jane Johnson archive these writings continue to throw light on the cultural significance of reading and writing in childhood.

By examining this rich juvenilia in a unique and child-centred way Glen shows that Charlotte Brontë's reading and her knowledge of the closed social world around her are both understood and transformed in her imagination through the children's complex 'play' with the toy soldiers who are the central characters in their fictions. Glen shows how the young writer plays with the radical ironic idea that the figures of power and pretension who inhabit this world are in reality mere fictions, an idea that is developed in her highly elaborated, wittily self-reflexive writings. Far more than this, however, Glen suggests that the young Charlotte Brontë is in fact playing with questions about the relation between power and reality: 'about what it means to be an object as well as a subject', questions which her own disempowered circumstances, the childhood of a girl within a nineteenth-century patriarchal family, make particularly acute. Thus in this ironic 'entertainment' of differing possibilities and perspectives Glen traces Brontë's questioning of reality where power lies elsewhere, and explicates the ways reading and writing enabled this child to imaginatively configure and ironically develop the meanings of her world.

Opening the Nursery Door contributes at all levels and in many different ways to a reconsideration of the central importance of literacy practices in childhood. How children come to read and write is not a neutral and unimaginative process divorced from the real business of life, but rather one which is interwoven with their growing consciousness, intimately involving the people around them in their domestic worlds. Through a study of literate practices within these private and intimate worlds, we begin to see in close detail how, on the one hand, children have integrated the texts that they were presented with and, on the other, the ways adults in all classes have attempted to create moral and knowledgeable people out of the infants they have bred. Light at last is beginning to be shed on the close and yet vital early role that women have played with regard to children's literacy, many finding a tradition of creative writing for themselves. Eventually by the eighteenth century women were opening up a public space in the world of letters in which their rational and didactic voices could help moralize the population, a space which was eventually eclipsed again by a powerful male literati.

We trace in this book the lack of understanding the nineteenth-century state brought to the schooling of the working class, crudely adapting reading materials in an effort to increase literacy on the cheap, combined with a massive effort in top-down moralizing which, being blind to questions of affection, craft, knowledge and gender, marginalized the domestic curriculum of poor children and helped to make public education meaningless and ineffectual for them. Only when a proper consideration of the words and domestic worlds of the poor were taken into account, when their wishes for a functional and empowering literacy were beginning to be listened to, was the school reading curriculum adapted in ways that began to make some sense and to enrich the children's imaginative landscape through new approaches to textbooks and anthologized literature.

Over three hundred years from 1600 to 1900 in English cultural life children have been encouraged, coaxed and bullied into reading and writing. Those practices are at last getting the historical and cultural scrutiny they deserve. The small shoebox, the handwritten story and commonplace book of Jane Johnson is an archive that has opened up this rich field of domestic literacy, the reappraisal of many different texts written for children and the ramifications the domestic curriculum had for the construction of public educational practice. Jane Johnson's handmade materials and her children's story, expressions of her love and constructive hopes for her children, will 'live forever' within our shared intellectual life.

NOTES

1 R.A. Houston, *Literacy in Early Modern Europe, Culture and Education 1500–1800* (London: Longman, 1988). Margaret Spufford, *Small Books and Pleasant Histories; Popular Fiction and its Readership in Seventeenth-Century England* (Cambridge: Cambridge University Press, 1981).
2 Leonore Davidoff and Catherine Hall, *Family Fortunes: Men and Women of the English Middle Class 1780–1850* (London: Hutchinson, 1987), p. 25.

3 Paul Langford, *A Polite and Commercial People: England 1727–1783* (Oxford: Oxford University Press, 1992), p. 565.
4 Ibid., p. 606.
5 Linda A. Pollock, *Forgotten Children: Parent–Child relations from 1500 to 1900* (Cambridge: Cambridge University Press, 1983).

Part I

HANDMADE WORLDS

1

CHILD'S PLAY OR FINDING THE EPHEMERA OF HOME

Shirley Brice Heath

Philosopher Gaston Bachelard[1] wrote in *The Poetics of Space* (1958) about the primacy of home in adult memories of childhood. He wanted readers to acknowledge that this 'corner of the world' we remember as home becomes in many ways every individual's first universe. Throughout life, in memory and deed, we follow the old saying 'We bring our *lares* with us.' In our memories, we comfort ourselves by reliving a sense of protection, play, and discovery that so often comes to be linked with home and its secrets kept since childhood.

To adults, no scene appears more peaceful than that of the sleeping child tucked away in the nursery, kept company by favourite stuffed animals, books, and toys and covered with a blanket that even by day accompanies the child as a source of comfort. The scattered items about the nursery that have given pleasure in daytime play now seem woven into the fabric of the peaceful nursery. Memories contrast this quiet evening scene with lively events of the child's day – the games played, the choice of playmates, the improvised items necessary to the drama of imagination. Persistent in such recollections lie the ephemera of childhood – the bits and pieces of temporary use, the sets of items that over the years lost some of their original pieces, and the scattered small scraps of handmade materials easily left behind as children grew older.

These ephemera creep into memories of childhood and houses far more freely than students of childhood can acknowledge, for traces of such ephemera reside almost entirely in memory. Blocks, card sets, small chips and game parts, and pictures torn or cut from magazines, unlike expensive sets of books, favourite toys and dolls, and special family board-games, lose their value and are thrown out. But what might such ephemera tell us of what went on in the nursery, before the hearth, or in the corner of rooms where children were sent to be entertained or to entertain themselves with sets of cards or building blocks?

A partial answer to this question comes from a remarkable 'manuscript nursery library'[2] created in the early eighteenth century by a vicar's wife who lived in Lincolnshire, England. Jane Johnson (1706–59), mother of one daughter and three sons, created hundreds of items arranged in card sets, crib mobiles, and little books. These materials reflect numerous themes aside from the expected learning of the ABC's, and they open a door of interpretation on play with children and early literacy expectations several decades before the publication of children's books began to flourish in the mid-eighteenth century. Jane Johnson and, no doubt, other women of the period, created ephemera for reading and playing with and for their children. They drew on the few books and materials of their youth, intuitions and common sense about the young, as well as on the writings of eminent figures such as John Locke. Jane Johnson's letters to her children and to female friends suggest that these women played out their sense of fashion, design, colour, and texture, as well as some of their reflections on contemporary life, in artistic creations made for their children's delight and instruction.

JANE JOHNSON AND HER CHILDREN

The early history of Jane Johnson is somewhat shrouded in mystery, but we know that she was coheiress with her sister, Lucy, of Richard Russell, Esquire of Warwick, who had married a woman descended from the family of a Lord Chief Justice in Warwickshire. When she died, Richard raised the girls and at his death willed his estate to them. The girls maintained themselves, most probably primarily in London after their father's death until 1727, when they sold the estate to Sir Horace Mann. We know almost nothing of Jane Johnson's life for the next ten years, until she married Woolsey Johnson in 1737 in Olney, Buckinghamshire. He had been educated at Clare Hall, Cambridge, receiving his BA in 1717 and his MA in 1721. In addition to being vicar, he was the patron and improprietor of his inherited estate Witham-on-the-Hill in Lincolnshire, for which he built the manor house and enclosed the Park in 1752. In the cemetery of Witham-on-the-Hill lie both Jane and her husband under a white marble pyramidal tablet set against the north wall of the chancel with the inscription:

> Sacred to the memory of the Revd Woolsey Johnson clerk who died April 21 1756 in the sixtieth year of his age, and Jane his wife daughter of Richard Russell esq. of Warwick, who died February 9 1759 in the fifty second year of her age. Also of George William Johnson, esq. eldest son of the above Woolsey Johnson and Jane his wife who died February 8, 1814, in the seventy fourth year of his age. Through life beloved.

Nearby in the same cemetery is buried George's brother, the Rev. Robert Augustus Johnson (1745–99), who became rector of a nearby parish and was the only child of Jane's who had children of his own. The remaining son Charles became vicar of the village church in Witham-on-the-Hill.

Barbara (1738–1825) was the eldest child in the family. She never married but remained close to childhood family friends of Lincolnshire and London. She became a member of moderately prominent social circles in London and often visited Witham-on-the-Hill, as well as the family homes of her brothers, especially Robert, with whom she maintained a frequent correspondence until his death in 1799. It is from her letters and memorabilia that we can draw many inferences about the kind of mother Jane Johnson must have been. Barbara kept throughout her life an album of her own fashions and occasions for acquiring and wearing many pieces of her apparel. She also tucked into her album pages and plates she had torn from various Pocket Books, leather-covered calendar books popular with women in the second half of the eighteenth century. Barbara's complete album, along with brief quotes from letters recalling moments of her childhood, is reproduced in *A Lady of Fashion: Barbara Johnson's Album of Styles and Fabrics* (1987).[3]

We may safely assume that Barbara's mother was educated primarily at home, but perhaps also at some nearby girls' school in music, reading and in manners befitting a lady of a country manor similar to that of females portrayed later in the century by novelist Jane Austen. *Emma*[4] (published in 1815) in particular gives considerable insight into the education of such women three-quarters of a century later: 'light' but considerable reading, facility with the piano and needlework, 'elegant, agreeable manners', and a range of knowledge about how to run a household and estate, and to entertain guests. We may assume that Jane Johnson was perhaps not quite so wealthy and comfortable as Jane Austen's heroine Emma Woodhouse, but she was certainly not so dependent on a vicar's salary as Mr Elton in the same novel. Emma reports conversations, thoughts, and perceptions of the characters of her countryside society. She also lets her readers in on their leisure reading of books and letters and pastimes of playing games with handmade alphabet cards created by women of the household for word games.

We know from the letters of Barbara and Jane that the Johnson children and their friends must have had much in common with Jane Austen's Emma. They too had books, wrote and received letters, played alphabet games, and had sets of cards and small handmade books created for their pleasure and for occasional use in the pastime of adults. As children, Barbara and her brothers were expected to be performers, listeners, reading audience, and reading and writing partners. The children wrote, did paper cuttings, painted, told stories, sang, and created a range of types of written and artistic records of their lives, many of which have been

19

lost but receive mention in letters written by Jane[5] to her children as well as being recalled by Barbara in her letters years later to her nieces and nephews, children of her brother Robert. The family kept a memorandum book to which Barbara refers, and Barbara herself noted on scraps of paper bits and pieces of knowledge about social events of her life and her fashions. In addition, her sense of continuity of the family's art of collecting, illustrating, and documenting must have been at work when she acquired years later the account book kept by a young merchant, George Thomson, between 1738 and 1748 of fashions and styles, as well as the occasion for which they were created. Barbara's album incorporates this account book (simultaneous with the first decade of her own life) and includes as well scraps of her gowns, pinned to album pages with brief notes and plates from various Pocket Books. Fashion illustrations, along with announcements of the 'fashions of the year', receive notice from Barbara who often adds to her album mention of special events in the life of her family and friends as well as well-known figures of the day. These accounts, notes, and illustrations add depth and a sense of continued habits of the home to the next generation from the handmade nursery library of Jane Johnson.

THE NURSERY LIBRARY

Discovered in 1986 in the private collection of Elisabeth Ball, children's book collector, of Muncie, Indiana, the nursery library that Jane Johnson created for her children is now in the possession of the Lilly Library of Indiana University. The collection tells much about expectations of literacy for children, types of activities in the home that revolved around written materials, and ways in which the production of these materials served as literary outlet for their producers – mother and children together. These fragile and tiny materials made by hand from bits of paper, cuttings from newspapers and magazines, and glued together with paste made from flour and water, suggest certain long-running patterns and values of literacy for children of families with upwardly mobile aspirations much like the Johnsons.

Included in the collection are ten series of alphabet cards, two hand-made books, six sets of religious lesson cards, and six sets of social commentary cards; the remaining assortment is of word and verse cards organized around syllables, parts of speech and categories of common items from daily life. Most of the cards are approximately 8.5 × 5.3 cm with a backing of Dutch flowered gilt paper; many have woven hangers on one side, suggesting their use as replaceable adornments in the household nursery. Also included in the collection is a handmade square box (4.5 × 4.5 cm) that holds seventy-eight word chips, all of which are about 1.2 cm in height. One side of each of these chips contains a playing-card symbol cut from brown, orange, and green Dutch gilt paper; the other side contains a single word, mostly from categories of food products, common household furnishings and animate beings about the house and farm (e.g., ale, almonds, bacon, bread; basket, chair, fork, knife, spoon; boy, dog, horse).

Of the two little handmade books in the collection, one gives the primary bit of information in all the materials that identifies Jane Johnson as their creator. This little book (8.5 × 5.3 cm) includes a page on which is inscribed: 'George William Johnson his Book. Printed and Bound by his Mamma 1745', followed by the signature of Jane Johnson. This book contains thirty-six numbered leaves; the words are in black on recto, the lessons are in a now-faded red ink on verso. The lessons are of a religious nature, for example: 'Whoso feareth the Lord it shall go well with him; he shall find favour with God and men.' The lists of words that face each page of lesson fall into categories according to syllabic regularity with each line often, but not always, in alphabetical order with no punctuation marks between them: Beam cream dream.

On the opening pages are pasted exquisitely intricate cut-outs of figures from tear sheets then available from booksellers in London. The cut-outs on these pages are of an elegantly dressed woman with calipers; and on the facing page is a peasant woman with a sheep. The page that is opposite the title page portrays a man holding a large book in his hand. On various pages of the book, apparently at random, are cut-outs of single items, such as a red flower (p. 16) and a yellow fish (p. 17). By about the end of the first third of the book, some lessons are prefaced by 'My son', and these are not of Biblical derivation, but of what we might think of as common sense or daily rules of living: 'My Son, if you value health, drink very little wine or strong Drink of any sort'. A series of lessons on wealth ends the book (pp. 32–6):

Health is better than Riches, but to be good is better than both.

In the first place, take care to be good; and in the next take care to be Rich.

Never part with one half-penny without a very good reason.

A Fool and his Money are soon parted.

He that will not take care of two pence, will never be worth a groat.

The final pages, unnumbered, include the words: 'The end of this Book', with a picture on the facing page of a woman seated beside a child in the cradle, and another woman standing nearby. The final two pages of the book include the following message, spread across both pages:

My son, so long	would they
as you live,	should do
never forget	Unto You.
the following	Remember
Rule,	this when I
Always do	am dead and
unto every	gone.
One, as You	

A second book, entitled 'A New Play Thing', is covered with the same Dutch gilt paper used as backing for most of the lesson cards of the collection. This book includes primarily letters of the alphabet in upper and lower case, with a single word on the left page (A Arm a), and on the right, a collection of consonant and vowel combinations (ba, be, bi, bo, bu). It bears no indication of author or the name of the child for whom the book was made.

Numerous series of cards in the collection bear little relation to alphabet cards, in that each of these cards contains commentary on the social life of the times. Some of these refer to distant events and places; most take in the sweep of everyday life that might have been seen from the window of a country home. For example, one set of cards includes such a description on one side of the card with an appropriate picture cut-out, delicately painted, on the other side. One such example is:

An Oxford Scholar in his Study, sitting by a Table with Mathematical Instruments before him, and a Globe of the World standing on the ground by him.

Other descriptions of distant scenes ring with a much more personal touch and suggest a rendering of news items referring to men of local renown in a simple country scene:

Two tame Swans swimming in the River they are the property of George Wrighte Esquire, Member of Parliament of Gothenurst, or Gay-Hurst near Newport Pagnel in the County of Bucks.

The backing picture is of two swans swimming together in a body of water with no identifying landmarks nearby. Yet another of this type refers to George Berkeley, Bishop of Cloyne, who advocated the curative powers of tarwater.

Doctor Berkley the good Bishop of Cloyne in Ireland, advising Mrs Wilson who has got a Cancer in her Breast to drink Tarwater, and he is likewise sending Patrick Norway his Servant with a Pitcher of Tarwater to a poor woman in Schoolhouse-bae that has got an Ague and Fever.

Backing this card are two pictures: one of an older man giving advice to a woman and another of a man carrying a pitcher.

Others of this series appear to be scenes from a carriage window on rides to nearby shires:

> David Morris, one Farmer Nicholas Bagshaw's Shepherd, with two Sheep, in Orton Field in the County of Westmoreland; he is driving one of them along, with his Hat, to Burton market to sell it.

The picture on the back is of a shepherd tipping his hat, accompanied by two sheep. Still other scenes within this series and several others could be of views from the window of Jane Johnson's own home. Others may come from travels she and her children made to take part in countryside events portrayed in pictures the children and their mother later cut from tear sheets and glued to the cards.

WINDOWS ON THE NURSERY WORLD

The nursery library that Jane Johnson made for her children stands in considerable contrast to the few remaining commercial materials made for children in the same period. These materials consist primarily of battledores (early versions of Hornbooks), ABC tracts or primers, and a few books of fables. Characteristic of all of these was a listing of letters of the alphabet in upper and lower case, with portions of a syllabarium (ba, be, bi, bo, bu, etc.). Portions of Bible verses, didactic sayings, and occasionally a quote from a fable were interspersed with these letters. Some listings of the letters of the alphabet included words that began with each letter, and some of these were internally meaningful ('A apple pastry, B bak'd it, C cut it, D divided it, E eat it, F fought for it, G got it', etc.), though most simply listed words.

The Johnson collection shares with the commercial children's literature available at the time three primary characteristics. The first of these is its use of the alphabet in various forms of representation (capital and small letters, in association with single words or opening words of phrases, and in combinations of consonant plus vowel to create syllables arranged alphabetically). The second is its use of Biblical admonitions to good behaviour and warnings of the evil results of bad behaviour, though Jane Johnson never used direct quotations from the Bible as did many of the battledores and hornbooks of the time. She also selected admonishments that might pertain to children (honouring parents, refraining from stealing and lying, and holding thrift, hard work, and honesty in high value) and omitted any that could refer only to the sins of adults (fornication and murder). The third similarity is in the use of maxims or brief sayings advising ways to achieve a good life.

Several features of Johnson's collection seem to foreshadow characteristics that were to come in commercial children's literature only much later in the eighteenth and early nineteenth centuries. Of these, four deserve particular mention: observations of daily life, observations on the role of women in society, observations of social critique, and categories created by both semantic and grammatical criteria.

Observations of daily life

Many of the writings on the cards were sentences that might have been uttered in ordinary conversation about daily life. These compare in several ways to the conversation among familiar neighbours portrayed in Austen's novels. Individuals mentioned are identified by either occupation or kin ties. Descriptions of places or inanimate beings are also located by ownership or connection with particular estates. Specifics of dress, especially of women, come in details of colour and particular styles of fashion.

Lady Margaret Mordaunt, Daughter to the Earl of Peterborow, in a Red Lutestring Coat.

Simon Frankland, a Butcher of Enfield in Middlesex, carrying a Sheep before him upon a horse nam'd Ball.

A pretty dark grey Doe, in a Park belonging to William Cavendish, Duke of Devonshire.

In addition to these simple conversational statements, numerous cards contain verses referring to scenes of daily life. These show an empathetic association with both animals and peasants and other non-landholding figures of the time. Each of these is accompanied by a picture that matches the verse.

A Cow and a Bull one day for their good,
Would try change of Air, and walk to the Woods:
But when they came there, they found little ease,
Their feet were so hurt, with the stumps of the Trees.

Give some Bread to my children I beg and I pray
Or they will be starved having had none today.

This latter verse is accompanied by two pictures, pasted separately: one of a woman dressed in fine attire and displaying a haughty manner, and another of a poor woman with two children reaching out in the direction of their hoped-for benefactress. This selection comes from a set of cards based on London street cries, several of which feature women.

Observations on the role of women in society

Women throughout the series of lesson cards are portrayed primarily as attempting to live good lives, restraining the forces of evil in society, and doing the work given to them with diligence and care. All of the listings based on categories of humans illustrating letters of the alphabet include references to women. Many of the verses call attention to women as individuals and to their various kinds of work.

> At a house by a Gate,
> Did live without state
> A little old woman
> and man.
> They did work for
> their bread, and were
> very well fed, and the
> old woman's name, it was
> Nan.

The accompanying picture is of a woman and man, each with a garden tool, against a scene of a farm.

> How wicked these
> men are to Quarrel
> and Fight:
> They surely forget
> that they are in
> God's sight.

Accompanying this verse is a picture of a woman attempting to stop two men who are in a fight.

> Good Girl Make
> haste and have
> done with your broom
> Of all things I hate
> such a dust in the
> Room.

The commentary on this verse comes in large part through the picture which is of a haughty disdainful mistress and a young pretty peasant girl with a broom. The two pictures are cut separately, indicating Jane Johnson's choice of the countenance and social bearing of each of the characters.

Certain verses related to women must be included also among those bearing the next feature.

SHIRLEY BRICE HEATH

Observations of social critique

Satire and irony mark a small percentage of the verses, as well as the particular combinations of pictures and verses. Many closely resemble the humorous and descriptive captions that accompany family photograph albums of today. For example, several verses and pictures show men looking like fools in pursuit of their pastimes of drinking, hunting, and entertaining women.

> The Man with his Dogs
> went out to kill Game,
> His Gun it went off,
> and shot the Dogs
> lame.

> It is wicked to get
> drunk, to swear, lye, or
> steal.
> And those that do such
> things will Hell's
> Torments feel.

Accompanying each of these verses is an appropriate picture of males; the second contains both a young boy and an older man who have obviously enjoyed much drinking.

But men are not the only ones captured with the wit of Jane Johnson: the French, and particularly French women, come in for particular criticism.

> Such short Gowns as these, are much used in France,
> And the Men and the Women cup capers and dance.
> The Ladys they Paint, and their backsides they show,
> The Men hop, and skip, and each one is a Beau
> Would you see men like monkeys; to France you must go.

The picture accompanying this verse is of a gentleman between two ladies in long full hoop skirts. All are finely dressed and their gestures exaggerated.

Categories created by both semantic and grammatical criteria

Most presentations of the alphabet used in hornbooks and the few books available for children before 1745 listed items only according to their first letters and their membership in a particular semantic category: animals, foods, birds, etc. Jane Johnson, however, created semantic categories of more abstract relationships. For example, several of the square card sets she designed with small hangers attached so that they could be hung

26

from one corner bore themes that were by no means immediately obvious. For example, one contained words such as flea, bee, fly, gnat, worm, leech, lice, snake, and was presumably organized around a theme such as 'unpleasant critters about the house and lands'. Others included only function words, such as *in*, *of*, *for*, mixed in with pronouns. Still others mixed categories, but grouped words of the same category together (colours on one side of a card ending with the words *light* and *dark* and on the other side utensils for eating plus the words *cup*, *mug*, and *glass*. Throughout the sets, Jane Johnson displays her keen attention to matters of grammatical structure, building blocks of language, and possible segmentation and arrangement of words. Some were listed in what might be described as a chiasmic relationship; for example, *where*, *there* was followed by *their*, and *were*, with *where* and *were* resembling each other in spelling but differing in pronunciation, and *there* and *their* having their similarity in pronunciation but not in spelling.

READING AND UPWARD MOBILITY

Jane Johnson's desires for the role of reading in her children's lives come through in several ways in this nursery manuscript. Though these artefacts do not allow us to reconstruct the precise ways in which she might have used these with her children or the talk that might have accompanied any recitation from them or reading by her, we can infer some expectations she associated with reading. Those most clearly stated come in the book that bears George William Johnson's name. Jane Johnson, like others of her time and station, linked the ability to read with increases in judgement, rationality, will-power, and knowledge. These qualities of character derived from access to accumulated wisdom from the past as well as from the sharpened insight gained through reading and writing. The morals, as well as the observations, offer so little in narrative and context, that we must imagine some kind of talk surrounding them. The children would have known some of the names, many of the scenes, and most of the listed items and could have easily giggled over members of their card sets that mentioned their friends and neighbours.

A few move the children themselves into the literate frame. For example, one card's observation refers to Barbara Johnson, George's older sister:

Lord Mountjoy, and Miss Barbara Johnson, Dancing a Menuet together at a Redotto in the Hay Market.

The accompanying picture is made of two separate cut-outs, one of a man and the other of a young woman, facing each other. Presumably, with any one of the children, this card would have provoked comment. Others mention family friends, and one card that contains nouns also includes the proper name *George*. It is easy to assume that these cards were prompts to which the children responded with sentences that used as many words from the cards as possible.

We cannot know the extent to which the 438 extant pieces represent all the sets Jane Johnson created for her children during their childhoods. But we can judge from the range of types and gradations of complexity of pictures and verses presented that she constructed them with a continuing use in mind. It seems highly unlikely that this mother viewed most of the sets as merely beginning reading materials. Their flexibility for use in learning skills from sound and letter matching to word recognition to sentence and story creation is evident. In addition, many contain what must have been family jokes and bits of retold family tales that would have a life far beyond the early reading days of only one young child. For example, the mention and picture of young Barbara dancing may well have occurred when she was in her early teens, but her younger brothers would surely have enjoyed joining in the creation of this card and the accompanying pieces of its set, all of which bear some strong reference to ladies' fashions. It may be that Barbara herself created this set, which bears clear linkages to the notes and pictures she later included in her album of styles and fabrics.

Numerous cards reflect the view that maintaining a good life becomes possible through the leisure that riches provide. But this leisure, like money, must be well spent. The close association between the alphabet – and by strong implication literacy – and moral well-being could not have escaped any child exposed to these materials. But neither could a child have failed to see the many ways in which a visual scene could be read. The tight coordination of picture and words on the vast majority of the lesson cards calls for the same integration of reading pictures and words that published children's literature came to suggest by the end of the eighteenth century and still insists upon today in materials created for young children. The tiny details of facial expression, style of dress, and body posture portrayed in the small pictures Jane Johnson cut and glued for her lesson cards carried many points of emphasis for her verses and statements. She reinforced concepts of social class, occupational differentiation, separation of roles of men and women, and quirks of national character through her juxtapositioning of pictures and words. The tradition of including social critique within literature prepared for children has received much scholarly attention, and this home-made collection indicates that Jane Johnson was no exception as an author. Politics, fashion, gender habits, weaknesses of character and individual quirks of personality bear the brunt of Jane Johnson's wit.

It seems also clear, given the number of scenes, verses, and statements that reflect problem situations, that she expected some attention to ways of getting out of these dilemmas to emerge either from talk with her

28

children about these lesson cards or from their own thinking about the scene or situation revealed. Animals, men, women, and children encounter problems in her cards, and many of the morals offer advice on ways both to solve and to avoid problems.

THE PLAY OF WORDS FOR CHILDREN

Jane Johnson's materials allow children to come through as active, mindful, imaginative, and artistic conversationalists and performers. This early eighteenth-century collection of literacy materials from a country-side home gives us more than a glimpse into the shadowy origins of expectations about literacy, children's roles in their current households and in the future, and the merits of observing and recording with an eye for detail, category, and artistry.

Literacy is linked with goodness, the good life, well-spent leisure, and a sense of humour and wittiness. Patterns more specific to the content of children's literature itself include: close interrelationship of illustration and text, portrayal of adult life for satiric comment, and connection of children's literature with problem-solving. Insistent connections between reading and being good and also rational indicate that the experience of reading children's literature is intended to extend far beyond the actual moment of reading to character building, tenacious problem-solving, and observational acuity. Imagination and empathy as qualities essential to sustain vitality in and for life also come through in many of the card sets.

Following one's interest, curiosity, and reading into illustrations as well as events comes through as a prized quality for children. Ambiguity, not certainty, except in some religious matters, lies submerged in the tricks of word play in several verses of some card sets. Jane Johnson often gives notice of the importance of intertextuality – the need to know one text in order to use another well. Rather than the usual stratagem of simplifying materials for children, she sometimes buries in the cards complex ways to turn the cards into games that might include mathematics, design rearrangements, and puzzles or riddles. She rarely simplifies conditions of life or contradictions between appearing to be of one character while becoming another through submission to drink or negative personal influence. Though some sets tell her children what to think, most include opportunities to consider alternative ways to construct scenes and draw conclusions. Many texts are completely open-ended. Several sets celebrate individuality and difference within various textual communities – those of family first and foremost, but with strong foreshadowing of other textual communities to come for her children: those of the state and the church. She calls her children to reading and to reading early so that they might collect their shared experiences and unite around common goals and social responsibilities. She embodies in many of her materials the

29

short step from textual communities to rituals of everyday life and the rhythms of an oral society.

For Jane Johnson's children, the hearth and home of 250 years ago created images of their universes to come, but embedded these in strong visual and verbal representations of the familiars of childhood and home. These ephemeral bits that somehow miraculously escaped the ravages of fire, vermin, water, and careless disregard that usually come to such handmade paper items open up for us the rituals and routines of literate identities and literary value-building. They suggest the power of ephemera to carry some of the most valued habits and deepest strengths for managing everyday living. Jane Johnson's nursery library, along with the fashion album of her daughter Barbara, foreshadow in illustration and text what Jane Austen wrote half a century later of similar textual ephemera:

> These letters were but the vehicle for gallantry and trick. It was a child's play, chosen to conceal a deeper game ...
>
> (*Emma*)

ACKNOWLEDGEMENT

Acknowledgement is here given to the Lilly Library of Indiana University for permission to quote from the Jane Johnson Manuscripts, Elisabeth Ball Collection.

NOTES

1 Gaston Bachelard, *The Poetics of Space* (Boston: Beacon Press, 1958).
2 This 'manuscript nursery library' is housed at the Lilly Library, Indiana University, USA.
3 Natalie Rothstein (ed.), *A Lady of Fashion: Barbara Johnson's Album of Styles and Fabrics* (London: Thames & Hudson, 1987).
4 Jane Austen, *Emma* (Oxford: Oxford University Press, 1971).
5 Some letters of Jane Johnson were in the hands of family descendants Mr and Mrs Blois Johnson who graciously allowed exhibition of selected portions of this material at Homerton College, Cambridge University, in April 1995 for the conference 'Scrapbooks and Chapbooks'; they are now housed in the Bodleian.

2

JANE JOHNSON: A VERY PRETTY STORY TO TELL CHILDREN

Victor Watson

Jane Johnson is central to *Opening the Nursery Door*. Her handmade teaching materials, her poetry for children, and the recently discovered story she wrote for her own two children, add significantly to our understanding of the ways in which mothers in the eighteenth century involved themselves in their children's 'nursery learning'. This chapter focuses on the unpublished story written by Jane Johnson in 1744, the manuscript of which was in private hands for a number of years until it was recently acquired by the Bodleian Library. Also in private hands are some of her letters, poems and notes, and a book of extracts which enables us to form some idea of what Jane Johnson read, and how she regarded her children and their education.

At first sight, her story's significance lies chiefly in its date. However, the more we discover about her, the further we are led into broader questions concerning the history of children's books, children's literacy, education, and – in particular – the role of mothers in their children's learning.

*

For anyone interested in children's books in the first half of the eighteenth century, there are two key dates. In 1693, John Locke in *Some Thoughts Concerning Education*,[1] offering some advice on ways of teaching a young child to read, recommended the provision of 'some easy pleasant book suited to his capacity'. This sensible suggestion seems to have provided a blueprint for the development of children's literature, a view apparently confirmed by the fact that, in 1744, John Newbery (see Chapter 5) published what came to be thought of as the first children's book, *A Little Pretty Pocket-Book*. Furthermore – to establish his credentials – Newbery made explicit his indebtedness to Locke and transformed with some precision the philosopher's recommendation into a realistic publishing venture.

But Harvey Darton was not satisfied with the notion of a direct continuity from Locke to Newbery, with its implicit assumption that together the philosopher and the printer set going 'the great tradition' of children's literature. He knew that this view was acceptable only if some important aspects of publishing history were set aside, and he took care in the opening chapters of his famous work[2] to do justice to those books for children written *before* Newbery.

He was right to be sceptical; there are too many unanswered questions. What happened in the intervening years between 1693 and 1744? Why did it apparently take half a century for Locke's blueprint for a children's book to be acted upon? Were other things going on which we know nothing about? How did children learn their letters *before* Newbery – and who taught them? And why 1744? Other contributors to this book provide answers to some of these questions; and the discovery of Jane Johnson's story, along with her poetry and home-made reading materials, have enabled us to identify further areas for reconsideration.

*

It seems an extraordinary coincidence that, in the same year that Newbery published *A Little Pretty Pocket-Book* in London, Jane Johnson in the rectory at Olney in Buckinghamshire was writing a private story for her own children, George and Barbara (Bab), aged five and six. An unpublished story written for children in that 'special' year 1744 must be of considerable interest to anyone interested in the history of children's books. She called it 'A very pretty Story to tell Children when they are about five or six years of age.' 'Pretty' *might* indicate that *A Little Pretty Pocket-Book* had arrived at the Olney rectory hot from Newbery's press and given Jane Johnson the idea – but it is more likely that the word was already highly charged with connotations of childhood. The title has a pragmatic quality, too, as if Jane Johnson had it in mind to make the story available for other parents to use.

We can see from the opening that Jane Johnson did probably the most magical thing any storyteller can do for young readers or listeners – she has *put them into their own story*.

> There was a fine Gentleman & a fine Lady & they Lived in a fine House; & they were call'd Mr & Mrs Alworthy: They had one little Boy & one little Girl, the Little Boys name was George, & the little Girl's name was Bab. & Mr & Mrs Alworthy were vastly fond of them both, & Lov'd them Dearly because they were both Good Humour'd, & did every thing in their power to oblige their Father, & Mother, & every body else. & they used every day to have a little Miss & Master of their own age come to play with them; this Miss & Master that came every day to play with them lived in the same Town, & their names were Miss Lucy Manly & Master Tommy

Manly. These four pretty children were so fond of one another that they were never so well pleas'd as when they were together, & were constantly trying which could oblige each other the most, & instead of crying for one anothers play things, & fighting, & hurting one another as most Children do that are so often together, they would part with any thing they had if the other had a mind to it: & Master George & Miss Bab would ask Mrs Alworthy when she gave them Sugar-Plumbs, or Plumb-cake, or any thing else that was good, to give Miss Lucy & Master Tommy some, & if Mrs Alworthy had none to give them, Master George & Miss Bab. would give Miss Lucy & Master Tommy half theirs; & thus they went on for three or four years, & all four learn'd to Dance together, & were always trying which could hold up their heads the best & which could turn out their toes most; & they all Learn'd to read their Books together, which they took so much pleasure in, & read so well that they were the admiration of all the Gentlemen & Ladys that Lived near them in the Country ...

There is a careful child-centred rhetoric here, along with hints of the elusive gestures of storytelling: almost certainly, for example, that reference to 'holding up their heads' and 'turning out their toes' was a shared nursery joke. Clarity of language and firm standards of conduct go hand-in-hand – and there may well have been some gentle parental irony in the voice of the teller as she stressed the children's extraordinary good behaviour and generosity to each other. But misfortune strikes swiftly.

But when Master Tommy, & Miss Lucy Manly were about eight or nine years old their Father & Mother were both taken sick of a Fever, & Died within a few hours of one another, this was a great concern to Miss Lucy & Master Tommy, & what made it still the greater, all the Fortune that they had was left in the hands of an Uncle that run away with it, & cheated them of all. So poor Miss Lucy & Master Tommy were left without a farthing in the World or, any body to take care of them.

The narrator has a good deal to say about death, going to heaven, the proper way to grieve and the importance of prayer – all done with a lightness of touch which indicates that Jane Johnson never lost sight of her young audience. The upshot is that the fictional Mistress Bab and Master George beg their parents to 'do as you would be done by' – an injunction repeated several times for reinforcement – and allow the two orphans to live with them. The benevolent parents had already privately planned the same scheme and the four children are delighted.

Then away they went & gather'd flowers & made Garlands, & Nosegays, & then they went up stairs & dress'd their Bird-cages, &

their Rocking-Horses, & their Dolls all over flowers, & they Danced, & jump'd & play'd about, & was as merry & as happy as possible.

The next incident is a trip to a local fair, for which each child is given half-a-crown. To a generation brought up on Bunyan, a fairground suggests moral danger; and, sure enough, on the way, Bab, George and Lucy give sixpence to some poor children who 'were all over Rags and had no shoes on their feet and the stones cut their feet till they bled'. But Master Tommy, although he has just been saved from poverty himself, is too mean to give to the poor. Here, though the narrative is to a large extent predictable, the telling is rich with a childlike attention to delightful detail.

> then they all went into the Fair; & when they were there they look'd at all the fine Play-things upon the Stalls to see what they liked best, & Miss Bab. bought her a mighty pretty Doll, dress'd like a Shepherdess, in a pink satten Jacket & petticoat, & a pretty Hat on, & a Basket of flowers in her hand; & Miss Lucy bought a tea-table & cups & saucers, & sugar dish, & tea pot: & Master Tommy laid out his whole half crown (none of which he would give to the poor Ragged Boys & Girls,) in Oranges, Sugar-Plumbs, Cherrys, Gooseberrys & such Trash & eat so much fruit & trumpery that it made his stomach ache . . .

There is no need for explicit moral comment here because words like *trash* and *trumpery* already carried a heavy weight of disapproval. The children discover 'several mighty pretty Horses to be sold cut-out of Ivory, with men and women riding upon them' and now Tommy bitterly regrets that he has spent all his money. So that night, 'up he gets like a Naughty Boy as he was, & steals the two shillings out of Master George's pocket'. Next day, Tommy claims that he found the money on the ground, goes to the fair, and buys one of the ivory horses. Anyone who has shared stories with young children can imagine the solemn faces of Jane Johnson's two young listeners as the story approaches this dramatic moral crisis. Finally, to greed, lying and stealing Master Tommy now adds an attempt to throw the blame onto Molly the Cook Maid, who is summarily dismissed for theft. (Was she also a real member of Jane Johnson's household?)

> So poor Molly was turn'd away; she cry'd bitterly all the time She was packing up her Cloaths, & said it was a sad thing to be thought a Thief; & a Lyar, & loose a good place, but however says she God Almighty that sees & knows all things that are done, will I am sure some time or other bring the Truth to light & punish Master Tommy for telling Lyes of me, but no body regarded what she said, for

34

every one believed Master Tommy too [sic] be too good to tell a Lye.

Many of the features of the story so far are recognizable, even perhaps predictable. Allegorical names were common in a culture familiar with a tradition that derived from Bunyan; five years later, in 1749, Fielding used the same name, Allworthy, in *Tom Jones*. The fair itself is reminiscent of Bunyan's Vanity Fair, the place of danger and folly where the sternest Christian will be subjected to temptation. And the grave view taken of lying, stealing and indifference to poverty would not have seemed strange to an age imbued with the principles and shibboleths of a culture of conduct-books. The two orphans cheated by a wicked uncle probably derive from *The Children of the Wood*, for we know from *The Spectator*[3] that this Norfolk tale was well-known long before 1744 – and we know that Jane Johnson loved *The Spectator*. Nor is there anything remarkable in her serious and explicit concern with death and heaven; her treatment of the subject is gentle compared with the grim insistence of, for example, James Janeway's *A Token for Children*[4] or some of the poems of Bunyan or Watts.

But what comes next cannot be so easily accounted for in terms of familiar English cultural influences; for when a magnificent magical chariot comes into the house, English Bunyan unexpectedly gives way to French Baroque.

> Some time after this as they were all at play together in a fine Great Parlour in Mr Alworthy's House the Door open'd & there came into the Room a fine Chariot all over Gold & Diamonds, & it was drawn by six fine White Lambs dress'd all over with flowers & Ribbonds, & the most beautiful little Boy that ever Eyes beheld set on the coach-box, & two charming pretty little Angels Rode on two charming fine Lambs by the Chariot side; as soon as they all came into the Parlour, Miss Bab. & Master George, & Miss Lucy & Master Tommy were quite transported at seeing so fine a sight, & they all ran to meet this fine Chariot, & as soon as they came near it the two fine Angels got down & took them by the hand & told them they were come with that fine Chariot to fetch them to the Castle of pleasure & Delight which stood about five miles of their house, & that there was a great many Misses & Masters there that wanted sadly to see them, & that if they pleased to go along with them Mr & Mrs Alworthy would give them leave to go & stay a month & then they would bring them back again.

Jane Johnson's young listeners would not have been surprised to learn that Master Tommy is not to be included in this visit to the Castle of Pleasure and Delight. Instead, he is told that if he looks 'upon the ivory horse' he will understand why. He throws the ivory horse out of the window in a great passion, wringing his hands, and saying:

> Oh! – how could I be such a fool to offend God-Almighty? Just as he was saying so the Door opened, & into the Parlour comes a little Dirty Chariot drag'd along by two Black-Hogs & a little ugly Man all over stinking Dirt, & he goes up to Master Tommy & told him he must go in that Black Chariot with him, & eat & drink & Lye with the Hogs, all the while his sister, & good Miss Bab. & Master George were in the Castle of pleasure & Delights. So he took him in his Stinking arms, & put him into the Dirty Chariot, & Drove him away to the Dirty Swine, & the two black-hogs went grunting on all the way for two or three miles & then stop'd at the great Hogsty & the little Dirty man open'd the Door, & took Master Tommy out, & then Lock'd him in amongst the Hogs.

Was there, perhaps, a real hogsty on the Johnson estate which the children were frightened of? This severe morality, with its emblematic use of the familiar and domestic, is then set aside as the journey to the Castle of Pleasure and Delights is lovingly described. The narrative is bright, almost radiant. There are summer fields and meadows, high and stately trees full of birds' nests, and angels bringing nests down for the children, while birds bring nosegays for them, and sit and sing on their hands and shoulders.

> When they came to the Castle the Chariot stop'd, & the Little Angels handed Miss Bab. Miss Lucy & Master George out, & lead them into a fine Garden full of all sorts of fruit, & such flowers as they had never seen before, & the Angels bid them gather what they pleased. & then they lead them to the fine House, & took them up Stairs into a very Large & most Beautiful Dining Room all hung round with Pictures, & there was above a Hundred Misses & Masters of different Ages all Dress'd in fine Cloaths, & playing at different sorts of Plays, in different parts of the Room; some little Misses were dressing & undressing fine Babys, some playing at cards, some at Ball, some at Marbles, some at shuttle-cock, some Dancing, some riding upon Rocking Horses, some swinging in fine Chinese Swings, some making fine Diners of sweet-meats, sugar-plumbs, Biscuits & all sorts of pretty-things, & others a going to visit them. Some playing with pretty little tiny Dogs, some with Parrots, that could talk as fast as themselves, some with Bull-finches & other pretty tame Birds that would fly about the room & come to them when they were call'd & sing when they bid them.

Jane Johnson's descriptions of this nursery-paradise are precise, evocative and colourful, crafted to make a rich provision for the imaginative appetites of her young listeners.

> & [the angels] gave each of them a very curious fishing Angle & in the evening they all went a fishing to a very Large fish pond within a mile of the Castle that was full of Chinese fish of different Colours all mighty pretty their scales shining in the sun like Gold & Red & Green & Purple & all sorts of colours.

When the three children in the story decide it is time to go home, they are taken to a stable to choose horses for themselves. In the description that follows, bright and colourful details are precisely and energetically celebrated in language which suggests the breathless yet controlled excitement of the storyteller.

> & Miss Bab chose a mighty pretty little Horse all over as white as snow, with a Red velvet side saddle trim'd with Gold: & Miss Lucy chose one all over white except the Ears, the Main, the tail, & feet, & they were Black with a Black star in the forehead, & her saddle was Blue velvet trim'd with Silver: & master George chose a pretty little Bay Gelding with a white Star in his forehead & a black tail & main, & his Saddle was finely Embroider'd with Gold, & his Bridle Bit, & sturrups were Silver.

On the way home, they pass master Tommy in his hogsty, who begs to be let out. He is released, washed and forgiven, and Molly the Cook Maid is restored to her position. Tommy, however, is so mortified because he can never go to the Castle of Pleasure and Delight, and because no one loves him as much as they love the other children, that

> in a few years he grew very dull, held down his head, fell sick of a Fever & Died.

Forgiveness is available, but wickedness is irrevocable.

The influence on Jane Johnson of the conduct-books, and of a long family association with Puritanism, is obvious. But her story is not just a didactic fable about the Wages of Sin; it opens up the possibility of a much wider range of influences. In particular, it is clear that she had read and enjoyed the translated fairy stories that were coming across from France, especially the distinctive tales of Mme D'Aulnoy.

The Comtesse d'Aulnoy's *Contes des Fées* had been translated in 1707, 1716, and again in 1721. Her stories were not written specifically for children. They were mostly tales about courtship, marriage, treachery and the unprincipled use of magic, and although they were not exactly indecent, they were certainly hedonistic. Marina Warner describes the French fairytales of the period as a women's 'genre of protest'.[5] These long novel-like romances, with their interpolated shorter fairy stories, were immensely popular in France. *The Arabian Nights* belonged to the same period and appealed to similar tastes. It had been translated into French between 1704 and 1717, and stories from it began to appear in English at about the same time. The climax of this French passion for fairytales was the eventual publication from 1785–9 of *Le Cabinet des Fées*, a massive series of more than forty volumes.

Many of the features in Jane Johnson's story clearly derive from the Comtesse d'Aulnoy's *Contes des Fées* – the generally fantastical country-side full of magical possibilities; the landscape of gardens, woods, palaces, trees and flowers; her baroque interest in ornamental details; the emphasis on colour and the vivid imagery of bright flowers, fruit and birds; and her focused attentiveness to the colour and brightness of clothes and jewellery. Finally there is an abundance of magical flying chariots and carriages, usually pulled by fantastical animals.

Mme D'Aulnoy made a great use of such devices. There are dozens of magical chariots in her stories. For example:

> Whereupon the Ram order'd his Chariot, and soon after appear'd six Goats harnessed to a Gourd-Shell, and lined with Velvet. The Princess plac'd herself in it . . .[6]

> and there came out a Chariot of Diamonds, drawn by six Swans, in which sat a beautiful Lady dress'd like an *Amazon*, with an Helmet on her Head of pure Gold, on which was a Plume of white Feathers; and her Visor, which was rais'd up, discover'd Eyes as bright as the Sun . . .[7]

> an Ebony Chariot drawn by Vultures, which flew in the Air with such Swiftness, that they soon gained her Palace.[8]

> The Chariot was of Gold richly wrought, and drawn by four fine white Horses harness'd variously. The first harness was cover'd with saphires; the second with several precious Stones, as Agats, Onyx, Topaz, and Rubies; the third was with Diamonds; and the fourth with Amethists of an inestimable Value. Four Fairies led the Horses with Silk and Golden Reins.[9]

Jane Johnson may also have been familiar with Cinderilla's magic coach in Perrault's *Histories, or Tales of Past Times*.[10] Although this collection was less well known than Mme D'Aulnoy's stories, it had been translated in 1729.

Jane Johnson's magic coach contained 'the most beautiful little Boy that ever Eyes beheld'. Who is he? Could it be that, along with Bab and George, she put into her story her baby son, Frederick Augustus, who had died the previous November?

Mme D'Aulnoy's baroque stories are characterized by a rococo imagery and an intensity of brightness and colour. This is especially associated with clothes, jewellery, and brilliant magical landscapes. When horses appear, their bridles and saddles are lovingly described. There are similar features in Jane Johnson's story too. We know she was interested in colour and design anyway,[11] and she would have enjoyed this kind of description in Mme D'Aulnoy's stories:

> The Three Princesses bespoke themselves every one a Robe of Sattin; the Eldest's was Green adorn'd with Emeralds; the Second's was Blue set off with Turquoises; and the Youngest White bedecked with Diamonds.[12]

> she discover'd a vast Plain enamelled with various Flowers, which exceeded all the Perfumes she had ever smelt of, surrounded with a large River of Orange-flower Water. In the Midst of the Plain were Fountains of Wine, Rosa-solis, and other exquisite Liquors, which formed Cascades and other pleasant purling Brooks, and here and there Holts of Trees, which served for Shelter to Variety of Choice Birds and Fowls, as Partridges, Quails, Pheasants, Ortolans, Turkeys, Pullets, &c. and, in some Parts, the Air was darkened with Showers of Biscuits, blanched Almonds, Tarts, Cheesecakes, Marrow-Puddings, all manner of Sweetmeats, both wet and dry; and in short, with all Necessaries of Life, with great Plenty of Crown-pieces, Guineas, Pearls and Diamonds.[13]

She would also have found in D'Aulnoy many examples of diminutive magic like this:

> The next Morning, when the Princess awaked, she saw twelve little Nymphs flying into her Chamber, who were all set on Bees, and brought in their hands little Baskets of Gold.[14]

What about Jane Johnson's *Castle of Pleasure and Delight*? That kind of naming was not uncommon in a post-Bunyan age; throughout the 1740s James Thomson was composing his poem, *The Castle of Indolence*, and in Mme D'Aulnoy's stories she would have found numerous other examples. One story has both an *Isle of Happiness* and a *Palace of Pleasures*. It is a curious story, in which the heroine is shut up in a Castle for her own safety:

> and the God [of Pleasures] my Father, to shew how dear I was to him, shut up with me the *Pleasures*, which were young children of an heavenly Beauty, who by their Presence inspire the most Sorrowful with Joy. He permitted them every Day to go out of the Palace, to shew themselves to Mortals; but commanded them always to return at Night to my delicious Prison . . .[15]

Jane Johnson would probably have liked that. Here the Pleasures are not *for* children; they *are* children. And perhaps she privately savoured that extra motherly significance in her own *Castle of Pleasure and Delight* full of happy fictional children.

I am sure Jane had read the stories of Mme D'Aulnoy. We know from her letters and extract-book that her reading was very wide. Her book of extracts shows a woman who was familiar with the classics and also read a wide range of popular fiction. She copied out extracts from *The Spectator*, *The Tatler*, Milton, the Bible, Juvenal, Pope's *Homer*, and many other works which we would expect a reflective and educated woman of the period to have read. She also quotes from *The Arabian Nights Entertainment*.

However, most of her extracts are quotations from what she calls the *Turkey Spy*. In fact, this was *Letters Writ by a Turkish Spy, who liv'd five and forty years undiscover'd at Paris*, an extraordinary eight-volume work of popular fiction by Giovanni Marana,[16] claiming to have been written by a Mohammedan spy, in Arabic, translated first into Italian and then into English. (A ninth volume, called a *Continuation*, is attributed to Defoe.) This work was constantly reissued and was clearly very popular. It was part thriller, and part historical fiction, offering an ironic commentary on the politics and wars of the time. Its general tone was wise, urbane and tolerant, and the extracts which Jane Johnson carefully copied out were invariably remarks about honour and good conduct. It is clear that her reading taste was wide and independent – perhaps wider than we would expect of a clergyman's wife – and that she selected from her reading anything which lent support to her own firm sense of morality and conduct.

*

The fact that Jane Johnson's story was written in the very year in which Newbery published his first children's book is perhaps no more than a coincidence. And yet, if we look again at the dates of some important publications, there is evidence to indicate that, in the period from 1740 onwards, there was for some reason a resurgence of interest in children and their education and reading.

It began with Samuel Richardson's *Aesop's Fables*, published in 1740. This work is rarely allowed any more than a brief mention in the Histories, but it was a major work. In many ways Richardson's thinking was strongly influenced by the conduct-books. His better-known *Letters Written to and for Particular Friends*[17] had, despite its title, been more concerned with conduct than with rhetoric. And in 1733 he had published *The Apprentice's Vade Mecum*,[18] another conduct-book. His *Aesop* was similar. In his Preface, he speculates at some length upon the nature of children's minds and explains that he wishes to 'reduce the work to such a size as should be fit for the hands and pockets for which it was principally designed'. (Richardson's *Aesop* is considered more fully in Chapter 4.)

This was a major contribution to children's books of the period and it is not clear to me why its importance has been neglected. The very fact that a writer and publisher of Richardson's eminence should have turned his attention at that time to children, and publicly ruminated upon their thinking, is itself significant. Jane Johnson would almost certainly have known the work; its approach would have appealed to her. But Richardson's interest in children and education was not confined to his *Aesop*. He described *Pamela* – also published in 1740 – as a work to 'cultivate the principles of virtue and religion in the minds of the youth of both sexes'.[19] That does not make it a children's book – but it is further indication of Richardson's interest in the education of the young. A more remarkable feature is that in his continuation of *Pamela* in the following year, some forty or fifty pages are devoted to an analytical account of Locke's *Some Thoughts Concerning Education*. This is as surprising as it would be today if a character in a novel by Mary Wesley spent forty pages introducing Piaget to the general reader! Why, half a century after Locke,[20] should Richardson have revealed an interest in the philosopher's views on the education of children? It indicates Richardson's own concern, but it also suggests that he knew his readers would be interested too.

Pamela was much disapproved of, but it *was* widely read – and it is inconceivable that Jane Johnson did not know of it. Her surviving letters and notes make no mention of *Pamela* – but we do know that she later read *Clarissa*[21] and very much approved of it. In a letter dated 17 October 1749, she wrote rather tartly:

> But being almost come to the end of my paper, 'tis time that I shou'd come to the end of my story or I shall not leave room to express my opinion of Mrs Hackshaw's Fine Taste & Judgement, which possibly may be very good, tho' she does not approve of Miss Clarissa Harlow, for perhaps her dislike of that story may proceed from a consciousness of its reproaching her own conduct, which you know has not always been with the strict regard it ought, to Parental Authority especially in matrimonial affairs, if this is not the reason of the dislike I don't know what is, for I believe she is the only Person of fine Taste & judgement upon Earth that does not approve of it, & I am only sorry she will not read it through, for my part I think it will do great things towards reforming the world, & shall never meet with any person who after they have read it quite through, & do not commend it, but I shall conclude that they have either a bad heart, or a bad head, or both, for in such case the fault must be some where & I am sure there is none in the Book ...

41

The evidence suggests that the notoriety surrounding Richardson's *Pamela* provoked or revived a quickening of public interest in childhood, to which his *Aesop* also contributed, that John Newbery recognized its market potential, and that Jane Johnson composed her story in the midst of this debate. It is also worth bearing in mind that several other children's books were issued in the period between 1740 and 1744, including Mrs Cooper's *The Child's New Plaything*, J. Robinson's *Little Master's Miscellany* and the ten volumes of Thomas Boreman's *Gigantic Histories*.

But that is not all. Richardson's final volume concludes with Pamela giving an account of herself telling two stories to her children. She calls this 'a little specimen of my *nursery tales* and *stories*' – a phrase which seems to indicate that nursery stories were a commonplace fact of domestic life.

> Then, Madam, we all proceed, hand-in-hand, together to the nursery, to my Charley and Jemmy: and in this happy retirement, so much my delight in the absence of my best beloved, imagine you see me seated, surrounded with the joy and the hope of my future prospects, as well as my present comforts . . .
>
> . . . I began with a story of two little boys, and two little girls, the children of a fine gentleman, and a fine lady, who loved them dearly; that they were all so good, and loved one another so well, that everybody who saw them, admired them, and talked of them far and near; that they would part with anything to one another; loved the poor; spoke kindly to the servants; did everything they were bid to do; were not proud; knew no strife, but who should learn their books best, and be the prettiest scholar, that the servants loved them, and would do anything they desired; that they were not proud of fine clothes; let not their heads run upon their playthings when they should mind their books; said grace before they eat, their prayers before they went to bed, and as soon as they rose; were always clean and neat; would not tell a fib for the world, and were above doing anything that required one . . .[22]

The account goes on in this vein for some while, an inventory of righteousness rather than a narrative for children. There is no action in Pamela's story; it simply stops.

> And they married, and made good papas and mamas, and were so many blessings to the age in which they lived.[23]

It is very probable that Jane Johnson was familiar with that, used it as a model – and developed it far beyond anything Richardson could do. Richardson creates an idyll of the nursery, a domestic pastoral of motherhood, very self-conscious and sentimental, and completely lacking that genuine quality of the affectionately oral to be found in Jane's tale. Her tale is genuinely child-centred; Richardson's account is Pamela-centred.

Nevertheless, a writer so revered – and controversial – as Richardson would probably have been very influential, and it is by no means unlikely that this closing account – together with Pamela's earlier consideration of Locke – contributed a great deal to articulating assumptions *about the ways in which mothers saw themselves as having a central educative role in the nursery*. His *Aesop's Fables* would have been part of the same interest. I doubt if Richardson single-handedly created this public interest in childhood. But it does seem that there was one – and that Richardson was in some way implicated in it.

There is, of course, another quite different possibility – that this kind of 'nursery-storying' was common in the middle-class homes of the period and that there existed an extensive oral tradition from which both Richardson and Jane Johnson in their different ways drew – and that Richardson became interested in it for no other reason than that in the early 1740s his own domestic life was dominated by four little girls under eight years old.

*

Jane Johnson ends her story by taking her three fictional children – and her two real listeners – into their own future.

But Miss Bab. Master George & Miss Lucy were beloved by every body because they were so good, & they all grew up to be very tall & handsome, because they constantly held up their Heads & turn'd out their toes, & that made them all look perfectly Genteel, & be admired by every body! & when they were old enough they were all married, the two Ladys to two of the Richest & Handsomest of the little Masters as they used to play with at the castle of Pleasure & Delights; & Master George was married to a Little Miss that had the best sense, & the most good nature of any one there, & her that he admired the most the first time he went there. & Mr & Mrs Alworthy kept all their Weddings in a Very Genteel & Hansome manner & gave a vast deal of money away to their Poor Neighbours to buy new Cloaths for themselves & their poor Ragged Children so that all the Town & neighbourhood were Dress'd clean & neat, & rejoiced at their Wedding & pray'd to God to Bless & Prosper them in every thing, & God Almighty granted their Prayers & did Bless them in every thing, because they were very good, & said their Prayers & went to Church & behaved themselves Handsomely there, & were very good to poor people, & to every body, so they all Lived very happy, & Loved one another Dearly till they were very old men & women & then they all Died & went to Heaven to live with God Almighty & all the Good Angels for ever & ever. Amen.

For a devout Christian believer, this is the ultimate happy ending to the only kind of narrative that matters, the story of personal salvation. Deftly, Jane Johnson turns her Children's Progress into a prayer and a blessing. Then there is a footnote:

> This story was made in the year 1744 on purpose to tell Miss Barbara-Johnson & her Brother Master George-William-Johnson who took vast Delight in hearing it told over & over again a vast many times by Jane-Johnson.

Although it is possible to identify the cultural influences that acted upon Jane Johnson, we should not undervalue her originality. She boldly put her children into their own story, and, although her tale has a strong moral and didactic purpose deriving from a tradition of pious works, she has brilliantly combined this with some of the features of the recently translated and fashionable magical fairytales from France. This was a considerable achievement: she took features from stories deriving from two radically different cultures and transformed them into a new narrative expressing her care of her children's spiritual and moral well-being.

Most important of all, and totally missing from Richardson's rather self-conscious account, is the inimitable *oral* character in the language, its intimate and loving child-centred rhetoric. It seems clear that it originated as a 'told' story, or was written with the 'oral voice' in mind. In Newbery's publications there are inconsistencies of tone and an arbitrariness in the construction of the narratives; but in Jane Johnson's story there is a simple and sensible coherence centred entirely upon the two actual children it was made for. Their presence as listeners, and their needs as Christian children, seem to have guaranteed a unity in the telling. Two-and-a-half centuries later, her story gives us a sense of the authentic intimacy and affection which was a feature of her relationship with her two small children.

No one would dispute that we have in Jane Johnson's 1744 story an 'easy pleasant book suited to her children's capacity'. But in addition to paying tribute to her qualities as a mother and a story-teller, I believe we must reconsider the history of children's books in the eighteenth century. We need to take account of the fact that the translated fairytales were more widely read, and exerted perhaps a greater influence, than we have realized; and that for some reason there was in the 1740s a cultural focusing of interest upon education, and upon children and their reading – and that Samuel Richardson played a central part in this, along with John Newbery.

What remains uncertain is the extent to which Jane Johnson was exceptional – or whether there were hundreds of forgotten mothers creating living nursery cultures like hers. Almost certainly we must revise the old orthodoxy that children's literature began because a philosopher had an idea and a printer put it into practice. That view fails to take account of the powerful need of a developing print-based culture to take its materials from oral practices. We must begin instead to think of an abiding and continuous parental provision for the moral and social well-being of children, and an unrecorded tradition of adults writing and speaking to children that may go back centuries. It is likely that what occurred in the eighteenth century was not the 'beginning' of children's literature but the emergence into public scrutiny (literally the *public*-ation) of a traditional private and domestic nursery-culture – undervalued, orally transmitted from one generation to the next, responsive to changes in contemporary thinking, making a pragmatic use of available materials, and mostly sustained by mothers.

ACKNOWLEDGEMENT

I am grateful to the Bodleian Library for permission to quote from the Jane Johnson manuscript (MS. Don. d. 198).

NOTES

1 John Locke, *Some Thoughts Concerning Education*, eds John W. and Jean S. Yolton, (Clarendon Press, 1989), p. 211.
2 F.J. Harvey Darton, *Children's Books in England*, revised by Brian Alderson, (Cambridge University Press, 1982).
3 See [Richard Addison] *The Spectator*, No. 85, Thursday, June 7th, 1711: 'the old ballad of the *Two Children in the Wood* which is one of the Darling Songs of the Common People'. In fact the story had been registered in 1595 and was available as a chapbook story from c. 1700.
4 James Janeway, *A Token for Children* (published ?1672).
5 Marina Warner, *From the Beast to the Blonde: On Fairytales and their Tellers* (Chatto & Windus, 1994), p. 163.
6 *A Collection of Novels and Tales of the Fairies. Written by that celebrated Wit of France, the Countess D'Anois, vol. 1 The Royal Ram*, p. 29.
7 Ibid., vol. II, *The Story of Princess Carpillona*, pp. 186–7.
8 Ibid., vol. III, *The Fair Italian*, p. 104.
9 Ibid., p. 128.
10 Charles Perrault, *Histoires, ou Contes du temps passé, avec des Moralitez*, first published in 1697, translated by Robert Samber as *Histories, or Tales of Past Times* in 1729.
11 See Natalie Rothstein (ed.), *A Lady of Fashion: Barbara Johnson's Album of Styles and Fabrics* (Thames & Hudson, 1987).
12 Op. cit. vol. 1, *The Royal Ram*, p. 24.
13 Ibid, p. 30.
14 Ibid, *The Palace of Revenge*, p. 94
15 Ibid., vol. III, *The Fairy of Pleasures and the Cruel Amerdin*, p. 95.

16 Giovanni Paolo Marana, *Letters Writ by a Turkish Spy, who liv'd five and forty years undiscover'd at Paris...*, 1694, in 8 volumes, a 9th being attributed to Daniel Defoe.
17 Samuel Richardson, *Letters Written to and for particular friends on the most important occasions...*, 1741.
18 Samuel Richardson, *The Apprentice's Vade Mecum*, 1733.
19 Samuel Richardson, *Pamela: or Virtue Rewarded*, 1740/1.
20 By 1744, there had been ten editions of *Some Thoughts Concerning Education*, and four editions of the *Collected Works*.
21 Samuel Richardson, *Clarissa, Or the history of a young lady*, 1747/8.
22 Samuel Richardson, *Pamela: or Virtue Rewarded*. The edition quoted here is the Everyman (ed. Mark Kinkead-Weekes), 1974, Volume II, pp. 461–2.
23 Ibid., p. 463.

3

WOMEN TEACHING READING TO POOR CHILDREN IN THE SIXTEENTH AND SEVENTEENTH CENTURIES

Margaret Spufford

The historians of education sometimes seem still to be partially befogged by the last remaining tatters of an old myth that education for the poor really began with the Charity School movement. Although I hope to focus this chapter on the subject of women teaching both their own, and also other people's children to read, I wish first to blow away these remaining wisps of fog for good, if I can.

Brian Simon wrote a splendid article on 'Leicestershire Schools, 1625–40' as long ago as 1954.[1] When I wrote *Contrasting Communities*, which appeared in 1974, I mapped the references to masters teaching between 1570 and 1620,[2] when the episcopal licensing system was working well. These masters were licensed to a variety of functions, but very frequently to teach 'to write, read and caste an accompte'.[3] Girls, on the other hand, were normally taught 'only' to read, and those gainful occupations, knitting and spinning. One of the very rare school curricula we have for such a school, for Orwell in Cambridgeshire, specified boys were taught to read, write, and cast accounts, girls to read, sew, knit and spin.[4] I was astonished by what I found (see Figure 3.1). Schooling was available within walking distance all over much of the county of Cambridgeshire, although, since most of these schools were unendowed, it was an ephemeral business: the teachers were young men trying to stay alive, just down from university, and seeking their first benefice, here today and gone tomorrow. Oddly, though, the old market towns which today have village colleges also had permanent schooling: the Sawstons and the Lintons and the Swaveseys were not newly equipped when Henry Morris came along in the 1930s with his great new idea of schools that acted also as rural community centres.[5]

I thought Cambridgeshire might be abnormal; its proximity to Cambridge University made it obviously accessible to these young men. However, Peter Clark carried out a similar exercise for Kent in 1977[6] (see Figure 3.2). Cambridgeshire was not abnormal at all. Kent also had this pattern of sporadic, but commonly found, schooling, with some centres when it was always to be found. And we already had the Leicestershire evidence. So I would like at the start of this chapter to correct the persistent and erroneous notion that 'schooling for the poor' was a new phenomenon in the eighteenth century.[7] Indeed, it is beginning to seem likely that the S.P.C.K. Charity School movement adopted and set on firmer foundations village schools already in being in the seventeenth century.

The fog has, I hope, vanished. Yet there remain major difficulties with my subject of women teaching reading before 1700. I need to approach it via the schooldames who probably taught reading only, and who are not only elusive, here today and gone tomorrow, like the schoolmasters, but nearly, if not quite, impossible to find. This is because the Bishops, who ought to have licensed them, very rarely, if at all, did so. Mrs Karen Smith-Adams, during her period as a research-student in Cambridge, was working on midwives. They, like schoolmistresses, were supposed to have episcopal licences. She very kindly carried out a parallel search for schooldames for me. They are not, with highly unusual exceptions which she diligently collected, to be found in the ecclesiastical registers.[8] But we know they were there, working alongside mothers, teaching reading. The fullest example comes from outside my period. James Raine, who was indeed a very poor boy, son of a village blacksmith and a dressmaker, founder of the Surtees Society, wrote an autobiography which describes his early schooling, by schooldames and both his grandmothers between his birth in 1791, and 1797.[9] By the time he was six he was in the hands of a 'superior master', by which time, he wrote, 'for two or three preceding years I had been able to read almost anything that fell my way'.[10] He could already write too – and that was abnormal for a six-year-old. He had been taught that skill by a master, which was normal for England.[11] But what really interests us is how he had been introduced to print. In the mental worlds of his grandmothers, print and oral tales fused. The picture is necessarily confused, however, because his maternal grandmother, who was poor enough to live in an almshouse, was blind. She took 'a particular pleasure in teaching me Watts's Hymns, which I was not slow in committing to memory'. She had these by heart. But also 'many a tale would she tell me with a moral at its end'.[12] Despite her earlier extreme poverty as a wife, she had managed to send her daughter, James's mother, to school for a long period.

James's mother was a highly unusual girl, because she had learnt not only to read, as was normal for girls in England, but was also, in her son's words, 'the writer of a very beautiful hand, and an excellent arithmetician'. This was rare indeed.[13] James Raine describes her as the 'great scholar of the village, writing letters for fathers and mothers to their

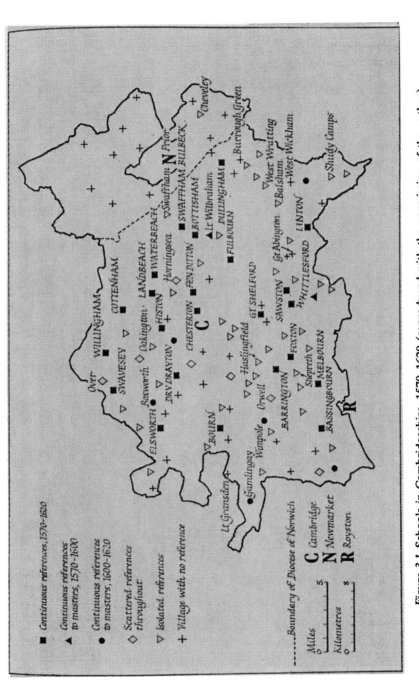

Figure 3.1 Schools in Cambridgeshire, 1570–1620 (reproduced with the permission of the author)

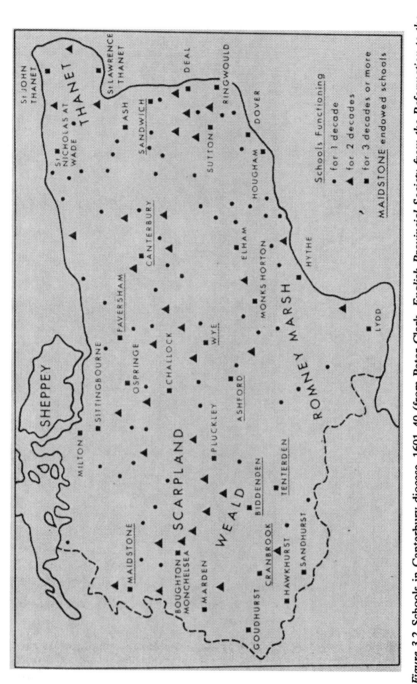

Figure 3.2 Schools in Canterbury diocese, 1601–40 (from Peter Clark, *English Provincial Society from the Reformation to the Revolution*, Harvester, reproduced with the permission of the author)

absent children and their relations'.[14] To our great loss, he simply assumes her effect on him and does not describe either the school she had gone to, or the help she undoubtedly must have given him. But he waxes lyrical about his paternal grandmother, by whose spinning-wheel he spent all the time he could as a very small child. She had few books, but two in particular caught his fancy: she had a 'life of Christ ornamented at the head of each chapter with a rude [i.e. crude] woodcut . . . It belonged to the earlier part of the seventeenth century. She also had a copy of Aesop's Fables, tattered and torn and imperfect, equally ornamented with woodcuts, over which I used to pore with infinite delight. This book . . . was of an earlier date.' But she also had an 'immense bundle of penny histories and ballads [so I] made myself intimately acquainted with giants, witches, fairies and their doings, and had the Seven Champions of Christendom and the ballads of Robin Hood at my fingers' ends.' But his grandmother had a 'very considerable' stock of tales, as well.[15] We are vividly reminded of the mental world of John Clare.[16]

James was formally taught his letters from a 'battledore', which had just taken over from the hornbook as the basic piece of first-reading equipment, by a schooldame in the village, with whom he remained for a year. He probably started at three and a half. Two other schooldames taught him next, both of whom were the wives of day-labourers. The second had been a maidservant before her marriage. Yet he makes it plain they did actually *teach*.[17] There is no ambiguity.

He went on to describe his teaching by two schoolmasters, beginning when he was still only five. The first, an ex-manual labourer,[18] worked in a tumbledown shack, covered with thatch and open to the roof. There he taught 20–25 boys and girls. By the time he was six, James had been taught to write, which was highly unusual.[19] The Dutch genre painter, Egbert van Heemskerk, whose paintings suddenly became so very popular in the 1680s and 1690s, painted such men at work (see Figure 3.3). So did his followers. They sold: they were of familiar, identifiable subjects. Again from the 1690s comes a piece of quantifiable evidence. The Brewers' Company of London ran a school at Aldenham, in Hertfordshire. Three times, in 1689, 1695 and 1708 a survey of the *reading*, not the writing, abilities of the incoming boys was carried out. It showed that together, out of the 127 boys covered, 10 per cent of the incoming 3 and 4-year-olds could read, but almost one-third of the 5-year-olds and just over half of the 6-year-olds could.[20]

Now, if children as young as 3, 4 and 5 years old were reading, the argument that some of them had been taught by their mothers is a very likely one. Of course, it is just possible that they had come in to the Aldenham school via a schooldame. Dr Samuel Johnson, no less, was taught to read by a woman before going to the Free Grammar School at Lichfield. He bitterly repented, as many others did, that as a boy 'he was

Figure 3.3 Egbert van Heemskerk: *Schoolroom*, present location unknown (reproduced with the permission of the Courtauld Institute, the University of London)

inordinately fond of reading romances of chivalry'. They sold well on his bookseller-father's stall at Uttoxeter market.

In the 1690s, too, the then Bishop of Lichfield had a highly eccentric survey made of his own manor of Eccleshall, in Staffordshire, which lay surrounding its own little market town. The insight this survey gives us of the women who taught reading in it is unusual: the pity of it is that we cannot tell, for lack of other evidence, whether the women were unusual, or only the insight. For they were not women from the higher social orders at all: they were labourers' wives, who had this skill to sell to help them eke out the family budget. One of them 'Stephen Dimock's wife' was the wife of a day-labourer living on the common. Thomas Alsop's wife, 'the best knitter in my parish', a valuable gainful skill she would have taught girls, was also the wife of a day-labourer. 'Barnet's wife' was married to a shoemaker, and 'Curly Wollam's wife' was married to a labourer who thrashed and thatched part-time, was a weaver the rest of the time, and earned the Bishop's approval as a 'very honest man, laborious and religious, sings Psalms in Church'. It is highly improbable that all these schooldames merely acted as childminders, which is one aspersion commonly thrown at them.[21] We have already seen that the day-labourers' wives who taught James Raine were not. Without any extrapolation through time, the shop of the Eccleshall mercer, Jeffrey Snelson, which would have supplied these women at the time, carried a large number of hornbooks (see Figure 3.4) and primers.[22]

No one who runs a business keeps useless stock. Also, inspection of the wills of Eccleshall people shows that a larger proportion than normal of poorer men went on to learn the ancillary skill of writing there. There is also a thesis in progress which, very excitingly, shows the enormous volume of hornbooks and ABCs being produced by the monopolists, the Stationers' Company, after the Restoration.[23] From these numbers, England was saturated with the basic equipment for learning to read: and once again, the Stationers' Company was a hard-nosed company, in business to make profits, not losses. We saw the fruits in Aldenham School, in those 3-, 4- and 5-year-olds who could read. And lastly, there are just too many odd anecdotes, casual, incidental comments, demonstrating, by accident, that yet one more child had learnt to read from a woman, before going to a formal school. Oliver Sansom, a yeoman of Berkshire, was one of these. He was born in 1636, and wrote:

> when I was about six years of age, I was put to school to a woman, who finding me not unapt to learn, forwarded me so well that in about four months time, I could read a chapter in the Bible pretty readily.[24]

It may be that this Berkshire woman was more able than her counterpart in Yorkshire who taught James Fretwell, the son of a timber merchant born right at the end of the seventeenth century: or it may just be that James Fretwell's mother was a more ambitious parent. For, James later wrote:

> As soon as I was capable of learning [my mother] sent me to an

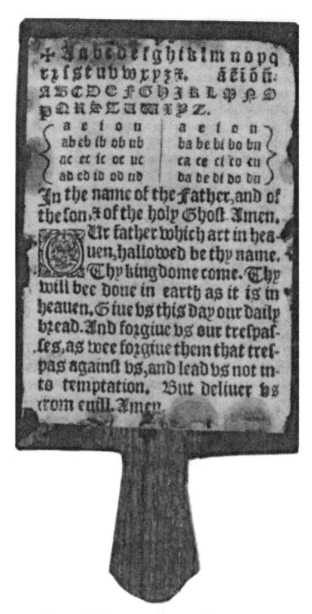

Figure 3.4 Seventeenth-century hornbook

old schooldame, who lived at the very next door. But I suppose I did not continue here but a few days, for growing weary of my book, and my dame not correcting me as my mother desired, she took me under her as pedagogy until I could read the Bible, *and thus she did afterwards by all my brothers and sisters* [emphasis added].[25]

So we reach the heart of the matter. Jane Johnson, gentlewoman, was not alone in the 1730s and she did not, by any means, set a precedent. Mrs Fretwell of Yorkshire was a highly successful teacher. When James was only four and a half he was admitted to the small local grammar school

> my dear mother being desirous that I should have a little more learning than she was capable of giving me ... when the master placed me among some little ones, such as myself ... when he called me up to hear what I had to say for myself, he ... removed me higher, asking my mother whether she had brought me an Accidence, which I think she had; so she had the pleasure of seeing me removed out of the horn-book class

It is hard to find other examples like Mrs Fretwell, teaching all her children. But Thomas Tryon, born in 1641, who is in so many ways the best example we have of seventeenth-century literacy, was not only the poorest boy, son of a Gloucestershire tiler and plasterer, to write his *Autobiography* (*and* wrote the most detailed and vivid account of how he learnt to read *from his own workmates*),[26] but also tantalizes us further, for he went on to write a series of treatises which are fascinating, set in the context of this poor background. One of them gives us the most mouth-watering glimpse of a whole possible group of mothers teaching reading.

Tryon founded a religious sect. He wrote not only a treatise called *A New Method of Education*, but probably was also the 'TT' who, together with 'GF' and 'GC' also produced *The Compleat School Master or Child's Instructor* of 1700. In the 'Principles' for his religious group, he wrote a section called 'Laws and Orders proper for Women to observe', giving them detailed directions on how they should teach their young children to read, pleasurably. 'Pleasure' in education was extremely important to him.

> At a Year and a Half or Two Years Old, shew them their Letters, not troubling them in the vulgar way with asking them what is this Letter, or that Word; but instead thereof, make frequent Repetitions in their hearing, putting the Letters in their Sight. And thus, in a little time, they will easily and familiarly learn to distinguish the Twenty Four Letters, all one as they do the Utensils, Goods, and

Furniture of the House, by hearing the Family name them. At the same time, teach your Children to hold the Pen, and guide their Hand; [this is, of course, extraordinary for the seventeenth century, when writing began at seven] and by this method, your Children, un-accountably to themselves, will attain to Read and Write at Three, Four, or Five years old...[27]

So, if these women actually carried their instructions out, there were women in the 1680s and 1690s who were building up their own little collections of seventeenth-century 'flash cards' and materials to teach their children to read, forty years at least before Jane Johnson. Maybe, some day, someone will find another shoebox, complete with the contents from a slightly different social background and an earlier period. It is by no means impossible. James Raine's grandmother had had a collection spanning two centuries.

*

So, if schooldames and mothers taught reading, what was there available to read, after the ubiquitous hornbook and primer, which always taught the child the basic tenets of religion, as well as reading?

Evidence mounts up to show that the 1620s marked a revolution in the cheap print trade. The ballad had existed for well over a century in affordable form. Now the chapbooks made their appearance as a genre, both those called 'small merries' and those called 'small godlies'.[28] So also did the serial newsbook.[29] Not only did the Ballad Partnership form, to market these things: even the Worshipful Company of Playing Card Makers made its first appearance. This is more serious a matter than it sounds: playing-cards were ubiquitous, and used by all social groups. They made alphabetical symbols familiar, they spread political news and satire as the 'Armada' pack and the Rump Parliament pack did, and pilloried famous persons and types, as the 'South Sea Bubble' pack did. They also educated: they made familiar the form of the map, both in John Ogilby's pack of 1676, and the 'New England' pack.

However horrified she might have been by playing-cards, even out of service time, we know the basic books Hannah Gifford taught from in the school newly established by the reforming Dorchester Corporation in the town Hospital. They set up Hannah there to teach in 1651, with the very considerable salary of £10 a year for less than thirty children, £12 if there were more. She was still there in 1668, and for most, if not all, of that time, she had been paid £12 a year. The most exciting thing is that we know something of her teaching material. In 1658, she was sent bibles, testaments, primers 'and other small books' to the value of £3.5s.7d by the local bookseller.[30] In May 1666, she was supplied with twelve hornbooks at 1d each, thirteen Primers at 3d each, eleven single

Psalters at 1/- each and eight Testaments at 1/6d each. The total was £1.7s.3d. At the end of April 1668, the local bookseller was paid for six hornbooks at 1d each, twelve Primers at 3d each, nine single Psalters at a total of 10/6 and nine Testaments at a total of 15/-.[31] It was, as I have said elsewhere, impossible to learn to read without being also taught the basics of religious belief: this was true quite separately from the Puritan nature of this school, the woman who ran it, and the Corporation which set it up. What we long to know is what were those 'other small books' of 1658? Did Goody Gifford permit her most virtuous pupils a glimpse of a 'small godly book' as a reward? Dr Michael Frearson's important evidence of the book-list of a 'godly' shoemaker in the 1620s is relevant here: *The Rich Cabinet* and *A Godly Garden of Comfortable Hearbes* and *Smug the Smith*[32] do not all sound forbidding. There was an ingenious plea in the 'Preface' to the chapbook *The Wise Mistresses*,[33] that

> History ought to be praised, not condemned; for it doth encourage Youth through the pleasantness of the Story, whereby he doth sooner attain to his English Tongue, and is still more desirous to read further. For many thousands at School, in their innocency, are more naturally given to learn first Historical Fables, by which they sooner come to read perfect, then to begin first in hard Books appertaining to Divine knowledge; which made that rare and learned Scholar Æsop, to put forth his Fables in the Schools, which being composed with such incomparable and acute Wit, Jeast and Merriment, that each Scholar daily strove who should outvie the other in the Dispute and Rehearsal of them.[34]

This may not have appealed to Goody Gifford, but is it perhaps possible that Aesop's *Fables* might have passed her guardianship? We have already seen[35] what an effect a seventeenth-century copy of Aesop had on little James Raine: one large enough, indeed to justify this selling hyperbole.

We have scattered references all through the century to the reading matter beloved of the poor. It was picked from the whole medley of what was available. Young Richard Baxter repented of the love of 'romances, fables and old tales' which had 'corrupted his affections' in the 1630s. We know James Raine's grandmothers had collected a seventeenth-century book illustrated with woodcuts, as well as the hymns of Isaac Watts, which he was circulating in the late seventeenth century,[36] as well as a heap of ballads. The Old Testament was more popular than the New amongst seventeenth-century children, just as it is amongst twentieth-century children: young Thomas Boston was ashamed to recollect that nothing had moved him to read the Bible when he was seven but 'curiosity, as about the history of Balaam's ass'.[37] He hid underneath the bedclothes with it, and a candle-end. London schoolboys swapped the whole corpus of romances later collected by Samuel Pepys. Older, print-starved poor men were held captive by tougher meat. One pitiable unhinged journeyman, Arise Evans, stopped his walk from the Black Mountains to London at Coventry for six months, simply because the master he found there had a copy of a *History of the World*, which he wished to get by heart. The passion for print could consume these readers.

Women were affected as well as men. I have used my favourite character, Sister Sneesby, the Cambridgeshire Quaker who earned her living by day-labour in her widowhood, too often.[38] But she was such a shining example because she was deaf, and was converted from her General Baptist beliefs to Quakerism, in the 1650s, by what I myself found a peculiarly indigestible Quaker tract. Let me hastily set up against her Widow Robinson, who caused deep offence to her Open Baptist brethren by singing 'carnal' songs and dancing on the table, at the shoe-makers' feast fifty years or so later.[39] I don't know whether it was the contents of her ballads, which were almost certainly taken from print at that date, or dancing on a table when high-flown with ale that gave offence – but she should be noted, in case women are only thought to be readers of pious material.[40]

Let me finish with John Bunyan. For John Bunyan also repented his early reading, and gives us the best list, probably from the 1640s, of any of those who did so. He had, he wrote, thought

> give me a Ballad, a News-book, *George on Horseback* [a quarto chivalric romance – see Figure 3.5] or *Bevis of Southampton*, give me some book that touches curious Arts, that tells of old Fables: but for the Holy Scriptures, I cared not. And as it is with me then, so it is with my brethren now.[41]

Apart from covering the whole spectrum of cheap print that I outlined for you earlier, and thereby demonstrating it did percolate to the lowest social levels, the most telling thing about this quotation is the simple, easily overlooked statement *'so it is with my brethren now'* (my italics). My 'brethren' were presumably not Bunyan's own flock of Bedfordshire Open Baptists – who were, incidentally, the poorest group of post-Resto-ration dissenters we know about[42] – but his fellow-villagers and relations round about Bedford in the 1660s when he wrote the autobiography from which this quotation comes. Such stuff was common in men's – and women's – reading.[43]

In the circumstances, it becomes highly significant that John Bunyan wrote one of the first books deliberately aimed at children. His emblem book, *A Book for Boys and Girls or Country Rhimes for Children*, came out in 1686. My ignorance of the field is too great for me to say it was the first deliberate attempt to write suitable substitution literature for children, instead of all the fanciful histories John Bunyan and others had

THE
Life and Death
OF THE
Famous CHAMPION
O F
ENGLAND,
St. GEORGE.

Pinted by J. M. for J. Clarke, W. Thackeray and T. Passinger.

Figure 3.5 St George on Horseback (reproduced with the permission of Dr Richard Luckett, The Pepys Library, Magdelene College, Cambridge)

reported reading with such monotonous regularity. But it must have been one of the first.

However, the very concept of 'children's books' becomes suspect, and possibly meaningless, when the first version of *Tom Thumb* had been printed in 1621, and all the chivalrics that entranced young Bunyan, as well as the extraordinary *Old Women of Ratcliffe Highway*, which uniquely competed with Lewis Carroll for sheer nonsense, were in print.

So I will leave you with a picture of schooling relatively readily available, schooldames and mothers actively teaching the rudiments, a semi-literate society able to read, if not write, gulping up new trash from the presses. And perhaps amongst these people were the forebears of Jane Johnson, like Mrs Fretwell, diligently teaching their own offspring, and perhaps indeed collecting suitable material for teaching reading, just as Thomas Tryon advocated. There is 'very little new beneath the visiting moon'.

NOTES

1 Brian Simon, 'Leicestershire Schools, 1625–40', *British Jo. of Ed. Studies* III (1954), pp. 42–58.
2 Margaret Spufford, *Contrasting Communities* (1974), Map II, p. 185.
3 Margaret Spufford, 'The Schooling of the Peasantry in Cambridgeshire, 1575–1700', *Land, Church and People: Essays Presented to H.P.R. Finberg*, ed. Joan Thirsk (Reading: British Agricultural History Society 1970) p. 127. 'Casting an accompte' was the skill of arithmetic, taught by using counters on a cloth, board, or table marked in squares. It was also known as 'reckoning'. There is a rare survival of a very grand reckoning table in the city of Basle. 'Ciphering' was the much greater skill of using written arabic numerals. Continental teachers charged more to teach the latter. See Margaret Spufford, 'Literacy, Trade and Religion in the Commercial Centres of Europe', *A Miracle Mirrored: The Dutch Republic in European Perspective*, eds Karel Davids and Jan Lucassen (Cambridge, 1996), pp. 254–5, 265, 266–7 and n. 91, p. 277. For the importance of the earning capacity given by knitting and spinning, which might indeed keep a labouring family afloat and off the poor-rates, see Margaret Spufford and James Went, *Poverty Portrayed: Gregory King and the Parish of Eccleshall*, ed. Robin Studd (Keele, 1996), Table III, p. 63, and discussion on labouring women's work, pp. 64–6.
4 Spufford, *Contrasting Communities*, p. 203, n. 32.
5 Nikolaus Pevsner, *Cambridgeshire*, 2nd edn (Harmondsworth, 1970), pp. 413, 454.
6 Peter Clark, *English Provincial Society from the Reformation to the Revolution: Religion, Politics and Society in Kent, 1500–1640* (Hassocks, 1977), Maps 4 and 5, pp. 202, 203.
7 For the medieval period, see J.A.H. Moran, *The Growth of English Schooling, 1340–1598* (1985); and Nicholas Orme, *Education in the West of England, 1066–1548* (Exeter, 1976) and *English Schools in the Middle Ages* (London, 1973).
8 Margaret Spufford, ed., *The World of Rural Dissenters, 1520–1725* (Cambridge, 1995), pp. 67–8, n. 230. David Cressy in his vast thesis 'Education and Literacy

in London and East Anglia, 1580–1700' (Cambridge Ph.D., 1973) which lies behind his *Literacy and the Social Order: Reading and Writing in Tudor and Stuart England* (Cambridge, 1980) also found very few licensed schooldames in his exhaustive initial study. Professor Cressy's opinion that schooldames were often merely childminders probably lies behind much received wisdom. However, English schooldames were undoubtedly called on to do much less than those in the Low Countries (see n. 13).

9 James Raine was born in 1791 and had a 'village' education until he went to weekly boarding grammar school in 1804. 'A Raine Miscellany', ed. Angela Marsden, *Surtees Society*, CC (1989).

10 Ibid., p. 45.

11 Ibid., p. 43.

12 Ibid., p. 17.

13 Poor English girls were not officially taught, nor did schooldames teach, arithmetic. This is a very strong contrast with, for instance, the Low Countries. In Antwerp, after the decline set in, from 1595–1645, 122 men and 120 women teaching were examined on their skills. Thirty-three per cent of the men and 45 per cent of the women taught 'only' Dutch reading *and writing*: I have yet to find a single seventeenth-century woman teaching writing in England. But, much more remarkably, 38 per cent of the men, and as many as 25 per cent of the women, taught *arithmetic*. This was utterly unheard of in England: see Spufford, 'Literacy, Trade and Religion', pp. 253–4, 258, 259–61 and Plate 8.2. Note that in a Utrecht orphanage, the girls were apparently taught writing from 1600, as well as reading. Girls in Amersfoort Sunday School may very well have been taught arithmetic, as well as reading and writing.

14 Ibid., pp. 31–2.

15 Ibid., pp. 14–15.

16 Margaret Spufford, *Small Books and Pleasant Histories: Popular Fiction and its Readership in Seventeenth-century England* (London, 1981), pp. 3–6.

17 'A Raine Miscellany', pp. 36–41.

18 In 1606 in the Isle of Ely, Edward Browne 'labourer' faced the Ecclesiastic Court for 'teaching of Children without any licence.' His wife was accused with him. The pair were dismissed, Ely DR, B/2/66, fol. 121v. I owe this reference to the kindness of Dr Christopher Marsh.

19 'A Raine Miscellany', pp. 41–6.

20 I am greatly indebted to Dr Roger Schofield, who worked out the figures for me (personal communication) from an unpublished paper of Newman Brown's, held at the Cambridge Group for the History of Population and Social Structure. It is possible that the distribution of reading skills was much greater in wood-pasture areas: see Spufford, *The World of Rural Dissenters, 1520–1725*, pp. 44–7, elaborated on in Spufford and Went, *Poverty Portrayed*, pp. 50–2.

21 See, for instance, David Underdown, *Fire from Heaven* (London, 1992), p. 225. Professor Underdown is merely repeating a received wisdom, see above, n. 8.

22 Spufford and Went, *Poverty Portrayed*.

23 Helen Weinstein, 'Rudimentary Religion and National Identity in Late Seventeenth Century England' (Cambridge Ph.D in progress, 1996).

24 Quoted in Spufford, *Small Books*, p. 24.

25 Ibid., p. 24.

26 His account of learning to read and write and the prices of primers and hornbooks may be found in full in Spufford, *The World*, pp. 68–70.

27 *Some Memoirs of the Life of Mr Tho: Tryon, late of London, merchant: written by himself...* (1705), pp. 117–18, 122–3.
28 Tessa Watt, *Cheap Print and Popular Piety, 1550–1640* (Cambridge, 1991). David Harrison, Roehampton Institute London, has completed a Ph.D. (1996) on the antecedents of the chapbooks.
29 Michael Frearson, 'The English Corantos of the 1620s' (Cambridge Ph.D., 1994, to appear in the Cambridge *History of the Book* series, ed. David McKitterick).
30 Underdown, *Fire from Heaven*, pp. 225–6.
31 I am particularly grateful to Professor Underdown, who took the trouble to look these lists of books and prices out for me from his collection of materials.
32 Spufford, *The World*, p. 53. I am much indebted to Dr Frearson for allowing me to use this important find of his.
33 Thomas Howard, *The Wise Mistresses*, Penny Merriments, III(6), p. 634, (Pepys Library, Magdalene College, Cambridge).
34 Preface to Thomas Howard, *The Wise Mistresses*, Penny Merriments, III(6), p. 634.
35 See p. 51.
36 Spufford, *The World*, p. 95.
37 Spufford, *Small Books*, pp. 25, 73.
38 Spufford, *Contrasting Communities*, pp. 216–17 and n. 39, and *The World*, p. 64.
39 Spufford, *The World*, p. 86, n. 297.
40 Ibid.
41 Spufford, *Small Books*, p. 7.
42 Bill Stevenson, 'The Social and Economic Status of Post-Restoration Dissenters, 1660–1725', in Margaret Spufford, *The World*, pp. 334–6 and Table 9.
43 See also David Harrison, *An Ancestral Subject Catalogue of Chapbook Themes* (Scolar Press, 1996), an invaluable finding-aid to scholars interested in the topics available to those who could read.

Part II

'SOME EASY PLEASANT BOOK'

4

SAMUEL RICHARDSON'S *AESOP*

David Whitley

In 1740 a small, rather unobtrusive looking volume of Aesop's fables was published by the then little-known printer Samuel Richardson. This in itself was not a remarkable event. New collections of Aesop had been published every decade – several editions in some decades – for at least a hundred years before this date. The event – if we can bestow so grand a title upon it – has called forth very little comment from modern literary historians and scholars. John Rowe Townsend notes it in passing in his history of children's literature.[1] An article was published in *Smith College Studies in Modern Languages* in 1938 which makes a case for its importance in terms of Richardson's development as a writer. Otherwise there has been little interest.[2] It is not even mentioned in Harvey Darton's compendious and authoritative history.[3]

In some ways this neglect is perhaps not surprising. Richardson's *Aesop* is not in any ordinary sense an original work. It is a scaled-down version of Sir Roger L'Estrange's grand folio edition of Aesop's fables, published some fifty years earlier, and although only a proportion of the fables from this source are selected, Richardson retains much of the text of the original verbatim. Yet, scrutinized with more care, I want to show that Richardson's *Aesop* is actually much more than a straightforward abridgement of an earlier work. Far from being unoriginal, Richardson's *Aesop* shows a quite remarkable quality of thought and engagement with key issues in the development of literature for children.

Aesop was published in the same year as Richardson's notorious first novel, *Pamela*, and marks a point of transition in his own writing from work dominated by the advice format of the conduct-book tradition to writing centred more strongly on fictional narrative. Although the collection of Aesopic fables which constitute the 1740 volume is not his own invention, the distinctive turn which he gave to the project showed a developing awareness that even exemplary narratives could be complex and multilevelled. Perhaps even more important, though, is the relationship between this collection of fables and the fully fledged tradition of stories published distinctively for children which was about to emerge. Not only does Richardson's *Aesop* have much to tell us about the debates which surround the emergence of such new forms: it is also a remarkable contribution to the emerging tradition of writing for children in its own terms.

But before diving in to define the key terms of these debates, I need first to challenge one or two common assumptions that are likely to hinder any such enquiry. The first assumption we must put to one side – if not stand on its head – is the notion that fables, because of their long-standing association with pedagogy and schools, were a relatively safe, uncontroversial form which could be included in an unproblematic way in any newly constituted corpus of literature specifically designed for children. Like most useful myths this one has a grain of truth in it. The animal fable was, after all, virtually the only narrative form singled out by John Locke as inherently suitable for children. He formed this judgement on the grounds that Aesop's fables in particular were 'stories apt to delight and entertain a child' and would thus 'draw him on, and reward his Pains in Reading'. By implication, Aesop's fables would also avoid the potential dangers of other stories a child might be drawn to for entertainment, which could 'fill his Head with perfectly useless trumpery, or lay the principles of Vice and Folly'.[4] Also, the familiarity of the most popular fables, their near proverbial standing, and the well-honed moralizing tradition that surrounded them would seem to make them an innocent enough genre on which to ground children's developing knowledge and understanding. Yet we need to remind ourselves that this is only a partial view of the fable tradition. For not only had the Aesopic corpus been stretched extremely wide by the time Locke was writing (and had indeed always included a substantial amount of 'popular' material of an obscene or scatological nature), it also formed part of an overtly partisan, highly politicized discourse of writing and public oratory which, recent scholars in particular have been keen to argue, was running at its fullest tide during the course of the seventeenth century.[5] Far from being safe for children in any morally worthy, unproblematic way, then, the Aesopic fable stood at the centre of some of the most heated political, social and religious debates within seventeenth-century culture.

The second common assumption that deserves rescrutinizing is the notion that no separate category of *story* existed for children before Newbery's publishing enterprises took shape in the mid-1740s. As John Rowe Townsend puts it, prior to this date 'no distinction was made between stories for adults and children'. Victor Watson's chapter on the sophistication and range of influences brought together in Jane Johnson's story should itself sound a note of caution as to whether this view can any longer be held without qualification (see Chapter 2).

At first sight, however, the genre of the Aesopic fable would appear to be virtually a *locus classicus* within which the view that children had no narratives of their own might be held to be exemplified. The same stories, after all, turned up in the increasingly lavish folio collections clearly designed for an adult readership as appeared in the school primers that were the texts upon which generations of children practised their basic skills in Latin. But although the plots of the stories may be the same, it is apparent from at least the middle of the seventeenth century onwards that there was an increasing awareness of the different needs of child and adult readerships. And from the end of the seventeenth century this awareness manifested itself – more positively – as a wish to cater for the specific needs of child readers. The terms on which this should take place then began to be very actively debated. The collections of fables which came out of such enterprises may not be as consistently child-centred as Jane Johnson's unpublished story, but they established many of the most important principles that informed a separate category of literature for children when this eventually emerged into daylight. No one brought these principles to bear on the tradition of fable writing more comprehensively and with more careful reflection than Samuel Richardson.

*

Before looking in more detail at the ways in which Richardson brings these principles into coherent focus however, we need to trace something of the form in which such ideas begin to emerge and the kinds of debates that surround them. A good starting point for such an investigation are the prefaces to the collections of fables which precede Richardson's *Aesop*. It is particularly illuminating in this context to review the attitudes contained in humbler editions of the fables which have, in the past, received relatively little attention. For here the intention to serve the needs of a child readership was in fact more consistently, if uneasily, expressed than in the grander productions. Arguably from the middle of the seventeenth century one can see a pattern emerging in which a major new collection of fables, when published, set new standards for lavish production and literary quality and was then followed by a series of humbler editions designed to cater for other needs and readerships. I offer below a list of the editions I shall refer to in arguing that such a pattern exists: I have marked the editions which were recognized as setting new benchmarks for quality in bold type to differentiate them from the more minor collections which followed:

1651 **John Ogilby, *The Fables of Aesop, paraphras'd in verse, and adorn'd with sculpture.***

1673 *Aesop Improved or Above three hundred and fifty fables, mostly Aesop's, with their morals, paraphrased in English verse.*

1692 **Sir Roger L'Estrange, *Fables of Aesop and other eminent mythologists: with morals and reflections.***

1703 (John Locke – disputed attribution) *Aesop's Fables in English and Latin, interlineary.*

1708 J.J. (Joseph Jackson) *A New Translation of Aesop's Fables.*

1722 Samuel Croxall, *Fables of Aesop and others, newly done into English with an application to each fable.*

1740 Samuel Richardson, *Aesop's Fables. With instructive morals and reflections.*

The most important of the early lavish editions is undoubtedly the collection first published by John Ogilby in 1651. Ogilby was a staunch Royalist supporter. He served in Ireland within the household of the Wentworth family and wrote a – now lost – Royalist epic called the *Carolies*. His rise, in career terms, faltered during the Interregnum but he was reclaimed by the Restoration court to a position of very considerable prestige and eminence. His collection of fables was produced as an expensive folio edition with fine engravings (illustrations for the later editions were by Francis Barlow) and he gave the stories an overtly Royalist twist. Aesop's stories had always been – at least potentially – an oppositional form. In the period within which his own party had lost power, Ogilby was able to give a new twist to this tradition by reinventing the fable as a 'vehicle for protest and solidarity for the Royalist nobility and gentry who seemed to have lost the war and certainly, with the execution of Charles I in 1649, lost their leader'.[6]

John Ogilby's 'Preface' begins with a recognition of a workaday Aesop 'whose Apologs this day are read and familiar with children in their first Schools'. But then, taking up the theme that 'in these latter times [the fables are] dishonoured by unworthy translators' he cites an august list of readers, interpreters and imitators of the fables, going back to Socrates, to establish its high philosophical credentials. Clearly this is not a volume which, in any ordinary sense of the word, is designed for children. Indeed, although it begins by recognizing the common space which it shares with literary work for children, the main thrust of the Preface is to distance the work from its association with children as far – and as high – as possible.

Humbler editions of the Fables which followed Ogilby's collection reveal a strong need to establish a different niche from Ogilby's within which to assert their value. A 1673 edition *Aesop Improved or Above three hundred and fifty fables, mostly Aesop's with their morals, paraphrased in English verse*, for instance, makes much of the fact that, though smaller in size than the benchmark Ogilby text, and lacking its exquisite illustrations, it far outstrips its august predecessor in terms of the quantity of fables offered. The anonymous author seems indeed to be inordinately proud of this feature of his edition.

He starts by seeming to shadow Ogilby's line of argument, but with a much clearer assertion that a joint readership of both children and adults is perfectly acceptable:

> Men and children may read the same books, but for different ends and purposes. Men may read those books for their profundity which children read for their pleasantness. Or men may read the same books for their solidity, wisdom and judgement, which is in them, which children are taught meerly for their fancy, stile and language. Doubtless the famous Oglesby had never provided so elaborate a translation for but 120 fables, or thereabouts, or found encouragement to print but such a number in two volumes, with excellent sculptures at a very great charge, if notwithstanding the seeming prostitution of that book to the use of children, it had not had a very great esteem amongst the wiser sort of mankind.

That 'seeming prostitution' appears to betray a deep-rooted ambivalence underlying the apparently easy accommodation of child and adult readerships in the opening assertions. The author goes on to reinforce this 'very great esteem' in which the fables are held by their adult readership in similar manner to Ogilby, citing as examples Socrates and others. He then moves back to considering children as readers in a very distinctive manner:

> All which things consider'd, no man's profession can be too grave, solemn or sacred to permit him the reading, translating, or improving of Aesop's Fables. Yet I myself, I think, should hardly have done it, had I not been constrained to concern myself for sometime with the education of youth and thereby invited to it, both for their advantage, and my own diversion.

The word 'constrained' here seems to match 'prostitution' in the earlier passage, marking a point of particularly uneasy convergence between the projects of writing for adults and children.

As the author moves on it becomes clear that he is distancing himself from the claims of the Ogilby edition at the same time as paying homage to it. In so doing he is seeking to define new criteria which will distinguish his edition in a positive sense from Ogilby's, without diminishing the latter's claim to fame. He settles on price and easy comprehensibility, criteria which will become increasingly important in establishing a literature distinctively aimed at children. Ogilby's translation, he tells us

> is incomparably good, for such as can reach the sense and the price of it ... but certainly to understand so lofty a poem as that is, requires a better capacity and more skill in poetical phrases and fictions than the generality of those who are willing to read Aesop's Fables are endowed with ... And doubtless the price of his two excellent folios ... doth as much exceed most men's purses, as the

style and language thereof doth their capacities. Moreover there are
not above 132 fables of that excellent translation, whereas the book
which is now in thy hand containeth about 350.

More is definitely better! Finally though, again in contrast to Ogilby,
he justifies his choice of verse as making the fables easier to remember
– firstly, 'common experience shewing us that it is easier for men (and to
be sure for children) to remember metre than prose' and, secondly,
to 'insinuate grave sense into the minds of young and old with more
delight and pleasure.'

The publication of a second major 'landmark' edition, produced by Sir
Roger L'Estrange in 1692, was countered in a similar way in a series of
humbler editions within which a different sense of readership was articulated. L'Estrange, like Ogilby, gave his Fables a strong Royalist slant. Just
as the authority of Ogilby's edition cast its shadow over subsequent
productions, so too the collections which follow L'Estrange's tend to
relate themselves to the terms within which his was presented. A good
example of this tendency can be seen in *A New Translation of Aesop's
Fables*, published in 1708 by an author who signs himself 'J.J.' (probably
Joseph Jackson), adding the ascription 'Gent' to affirm his status as a
gentleman. Here though, the sense of a readership amongst young people
and children for whom the volume is designed is much less ambivalently
spelled out.

The aim of the *New Translation* is stated uncompromisingly on the title
page as 'being rendered in a Plain, Easy and Familiar style, adapted to
the Meanest Capacities'. L'Estrange's achievement is then both valued
and critiqued in similar terms to Ogilby's earlier: the author acknowledges
the 'high desert and equal applause' which L'Estrange's 'elaborate pile
of fable work' has justly earned. But he continues with the judgement
that, however, Lestrange's volume

> is swell'd too big for the purse of every common purchaser, and
> even his very Reflections, tho' so wonderfully ingenious, too much
> lengthened out for the reading, at least the capacity and apprehen-
> sion of youth; insomuch that his Book of Morals seems rather
> designed for part of the furniture of a statesman's closet, than the
> satchel of a school-boy; and consequently has not so fully attained
> the chief aim of their publication viz. the Instruction of Youth.

The new translation is designed to correct these 'faults' and is therefore
'set forth at a moderate price, to give it a larger currency' and attempts
to strike a happy balance 'betwixt the coarseness and grossness of the
former vulgar translations of Aesop, and the over-polite labour of Sir
Roger; as hoping the shorter comprehension of the true moral to each
fable may give it an easier reception into the understanding, or at least

root it deeper in the memory of every juvenile reader'. Illustrations are added to 'gain it a yet more favourable acceptance from every young hand'.

Three key issues have now begun to emerge as crucial if a positive emphasis is to be given to the project of fable writing specifically for children: style, price and, if possible, illustrations. Although there remains some doubt about the attribution, it is possible that John Locke put his recommendation of Aesop for children into practice with the publication in 1703 of *Aesop's Fables in English and Latin, interlineary, for the benefit of those who, not having a master, would learn either of these tongues.* Whether or not Locke personally supervised this project, the preface certainly brings together the main elements that were now beginning to distinguish writing which was consciously oriented towards a child readership. Interestingly, here though the 'plain style' is presented apologetically as a necessarily clumsy constituent of a volume whose principal aim is functional: for the untutored to be able to grasp basic elements of Latin.

> The English of these Fables cannot be expected to be very good, it being intended verbally to answer the Latin as much as possibly it could, the better to obtain the end for which this translation was made.
> There is added to this, the pictures of the several beasts treated of in these fables, to make it still more taking to children, and make the deeper impression of the same upon their minds.

The illustrations which accompany this text win high praise from Harvey Darton as being designed with a clarity and simplicity which, for the first time he argues, make them genuinely suitable for children.[7] Yet, though they are indeed striking, they are not designed to aid a child reader's engagement with the meaning of the narrative. Rather they have a mnemonic function, meant to aid recall of key animal participants in the stories in an iconic mode (see Figure 4.1). They are very different in kind as well as manner from the illustrations Samuel Richardson chose to include with his text which, though more cluttered, generally seek to interpolate central features of the narrative (see Figure 4.2).

*

Having traced the terms in which a debate was taking place as to the *form* collections of fables should take if they were to successfully engage children's attention, I want to turn now to consider the more contentious arguments which surrounded the content of Aesop's stories. It is here that the debate becomes consciously, and quite explicitly, ideological. The main contenders in the first stage of this debate are, in the 'right' corner, the heavyweight L'Estrange, and in the 'left', lighter but with a vicious line in polemic, an exponent of the Whig cause called Samuel Croxall.

71

Figure 4.1 From John Locke(?), *Aesop's Fables in English and Latin, interlineary* (1703; reproduced by permission of the Syndics of Cambridge University Library)

Croxall published an edition of the fables in 1722 with the avowed aim of countering, indeed reversing, what he saw as the appalling ideological bias of his grand predecessor. The terms within which he seeks to reappropriate the Aesopic tradition for what he calls the 'cause of Liberty' are both interesting and highly inflammatory.

In his own Preface L'Estrange had explained how he was drawn to making his own translation of Aesop through the dissatisfaction he had felt with the school versions currently available. These he judged roundly

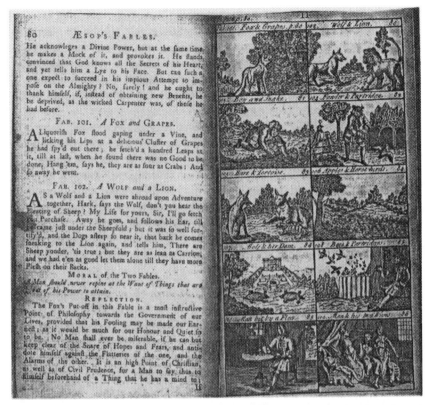

Figure 4.2 From Samuel Richardson, *Aesop's Fables With Instructive Morals and Reflections* (1740; reproduced by permission of the Syndics of Cambridge University Library)

to be flat and insipid: 'This Rhapsody of Fables is a Book universally read, and taught in all our schools; but almost at such a Rate as we teach Pyes and Parrots, that pronounce the words without so much as guessing at the meaning of them.'

Croxall takes Lestrange to task on two counts, first, the old one that the book was too expensive and large for children; and second, that the values it sought to inculcate were pernicious (words which Croxall has taken directly from L'Estrange's Preface are italicized):

Now the purpose for which he [L'Estrange] principally intended his book, as in his Preface he spends a great many words to inform us, was for the use and instruction of children; who being, as it were, a mere *rasa tabula*, or blank paper, *are ready indifferently for any opinions good or bad, taking all upon credit; and that it is in the power of the first comer, to write Saint or Devil upon them, which he pleases.* This being truly and certainly the case, what Devils, nay, what poor Devils, would Lestrange make of those children, who should be so unfortunate as to read his book, and imbibe his pernicious principles! Principles coined and suited to promote the growth, and serve the ends of Popery and arbitrary Power... What sort of children therefore are the *blank paper*, upon which such morality as this ought to be written? Not the children of Britain, I hope; for they are born with free blood in their veins, and suck in Liberty with their very milk. This they should be taught to love and cherish above all things... Let therefore Lestrange with his slavish doctrine be banished to the barren deserts of Arabia, to the nurseries of Turkey, Persia and Morocco, where all footsteps of Liberty have long since been worn out, and the minds of the people, by a narrow way of thinking, contracted and inured to fear, poverty and miserable servitude... But let the minds of our British youth be for ever educated and improved in that spirit of Truth and Liberty, for the support of which their ancestors have often bravely exhausted so much blood and treasure.

When Richardson came to consider a version of Aesop designed particularly with children in mind in the late 1730s he was very much aware of this highly charged debate. Politically more aligned to Croxall (but perhaps not overimpressed by the bombast) he is more drawn towards the style of L'Estrange's work. In his own Preface Richardson tries to adjudicate in more dispassionate terms. He finds Croxall's objections to L'Estrange just with regard to the 'Political Part, and the Bulk and Price of the Performance' but wants to preserve what he sees as the much higher *literary quality* of L'Estrange's work. His approach here seems much less functional than Locke's.

Richardson therefore bases his own Aesop on L'Estrange, confident that

> we should do an acceptable service if we could give [L'Estrange's] *exceptionable Reflections* a more general and useful turn; and if we could reduce the work to such a size as should be fit for the hands and pockets for which it was principally designed; and at the same time preserve to Sir Roger the principal graces and beauties for which he is so justly admired... Political Reflections [changed to] such as we hope will be found more general and instructive. For we think it no wise excusable to inflame children's minds with distinctions, which they will imbibe fast enough from the attachments of parents etc., and the warmth of their own imaginations. But nevertheless we must add, that wherever the fable compelled, as we may say, a political turn, we have, in our Reflections upon it, always given that preference to the principles of LIBERTY, which we hope will for ever be the distinguishing characteristic of a Briton.

As we are sensible to the alluring force which cuts or pictures, suited to the respective subjects, have on the minds of children, we have, in a quite new manner, ingraved on copper-plates, at no small expense, the subject of every fable; and presume that the little trouble which children will have to turn the cuts, as ten of them are included in one plate, will rather excite their curiosity, and stimulate their attention, than puzzle or confuse them, especially as the readers are distinctly referred to both page and fable in every representation.

Richardson signals the distinctive emphasis he has sought to bring to the use of illustrations in this quote. At first glance it is hard to see why he seems to be getting quite so excited about this issue. The engraved plates have been done 'in a quite new manner', he tells us, and 'at no small expense'. Is the evident pride which he feels in this aspect of his production simply an eighteenth-century version of what we would now call 'sales hype'? Richardson's initial emphasis would, at first, seem to make this likely as the motivation he describes in being 'sensible to the alluring force which ... pictures have on the minds of children', and would seem to draw him into line with earlier justifications of text for children being accompanied by illustrated material. Even if this remains unusual, it hardly warrants the revolutionary tag that this is being carried out 'in a quite new manner'.

But in fact there is a new emphasis here which, though subtle, is none the less far reaching in its implications. The earlier justifications I have quoted for the inclusion of illustrations were offered in phrases which placed children – syntactically at least – as passive recipients of the visual stimulus being offered. Illustrations are offered to make the morals 'still more taking', so that texts will 'make a deeper impression on [children's] minds', to 'gain a more favourable acceptance' and so on. It is the texts and didactic intentions of the authors which are the active subjects in these phrases: the children, even when being stimulated, are construed as essentially recipients. Richardson's opening phrase seems initially to reiterate this position but the second half of the sentence surreptitiously positions us, as readers, with the children as they apply themselves, actively, to make use of the pictures. What comes into focus here is no longer the impression – however deep – made *on* children by the pictures but the process whereby children, their curiosity engaged, make sense of the text. Richardson may have stumbled on this formulation as a way of justifying his cost-cutting exercise of gathering ten illustrations together into a single plate, a practice requiring more effort from the child reader in order to relate text with illustration. But the care and purposefulness with which he pronounces on the putative gains from such interactive reading suggest he is aware that more is at stake here than the price at which publishers can offer illustrated text.

75

DAVID WHITLEY

In his project for the fables then, Richardson brings together in an exceptionally coherent way, many of the strands of thinking about children and story in this genre that I have been tracing. The price, the size of the book, the inclusion and arrangement of illustrations and the underlying values/politics all come into view in his discussion. He wants to preserve the literary quality of the stories: they are not to be reduced to the narrow functionalism of books to teach reading or Latin. The value of pictures is endorsed – indeed he has thought very carefully about the experience of the child in trying to relate the pictures to the text – but he attempts to make the price and size of the volume more suitable. And he tries to settle the particularly heated debate over the political interpretation which is appended to these stories. He wants to take party politics out of the debate but political constructions are not (yet) excluded altogether.

But what of the stories themselves? Harvey Darton has argued that L'Estrange 'had tried, with some success, to see the child's viewpoint' in his version of the fables. If this is so, then Richardson undoubtedly develops the potential of the fable to speak for and about children even further. Not only in the terms of the project as a whole but within individual fables, Richardson advances a distinctive view of children and learning, carefully adapted from L'Estrange.

L'Estrange had already brought to the fable tradition a lively sense that sober moralizing needed to be quickened with a spirit of playfulness or fun. He may have derived this sense from the tradition of Cavalier writing which took its authority from Ben Jonson, or it may have been a personal inclination, sharpened through antagonism to the culture and politics of puritanism. In any event, the attitude manifests itself in the interpretation which is offered to a number of the fables. The values on which this attitude is based are perhaps best articulated in his response to the time-honoured story of the boy who cried wolf. L'Estrange entitles this 'A Boy and False Alarums' and uses a very succinct version of the well-known fable as a pretext for developing a keen sense of the value of what he calls 'raillery' – playfulness and wit – in social relations. 'Raillery', he extemporizes, 'is the very sauce of civil entertainment' and he goes on to suggest that 'without some such tincture of urbanity, even in matters the most serious, the good humour flattens, for want of refreshment and relief'. The boy who took such pleasure in raising false alarms is not then berated for fooling around *per se*. Indeed the value of fooling, or playful spirits generally, is strongly endorsed as being a central aspect of our whole humanity which it would be wrong to repress. The shepherd boy, in a far more generous judgement, is simply invoked as an example of a lad who 'went too far on a topic that he did not understand'.

Richardson edited down L'Estrange's work and left extremely detailed notes in his Preface as to both the principles on which he had done this and the specific fables he had left out. What is interesting about this fable is that Richardson included it with only the lightest of editorial pruning which appears designed, not to alter the slant L'Estrange gives to the story, but, if anything, to give slightly sharper definition to its core values. Despite having a much stronger affiliation with puritan-influenced thought than L'Estrange, in other words, Richardson clearly seeks to retain a sense of the value of playfulness for both child and adult in his approach to the Aesop project.

Perhaps this is not so surprising if we recall the extent to which 'raillery' is allowed to infiltrate the exemplary moral consciousness of Richardson's eponymous heroine in *Pamela*. But Richardson takes over other values from L'Estrange which, if not quite inimical, are at least more problematic to traditions of dissenting thought and moralizing. One of the most important of these is the representation of curiosity, especially in childhood, as a healthy, necessary and essentially innocent quality. The function attributed to curiosity in relation to the Fall had made it problematic in relation to most strands of religious philosophy, but its positive value was beginning to be asserted within the new empiricist philosophy, and more secular, scientific traditions of thought. John Locke had explicitly encouraged it. One of the clearest examples of its being worked up as a positive value in relation to children comes from the handling of a fable which L'Estrange entitles 'A Father and Sons'. L'Estrange's story is offered verbatim in Richardson's edition:

> A countryman that lived handsomely in the world himself upon his honest labour and industry, was desirous his sons should do so after him; and being now upon his death-bed; 'My dear children', says he, 'I reckon myself bound to tell you before I depart, that there is a considerable treasure hid in my vineyard. Wherefore be sure to dig, and search narrowly for it when I am gone.' The father dies, and the sons fall immediately to work upon the vineyard. They turned it up over and over, and not one penny of money to be found there; but the profit of the next vintage expounded the riddle.

The appended moral makes clear the particular value which is to be placed on curiosity:

> Good counsel is the best legacy a father can leave to a child, and it is still the better, when it is wrapped up, as to beget a curiosity as well as an inclination to follow it.

L'Estrange's 'Reflexion', most of which is repeated by Richardson, reinforces this point by making curiosity central to his theory of the Aesopic fable and its effects. L'Estrange's version runs as follows:

> Aesop very well understood that naked lessons and precepts, have

nothing the force that images and parables have upon our minds and affections: beside that the very study to unriddle a mystery, furnishes the memory with more tokens to remember it by. A tale in emblem sinks deeper where the life and spirit of it is insinuated by a kind of bias and surprise. It was a touch of art in the father to cover his meaning in such a manner as to create a curiosity, and an earnest desire in his sons to find it out.

That 'touch of art in the father' is beautifully put, and might well stand for the whole way in which L'Estrange seeks to ease the fable away from too narrowly conceived a utilitarian function in relation to either morals or reading. The positive value assigned to curiosity here is repeated in other fables, such as the story of the boy who puts his hand on a snake while 'groping for eels' and receives only a mildly admonitory caution. The opportunity for a sterner line of moralizing is passed up in favour of a perspective which sees in ordinary experience opportunities for learning that are treated non-punitively and without the smack of original sin.

But if Richardson, by incorporating wholesale such sections of the text, implicitly endorses many of the child-centred values which he finds in L'Estrange's work, then in some respects he seems also to be trying to move beyond his immediate source. Some of the fables, for instance, are reprised in a manner that strongly suggests John Locke's advocacy of children's faring best under mild tutelage, severer methods being called for only *in extremis*. In the fable of 'The Sun and the Wind', for instance, Richardson trims the story somewhat and offers his own, substantially revised, interpretation. Richardson's version runs as follows:

A controversy betwixt the Sun and the Wind, which was the stronger of the two, was agreed to be decided in favour of him which could make a traveller quit his cloak. The Wind fell presently a storming, and threw hail-shot, over and above, in the very teeth of him. The man wraps himself up the closer, and keeps advancing still in spite of the weather. The Sun then began his part, and darted his beams upon him so strong, that at last the traveller grew faint with the heat, put off his cloak, and lay down in the shade to refresh himself.

L'Estrange's version contained no hint of the moral which Richardson goes on to draw from this story: *Mildness and persuasion win upon ingenuous minds sooner than a blustering and bullying behaviour.* And the Lockian overtones are further amplified in the, again, completely original Reflection, where Richardson argues that the story shows us 'the effects of persecution on the minds of men, which generally hardens and confirms them in their principles, whether good or bad: while in that of the Sun we see the success of a mild and benign nature, which generally softens and overcomes the most obstinate spirits'. Richardson issues a similar qualification with respect even to stories such as that in which a nurse subdues her bawling infant charge with the threat of throwing it to a wolf, which would seem at first sight to justify the implementation of harsh discipline. Here Richardson admits in his moral that though 'an ingenuous spirit will be wrought upon by fair words ... a perverse one must be terrified into its duty, if soft means will not do'. But he adds the rider that this edict should be applied *only to adults* 'for, as to children or infants, there cannot be a more pernicious error than to terrify them'.

*

What then can we conclude? I would like to suggest that we need to remind ourselves, following Harvey Darton, that even before children's literature proper got under way, the genre of fables was a testing ground for ideas about what children needed from a story and the most appropriate forms for this to reach them. In studying some of the less-well-known editions alongside their more famous counterparts, the full extent of this debate and its particular terms of reference become more apparent. The debate was fuelled not only by the growing awareness that there was a profitable market for children's books (though this was undoubtedly a decisive factor) but also through a new awareness that children and their reading responses needed to be theorized. Such theorizing took place, often in highly contentious ways, across a whole range of issues: in relation to visual image, in arguments about the value of literary as opposed to functional dimensions of the stories, the legitimate scope for moral and political interpretation and so on. Richardson, in developing L'Estrange, had an exceptionally clear vision of the form children's literature in this genre should take. Within the format he both inherited and reshaped, he embedded a construct of children strongly related to the tradition of thinking about childhood which John Locke had brought into such sharp focus. In showing how this could be worked out in detail within a particular narrative form he took Locke's thinking a stage further.

NOTES

1 John Rowe Townsend, *Written for Children* (London, 1965).
2 Katherine Hornbeak, 'Richardson's Aesop' *Smith College Studies in Modern Languages* 19 (1937–8), pp. 30–50.
3 F.J. Harvey Darton, *Children's Books in England*, 3rd edn, revised by Brian Alderson (Cambridge, 1982).
4 John Locke, *Some Thoughts Concerning Education*, section 156, 1705 edition (London 1902).
5 See, for instance, Annabel Patterson, *Fables of Power* (London, 1991).
6 Ibid., p. 87.
7 Harvey Darton, *Children's Books*, p. 17.

5

JOHN NEWBERY AND TOM TELESCOPE

John Rowe Townsend

Harvey Darton, in the first serious history of children's books,[1] referred to John Newbery as 'Newbery the Conqueror', and to the year 1744, when Newbery published his famous *Little Pretty Pocket-Book*, as 'a date comparable to the 1066 of the older histories'. This was no doubt an echo of Newbery's own cheerful impudence when, for instance, he advertised the *Lilliputian Magazine*, or *Young Gentleman and Lady's Golden Library* as 'an Attempt to mend the World, to make the Society of Man more amiable, and to establish the Plainness, Simplicity, Virtue and Wisdom of the Golden Age, so much celebrated by the Poets and Historians'. Yet, allowing for the hyperbole, Darton's comparison is not totally outrageous. English history did not begin with William the Conqueror, and the history of children's literature did not begin with John Newbery, but each of them is associated with the start of a new age. After them things were different.

Recreational literature for children may be said (with admitted simplification) to have a dual prehistory. On the one hand, there was story material – legend, folktale, ballad, romance – going back into the mists of time. On the other hand were such forms as courtesy books, instructions from father to son and mother to daughter, moral exhortations from Puritans and others, which had flourished increasingly with the spread of printing. The first stream was, in a broad sense, entertainment, but was not devised specially for children; the second stream was devised specially for children but was not meant to entertain them. The little books published by John Newbery marked a decisive stage in the process of bringing the two streams together.

Percy Muir, writing two decades later than Darton, did not agree with the emphasis placed on Newbery as innovator.[2] He complained of the 'disproportionate regard for Newbery's importance' among historians of children's books, and cited several precursors, the most interesting being Thomas Boreman, who published, a few years before Newbery arrived on the scene, a series of tiny books which he called Gigantick Histories. There were also chapbooks and home-made books, but it was Newbery who established the publication of books designed specially for children as a serious and continuing part of the trade, and Darton's view of him as the founding father of children's books has in general prevailed, helped by the adoption of his name for the principal American children's book award, the Newbery Medal.

In the half-century before Newbery opened his first shop in London, views of childhood had been changing. Under the influence especially of the philosopher John Locke, the child's mind was beginning to be seen not so much as steeped in original sin but rather as a blank page on which the right messages could be written. In his *Treatise upon Education* Locke had commended teaching through pleasure rather than the rod, and in particular had expressed the need for 'easy, pleasant books' which would reward the child's effort in learning to read.[3] This was the opportunity that Newbery, an admirer of 'the great Mr Locke', exploited.

Darton defined children's books as 'printed works produced ostensibly to give children spontaneous pleasure, and not primarily to teach them, nor solely to make them good, nor to keep them *profitably* quiet'. The key word was 'pleasure'; and it is understandable that Darton and his successors placed their emphasis on this. Pleasure was the new ingredient, and the most significant one in terms of tracing the development of children's literature. It is understandable also that writers about Newbery (including myself) have been intrigued by the character of the man: Goldsmith's 'philanthropic bookseller' who was 'the friend of all mankind' and was also a vendor of quack medicines; whose humour and benevolence were coupled with an ever-open eye for the main chance. There is good clean fun to be had with his ways of puffing his own wares, such as the well-known fate of Goody Two-shoes's father, who 'died of a violent fever in a place where Dr James's Powder was not to be had'; and his innovatory advertising techniques. (*Nurse Truelove's New Year's Gift* was to be given free to all little boys and girls, at the Bible and Sun in St Paul's Churchyard, 'they paying for the binding, which is only Two Pence each book'.) Yet all this may have tended to obscure Newbery's real significance in his own day.

One need only look through the long list of his titles to see that, more than anything else, John Newbery was an educational publisher. His aim, whether in pursuit of profit or from a wish to spread the benefits of learning – or, most likely, a combination of the two – was to educate the rising middle class, to which he belonged, and its offspring with it. In an output that ran into hundreds, instructional titles, for both adults and children, are dominant. He brought out, among much else, a spelling dictionary, a world atlas, histories of England and the world, a *Gentleman and Lady's key to Polite Literature*, a set of descriptions of famous London buildings, Dr Johnson's *Idler*, a book called *The Polite Lady, or, a Course in Female Education* (which I would dearly love to see), an edition of

Plutarch's *Lives*, a number of play texts, and a guide to letter-writing. He was a writer himself, and there is a case for supposing he wrote all or most of the children's books – it is too complex a question for discussion here – but he cannot have written more than a fraction of his total publishing output.

Percy Muir thought that Newbery, whether as writer or publisher, could be credited with 'not more than half a dozen titles of a purely entertaining or recreational kind for children'. This is a matter in which judgements are bound to be subjective. Deciding which Newbery books are for children, and which of these are recreational, is a difficult exercise; but my own listing of his books for 'Little Masters and Misses' (children) and 'Young Gentlemen and Ladies' (adolescents) runs to twenty-four in all, of which the great majority could be said to have both recreational and instructional elements.

The *Little Pretty Pocket-Book* sets the tone, being said on its title page to be intended for 'the Instruction and Amusement of Little Master Tommy and Pretty Miss Polly'. Instruction was put first, no doubt with an eye on those adults who – then as now – liked to feel that a child's reading was teaching it something. The book consists mainly of alphabetically arranged pictures of children's games, each accompanied by a rhyme and a moral (frequently unrelated). Several other books announce a similar dual aim. In a few, which I assume would pass Percy Muir's test, the instructional content is minimal; for instance:

FOOD FOR THE MIND: or, a NEW RIDDLE-BOOK: compiled for the use of the great and little good Boys and Girls of *England, Scotland,* and *Ireland.* By JOHN THE GIANT KILLER, Esq; Adorned with Cuts. Price *Six-pence,* bound and gilt.

This book consists of rhymed riddles, one to a page and illustrated with crude woodcuts; there are no obvious lessons; and while the result seems less than riveting to a modern eye, the pages were no doubt pored over for hours in an age when there was not much competition. Other books, while intended to make learning as painless as possible, are clearly educational:

A PRETTY PLAY-THING for Children of all Denominations: Containing, I. The Alphabet in Verse for the use of Little Children. II. An Alphabet in Prose, interspersed with proper Lessons in Life, for the Use of great Children. III. The Sound of the Letters explained by visible Objects. IV. The CUZ'S CHORUS, set to Music; to be sung by Children, in order to teach them to join their Letters into Syllables, and pronounce them properly. The whole embellished with Variety of Cuts, after the Manner of Ptolomy [*sic*]. Price *Three-pence,* bound and gilt . . .

Both of these books, as it happens, offer elements designed both for 'little Children and great Children'. Newbery did occasionally classify his publications by age group, although, then as now, the borderlines were somewhat hazy. The books for Little Masters and Misses were frequently concerned, as above, with teaching children their letters; those for Young Gentlemen and Ladies with the 'Lessons of Life'. While he courted young readers with such devices as his dedications from 'their old Friend in St Paul's Churchyard', and no doubt hoped to please them, there can be little doubt that Newbery saw his books as being, at bottom, useful and instructional rather than entertaining for entertainment's sake.

Among the best-selling, and in their day best-known, Newbery books for the young were a sequence called *The Circle of the Sciences*, published in the late 1740s, and *The Newtonian System of Philosophy* (sometimes known as *Tom Telescope's Philosophy of Tops and Balls*) in 1761. The first announcement of *The Circle of the Sciences*, in 1745, said that 'for the sake of those who can't afford to lay out much Money at a Time, [the work] will be published in little Volumes, bound, at six-pence each'. The preface to the fourth book, on *Poetry* (in effect an anthology), observed that 'Literature should be an agreeable Amusement to young Minds', so 'we shall make it our principal Aim throughout our LITTLE CIRCLE to strew (if we may be indulged the expression) the Path to Knowledge, as it were, with Roses'.

Bibliographically, the *Circle* is rather confusing, because the books appeared in dribs and drabs, and titles moved in and out of the series, but it seems to have settled down to a definite list of seven titles, which were: *Grammar, Arithmetic, Rhetoric, Poetry, Logic ('with Ontology, or Metaphysics'), Geography*, and *Chronology*. To each of these titles were added the words 'made familiar and easy to young Gentlemen and Ladies'; *Grammar* had the additional words 'and Foreigners'. Most of the subjects were not what we now call sciences, but in conjunction with *Tom Telescope* the books add up to a body of knowledge, available at a modest price, which would enable any literate person to acquire a very decent general education, in terms of what was available at the time: perhaps more than could be counted on at one of the ancient universities.

Tom Telescope, however, is Newbery's triumph. Probably he was author as well as publisher, though this is not certain. The title page says that the book is 'the substance of six Lectures read to the Lilliputian Society by Tom Telescope, A.M., and collected and methodized for the Benefit of the Youth of these Kingdoms by their old Friend, Mr NEWBERY, in St Paul's Church Yard'. There was of course no such person as Tom Telescope: he was one of a gallery of imaginary characters such as Tommy Trip, Giles Gingerbread and Woglog the Great Giant who wrote or appeared in Newbery children's books.

The historian J.H. Plumb said of *The Newtonian System of Philosophy*

Frontispiece

THE
NEWTONIAN SYSTEM
OF
PHILOSOPHY

Adapted to the Capacities of young GENTLEMEN and LADIES, and familiarized and made entertaining by Objects with which they are intimately acquainted:

BEING

The Substance of SIX LECTURES read to the LILLIPUTIAN SOCIETY,

By TOM TELESCOPE, A.M.

And collected and methodized for the Benefit of the Youth of these Kingdoms,

By their old Friend Mr. NEWBERY; in St. Paul's Church Yard;

Who has also added Variety of Copper-Plate Cuts, to illustrate and confirm the Doctrines advanced.

O Lord, how manifold are thy Works! In Wisdom hast thou made them all, the Earth is full of thy Riches.
Young Men and Maidens, Old Men and Children, praise the Lord. PSALMS.

LONDON,

Printed for J. NEWBERY; at the BIBLE and SUN, in St. Paul's Church Yard. 1761.

Lecture on Matter & Motion ?

Figure 5.1 The Newtonian System of Philosophy: frontispiece and title-page

(see Figures 5.1 and 5.2) that it was 'crystal clear, the examples exceptionally apposite, and its attitude to the universe, to philosophy, to humanity, and to the natural sciences would have drawn prolonged cheers from the Encyclopaedists'. It was 'not only a brilliantly produced book for adolescent children, but it also gives us a novel insight into how the ideas of the Enlightenment were being disseminated through society'.[4]

The imaginary lectures are delivered by young Master Telescope, a diminutive prodigy, who is shown in the frontispiece standing on a table and whipping his top by way of demonstrating the laws of motion. The subjects are: No. 1 'Of Matter and Motion', No. 2 'Of the Universe, and particularly of the Solar System', No. 3 'Of the Air, Atmosphere, and Meteors,' No. 4 'Of Mountains, Springs, Rivers and the Sea', No. 5 'Of Minerals, Vegetables and Animals', and No. 6 winding the series up with what Pope described as the proper study of mankind, 'Of the five Senses of Man, and of his Understanding'. Obviously, after more than two centuries of additions to scientific knowledge, such a work must be irredeemably out of date, although I have to say that, as a person whose own scientific education was defective, I have learned quite a lot from it.

(115)

ture ; for by a due temperament of thofe two oppofite qualities moft of her productions are formed.

What we call *heat* is occafioned by the agitation of the infenfible parts of the body that produces in us that fenfation ; and when the parts of a body are violently agitated, we fay, and indeed we feel, that body is *hot*; fo that that which to our fenfation is *heat*, in the object is nothing but *motion*. Hey-day, fays Lady *Caroline*, what fort of Philofophy is this ? Why, Madam, fays Sir *Harry*, this is a pofition which has been laid down by thefe airy Gentlemen for a long time, but which never has been proved by experiment. Take care, Baronet, fays the Marquis, or you'll forfeit all pretenfions to Philofophy. The forfeiture, my Lord, is made already, fays the Philofopher ; Sir *Harry* has been bold enough to deny that which experience every day confirms for truth. If what we call Heat is not motion, or occafioned by the motion of bodies, how came my Lord's mill to take fire the other day, when it was running round without a proper fupply of corn ? And how came your poft-chariot to fire while running down *Breakneck-hill*, Sir *Harry* ? Confider, there was nobody with a torch under the axle-tree ;

Chariot fired by Motion.

Figure 5.2 The Newtonian System of Philosophy: inside pages

The book is illustrated with copperplate engravings, which no doubt helped, but the key technique used to make it digestible by young readers is that of fictionalization. It is framed in something resembling a story; and this outer story also incorporates some social and moral disquisitions that we can take as casting light on Newbery's own attitudes. (They are in line with the indications of attitude given by other Newbery books.) It is holiday time, and a group of little gentry, home from school, have met at the Countess of Twilight's to divert themselves. But they can't agree on how. One proposes Thread-the-Needle, another Hot-Cockles, a third Shuttlecock, a fourth Blind Man's Buff; then cards are mentioned. Now Master Telescope, 'A young Gentleman of distinguished abilities', jumps up and begs them to think of a more innocent amusement. 'Playing cards for money', says he, 'is so nearly allied to covetousness and cheating that I abhor it . . . Parents might almost as well teach their children to thieve as to game; for they are kindred employments, and generally terminate in the ruin of both fortune and character.'

Lady Twilight then says, in effect, 'Well, what do you suggest?' And Tom Telescope says that at *his* school 'we often play at Sham Orations, Comical Disputes, Measuring of Land and Houses, Taking the Heights

and Distances of Mountains and Steeples, solving Problems and Para-
doxes on Globes and Maps, and sometimes at Natural Philosophy, which
I think is very entertaining and at the same time extremely useful.' (It is
obviously a progressive establishment.)

The young visitors agree that Natural Philosophy would be a good
game, and Master Telescope, with the aid of his whip and top, begins his
first lecture. He tells his hearers how a body in motion would go on for
ever if nothing stopped it. At this point we meet the obstreperous Tom
Wilson, who dramatizes the proceedings with challenging but ill-founded
objections and says anybody can see that this isn't true: a ball stops
rolling, or a top spinning, of its own accord. So Master Telescope tells
him not to expose his ignorance and explains the effects of friction and
gravity.

Next day we all go to the Marquis of Setstar's observatory, to learn
about the universe, and particularly the solar system – here the book
has pictures of the Marquis's observatory and of various astronomical
instruments – and Tom Telescope tells us *inter alia* how the universe
contains many thousands of worlds as large as ours, suspended in ether
and rolling like the earth round the several suns. Here I think modern
astronomers would not support Master Telescope, who supposes these
other worlds to be filled with animals, plants and minerals, all perhaps
different from ours but all intended to magnify the almighty Architect.

The day after that, Tom's fame has spread, and the Duke of Galaxy,
no less, comes to hear him. This puts our group of young people into
confusion – they are in awe of so mighty a personage – but gives Tom
an opportunity to tell them they should look a superior straight in the
eye, and that whereas civility is owed to everyone and respect to the great,
'our affection is only to be obtained by worthiness of character. Birth
and fortune are merely accidental and may happen to be the portion of
a man without merit; but the man of genius and virtue is ennobled, as it
were, by himself, and is honoured not so much for his grandfather's
greatness as his own.'

And so we go on, with the lectures – themselves in good plain prose
– leavened with illustrations, homely analogies, interruptions by Tom
Wilson and others, and occasional clashes. There's quite a little cast of
characters, both young and grown-up. For the last lecture we have several
new adult guests, including a brash young baronet, Sir Harry, and the
Ambassador of Bantam, an imaginary country. The Ambassador is
shocked by the manners of the company, who come in to the lecture
talking and laughing and won't let Master Telescope begin; and now it's
time for some remarks from Lady Twilight, who says it's no good
expecting people in the polite world to behave on these occasions with
any sort of good manners or decorum ... 'Why, Sir, I have often been
interrupted in the middle of a fine air at an oratorio by a Gentleman's

whistling a Hornpipe; and at St Paul's it is no uncommon thing to hear both Gentlemen and Ladies laugh louder than the organ.' 'Hush, Madam,' says the Marquis, 'if your friends and neighbours are fools, you ought not to expose them, and especially to foreigners.'

Sir Harry gets his comeuppance when he asks obtusely why a looking-glass, of all things, should be used as an illustration of a scientific point. 'Because, Sir,' says young Master Telescope smartly, 'it is an object with which some people are the most intimately acquainted.' As Sir Harry is an egregious fop, this reply produces a loud laugh.

We also have some strictures on cruelty to animals and an interesting attack on slavery, when our young philosopher points out that a neighbour, Sir William, will not sell a horse that is declining, for fear he should fall into the hands of a master who might treat him with cruelty; but 'he is largely concerned in the slave trade (which, I think, is carried on by none but *we good Christians*, to the dishonour of our celestial Master) and makes no difficulty of separating the husband from the wife, the parents from the children, and all of them ... from their native country, to be sold in a foreign market, like so many horses, and often to the most merciless of the human race.'

However, after all this liberalism, the concluding passage of the book, when Master Telescope has completed his series of talks, is an appeal for the return of austere virtues, giving Sparta as the great exemplar in contrast to the wealth and luxury of Athens. The Spartan qualities, it appears, secured the felicities of the Golden Age, whose potential return is the subject of the book's last sentence.

This seems a startling preference: we now think of the example set to the world by Sparta as one of brutal militarism, while in Athens we see the founding fathers of Western philosophy, medicine, literature, and indeed in its broad sense Western civilization. But we must look at Newbery in his context: he was the industrious tradesman, making his way by continual hard work in a city which for many years had known political corruption and the self-indulgence of the ruling classes – the city excoriated in Samuel Johnson's poem *London*. It is perhaps not too surprising if John Newbery admired the Spartan virtues.

That the Newbery books filled a need is obvious from the fact that they sold in large numbers and stayed in print for many years: some into the next century. Newbery died rich. It is impossible to assess the contribution made by his books to education in the days before public provision, but it must have been considerable. And as the advocate of kindness in bringing up children, of making learning a pleasure, of conscience in such matters as slavery and the ill-treatment of animals, of reason and common sense in the conduct of affairs, and of religious tolerance (not mentioned here but indicated in his publications and in his life), he must be regarded as a copybook example of enlightened self-

87

interest. I summed John Newbery up in my recently published book as 'a great man in a small way';[5] but I now feel that perhaps I was underestimating him. Maybe his was not such a small way after all.

ACKNOWLEDGEMENT

This chapter was first published in *Signal*; it is reprinted here with the kind permission of the Thimble Press.

NOTES

1 F.J. Harvey Darton, *Children's Books in England: Five Centuries of Social Life*, third edition, revised by Brian Alderson (Cambridge: Cambridge University Press, 1982).
2 Percy Muir, *English Children's Books 1600–1900* (London: Batsford, 1954).
3 John Locke, *Educational Writings*, edited by J.L. Axtell (Cambridge: Cambridge University Press, 1968; and many other editions).
4 J.H. Plumb, 'The First Flourishing of Children's Books', in Gerald Gottlieb's *Early Children's Books and Their Illustration*, (New York: Pierpont Morgan Library with Oxford University Press, 1975).
5 John Rowe Townsend, *Trade and Plumb-cake for ever, Huzza! The Life and Work of John Newbery, 1713–67* (Cambridge: Colt Books, 1994).

Part III

WOMEN WRITING FOR CHILDREN

6

'THE CURSED BARBAULD CREW'

Women writers and writing for children in the late eighteenth century

Norma Clarke

In traditional histories of children's literature, the late eighteenth century and the early nineteenth century are identified as times of blight when children were subjected to painfully didactic stories and heavily moral tales, written, for the most part, by a 'monstrous regiment of women'.[1] These women included Sarah Trimmer, 'a preposterous woman'; Mary Sherwood, 'the most fiercely didactic of all writers of the moral tale', author of *The Fairchild Family* which Percy Muir dubbed, 'this truly appalling book'; and Mary Wollstonecraft, better known as the champion of women's rights, whose *Original Stories* for children was described by John Rowe Townsend as a 'repellent piece of English Rousseauism'.[2] As the tone of these comments might suggest, traditional histories have on the whole preferred not to dwell on moral tales of this era at all. They pass over them with a few urbane witticisms or hostile allusions *en route* to what is defined as 'real' children's literature; that which, in F.J. Harvey Darton's words, is 'produced ostensibly to give children spontaneous pleasure'.[3] This is what Mary Lamb was looking for when she went to Newbery's bookshop in 1802, hoping to buy *Goody Two Shoes*. But instead of books to delight, she found only books to instruct. Her brother, Charles Lamb, described the scene in a furious letter to Coleridge: 'Goody Two Shoes is almost out of print. Mrs Barbauld's stuff has banished all the old classics of the nursery; and the Shopman at Newbery's hardly deign'd to reach them off an old exploded corner of a shelf, when Mary ask'd for them. Mrs. B's & Mrs Trimmer's nonsense lay in piles about . . . Damn them! I mean the cursed Barbauld Crew, those Blights and Blasts of all that is human in man and child.'[4]

Lamb's emotional outburst – a veritable curse – has been much cited and rarely examined. Even today, the dichotomies established in the post-Romantic period continue to structure debates about children's literature; instruction is opposed to amusement, morality to fun, and the 'real' world to fantasy, as if these categories were guarded by impermeable boundaries. The powerful figure of William Wordsworth and his construction of the child, especially in Book 5 of *The Prelude*, endorsed Lamb's view and helped eclipse a whole generation of women writers whose prominence in their own time is obvious from the force of Charles Lamb's remarks. The Romantic myth of the child posits a boy child from whom an adult male self struggles to emerge, a process in which imagination and separation are paramount. For Lamb, Wordsworth and Coleridge, 'all that is human' was to be found in an Other world of fantasy, in stories of ogres and giants, fairies and elves: 'I know no other way of giving the mind a love of "the Great" & "the Whole",' Coleridge explained, discussing his own early enjoyment of fairy tales. In insisting on this in 1797, Coleridge was going against established convention: 'Should children be permitted to read Romances, & Relations of Giants & Magicians & Genii? – I know all that has been said against it . . .⁵ A very great deal was being said against it. The Edgeworths' preface to the *Parent's Assistant* (1796) put the matter succinctly: 'why should the mind be filled with fantastic visions, instead of useful knowledge?'⁶ But subsequent literary orthodoxy aligned itself with Coleridge. To be against magic and genii was to be against the human; the 'useful knowledge' of the didactic writers became synonymous with all that was dry, inhuman and dreary. Major literary figures like Anna Barbauld fell into obscurity. What remained was Lamb's extraordinary caricature of her, whereby one of the most humane, enlightened, rational and sensitive women writers of the period was depicted as a witch, bent not on nurture but destruction.

If one can talk at all of a 'Barbauld crew' it should be said at once that it did not consist only of women. Radical liberal figures like Barbauld's brother John Aikin, Richard Lovell Edgeworth, Thomas Day and William Godwin all concerned themselves in different ways with the cause of producing rational literature for children. These names should alert us to what Alan Richardson points out in *Literature, Education and Romanticism: Reading as Social Practice 1780–1832* – that debates on children's literature were highly politicized at this time. Those who urged the importance of fairyland in forming the minds of the young, were also tending towards conservative views of social and political affairs. 'The Romantic advocates of fairyland . . . had already turned from Godwin and their youthful radicalism toward the conservative social and political stances that would mark their later careers.' Wordsworth calls for magic in preference to rational cause-and-effect explanations:

> Oh, give us once again the wishing-cap
> Of Fortunatus, and the invisible coat
> Of Jack the Giant-killer, Robin Hood,
> And Sabra in the forest with St George.⁷

Such a call takes on a political edge when seen in relation to the radical ferment of the 1790s with its unprecedented upsurge in literacy and a hunger for ideas demonstrated by the popularity of political pamphlet literature. The mass distribution of Tom Paine's *Rights of Man* (1791–2) alarmed the establishment who took no pleasure in being told that, 'Our peasantry now read the *Rights of Man* on mountains, and on moors, and by the wayside.' In a similar way it can be argued that women who wrote rational literature for children were consciously or inadvertently offering those children, and the adults they would grow into, tools for reappraising their social and political situations.

Not all such women were radical in their politics and not all would have subscribed to views we might now label feminist. But any woman entering the public sphere – as many did – negotiated a complicated environment of mixed welcome, enablement, prejudice and closed doors which coloured their public pronouncements. Activist women of all political persuasions made use of the best available routes to effective power: Hannah More, for example, managed her high Tory churchmen with great skill. Some writers for children barely concealed their political agenda: Mary Wollstonecraft's contempt for what she viewed as a decadent model of womanhood – all idleness, vanity and empty-headedness – is plain in *Thoughts on the Education of Daughters* and *Original Stories*. Others were more covert in their expression: Maria Edgeworth, as Mitzi Myers convincingly shows, devised stories which dramatized a female ethic based on affiliation and gift exchange. Serious scholarly work on the women writers of this period is now appearing, but there is still a great gap to be filled and much thoughtless repetition of old stereotypes to be undone. Further, the critical paradigm which sets up a hierarchy of fairy tale versus moral tale compounds the problem. Few scholars have entered as deeply into this issue as Mitzi Myers whose work on Maria Edgeworth, Mary Wollstonecraft and Hannah More provides a stimulus for wider revisionary revaluations.[8]

*

Anna Barbauld first came to prominence with a volume of poems published under her maiden name, Aikin, in 1773. She was one of a new breed of professional women writers who were to dominate the last three decades of the eighteenth century. Her arrival on the literary scene was greeted with excitement. The *Monthly Review* congratulated its reading public on 'so great an accession to the literary world, as the genius and talents of Miss Aikin. We very seldom have an opportunity of bestowing praise with so much justice.' Young Coleridge walked forty miles from Stowey to Bristol to meet her, and even Wordsworth, not famed for paying tributes to other poets, praised her. *Poems* went through five editions between 1773 and 1777. In the course of a long and productive literary life, Barbauld was to go on to publish a substantial body of poetry. In addition, she helped to manage and taught in her husband's school, wrote the best selling *Hymns in Prose for Children* and *Lessons for Children*, engaged in political pamphleteering on such issues as the slave trade, public worship and warfare, and, amongst other miscellaneous editing and critical work, edited the letters of Samuel Richardson in six volumes and *The British Novelists* in fifty volumes. Her sheer productivity in mainstream literary endeavour makes a nonsense of Samuel Johnson's snobbish scorn. Johnson observed magisterially:

> Miss Aikin was an instance of early cultivation, but in what did it terminate? In marrying a little Presbyterian parson, who keeps an infant boarding-school, so that all her employment now is, 'To suckle fools, and chronicle small-beer.' She tells the children, 'This is a cat, and that is a dog, with four legs and a tail; see there! you are much better than a cat or a dog, for you can speak.'[9]

If to be closely associated with the young was to be damned out of hand, then few women writers could escape condemnation. Most, if not all, had experience of teaching and training up children, either in the capacity of older sisters, or as mothers, aunts, governesses and teachers. This was not new, of course; what was new was the expanding market in books written both by and for such women. In this period, a remarkable number of women emerged as respectable authors by writing books which stemmed directly from their teacherly roles. These books fulfilled their own need for helpful texts as well as providing for other women similarly situated within the domestic space of families or in schools. Sarah Trimmer, for example, began writing educational materials as soon as she started teaching her own children. She was encouraged by the example of Anna Barbauld's *Lessons for Children* (1778–9). Both women sought to write in a way which took account of the developing child's capacities, as they had observed it from their experience of mothering and teaching. Barbauld's *Lessons for Children* came out as a carefully age-graded series of books: *Lessons for Children of Two to Three Years Old*; *Lessons for Children of Three Years Old*; and *Lessons for Children from Three to Four Years Old*. Simple narratives of domestic life, these were texts devised to help children learn to read by presenting them with familiar objects in homely settings. Such writing was fed by and fed into the practical activities of everyday learning, was rooted in particular local or domestic events, and might even be written with a particular child in mind. Literacy was probably considered secondary to moral teaching. The concern for morals, however, led to the close observation of children which gave women like Barbauld and Trimmer their understanding of the processes of children's learning. Sarah Trimmer saw how the cat-echistic method of questions and answers could help make difficult material digestible for the young, and introduced this format in her natural history textbook, *Easy Introduction to the Knowledge of Nature* (1780). Questions and answers, dialogues between parents and children, or tutors and children, were to be the most widely adopted formula amongst juvenile writers of this period, who sought to develop it beyond the rote learning of the catechism. Sarah Trimmer also understood the importance of the visual, originating a series of prints on biblical and historical themes which could be displayed on nursery walls and for which she wrote an accompanying volume of notes.

Given that the second half of the eighteenth century saw a huge expansion in the numbers of women finding their way into print, it is not surprising that they should also do so in their capacity as teachers. Didactic or broadly educational texts, advice literature and conduct-books were – next to devotional meditations or sermons – the most commercially attractive genres for aspiring writers in an age dedicated to improvement. Hitherto, predominantly written by men and directed at women, such texts were clearly attractive to women writers since they carried none of the stigma of fiction and could provide a point of entry into the public sphere, as well as a possible income. Since the beginnings of printing, women had published books of every kind: as Ina Ferris has observed, by the end of the eighteenth century, 'the perception that the novel was a female field was well entrenched'.[10] The same can be said of drama and, to a less generally acknowledged extent, poetry. But the runaway successes were always likely to be serious works of a moral kind. Catherine Talbot, friend and correspondent of the scholar Elizabeth Carter, did not live to see the popularity of her meditative essays, *Reflections of the Seven Days of the Week*, for they were published posthumously. A first edition in 1770 of 25,000 copies sold out in months and there were three more editions in that year alone.[11] It is against this background, in the light of a public eagerness for such works, that Barbauld's *Hymns in Prose* (1781) should be understood. It, too, was immensely popular, was a standard classroom reader, and confirmed her literary celebrity.

Culturally, the authority invested in the figure of the teacher was implicitly male, but in the population as a whole far more women than men were engaged in teacherly activities because of their domestic roles. By writing books and thus extending their influence from the realm of the private to the public, women laid claim to some of that authority. In this sense, harmless-seeming and very proper books for the young like those of Barbauld and Trimmer signify an important shift. In various ways, they place women at the centre of the educational-cultural exchanges depicted. Writers who learned from Barbauld and Trimmer – like Mary Wollstonecraft, Hannah More and Eleanor Fenn – made female authority explicit through the use of idealized teacher-figures whose role was to lead children to knowledge. For their purposes, dialogue between pupils and teacher was an ideal form. By dramatizing the teaching situation in this way, the authoritative voice of the woman as combined teacher/writer could be foregrounded. She might be named Mrs Teachwell, or the Rational Dame, or the Moral Mother; or, more simply, Mrs Andrews, in Sarah Trimmer's *Instructive Tales*; Mrs Jones, in Hannah More's *Tracts*; or Mrs Mason in Mary Wollstonecraft's *Original Stories*. These benevolent figures who guide and direct their fictional charges and point the moral for the reader are self-confident, virtuous, helpful and high-minded, altruistic, and remarkably powerful within their communities of influence.

In Mary Wollstonecraft's *Original Stories* there are two such figures. *Original Stories* dramatizes what are essentially standard sermons of the conduct-book. It seeks to teach good habits and correct principles, presenting them in the form of 'conversations calculated to regulate the affections and form the mind to truth and goodness'. The affections and minds in question are explicitly female and it is an older female who is responsible for them. Mrs Mason, 'a woman of tenderness and discernment', takes charge of two young girls whose mother has died and who have 'caught every prejudice' of the times. The object is to change them: they need to be moved from vanity, affectation and selfishness (all seen as social constructions) into the realm of reason. Reason and virtue are synonymous. Further, reason is the source of independence: Mrs Mason tells the girls, 'It is the proper exercise of our reason that makes us in any degree independent'. Reason both speaks through the female mouthpiece, and also justifies her right to speak. The saddest of all sights, we are told, is 'the wreck of a human understanding' – the complete absence of reason. This is the destiny, it is implied, that awaits women who do not cultivate their minds. Such women are represented by Lady Sly. Lady Sly cares only for a fine carriage, house and clothes, has no regard for truth, got her fortune dishonestly, and is a back-biting, scandal-mongering discontent unloved by children or the poor. In contrast, Mrs Trueman with her easy, simple manners, accomplished and dignified mind, love of reading and ability to be by herself, is the true woman, loved by children and the poor. Her beauty having been destroyed by smallpox, she attended to her mind instead and was saved from those womanly weaknesses, affectation and vanity. Reason is a defence against 'vanity and those littlenesses which degrade the female character'. The writing enacts the virtues: it demonstrates responsibility, asserts authority in tone and substance, justifies assertiveness by usefulness and virtue, validates knowledge and enables a participation in the high social valuation accorded to learning in the eighteenth century.[12]

This emphasis on reason takes Wollstonecraft's didactic writing beyond the limits of the traditional conduct-book. Her object is not to make young women behave more appropriately; as she bluntly says in the Preface to her first published work, *Thoughts on the Education of Daughters*, 'I wish them to be taught to think'. In a series of short chapters under such headings as 'Moral Discipline', 'Artificial Manners', 'Dress', 'The Temper', 'The Treatment of Servants' etc., she offers the guidance of a rational mind, professional and detached. Education and rules 'to regulate our actions by' may be the responsibility of parents working together, but in real life such an arrangement doesn't always work: 'the marriage state is too often a state of discord; it does not always happen that both parents are rational'.[13] Hence the need for a professional discourse, for thought-provoking texts like *Thoughts on the Education of Daughters*, and helpful weighty tomes like Wollstonecraft's second publication, *The Female Reader*. *The Female Reader* is a collection of extracts with a preface 'containing some hints on female education'. It was published under the pseudonym of 'Mr Cresswick, Teacher of Elocution', though Wollstonecraft's full name had appeared on the title page of the earlier *Thoughts on the Education of Daughters*. As in *Thoughts on the Education of Daughters*, Wollstonecraft goes out of her way to acknowledge the importance of the work of Anna Barbauld, quoting from her at length in the preface and including a number of pieces. Barbauld's short poem, 'On a Lady's Writing', emblematizes the idealized rational writing woman:

> Her even lines her steady temper show,
> Neat as her dress, and polish'd as her brow;
> Strong as her judgement, easy as her air;
> Correct though free, and regular though fair:
> And the same graces o'er her pen preside
> That form her manners and her footsteps guide.[14]

This perfected woman contrasts with the various evocations of a non-rational, non-professional, unimproved woman that occur throughout *Thoughts on the Education of Daughters* and *Original Stories*. Mothers are figured as creatures of false impulses and faulty logic, undisciplined, and in dire need of teaching and correcting. In *Thoughts on the Education of Daughters*, we are told that 'indolence' has led many mothers to fail their children:

> Mama is only anxious that they should love her best, and perhaps takes pains to sow those seeds, which have produced such luxuriant weeds in her own mind. Or, what still more frequently occurs, the children are first made play-things of, and when their tempers have been spoiled by indiscreet indulgence, they become troublesome, and are mostly left with servants.[15]

And in the preface to *The Female Reader*:

97

It has been a custom too prevalent to make children learn by rote long passages from authors, to whose very expressions they could not annex an idea ... Parents are often led astray by the selfish desire of having a wonderful child to exhibit; but these monsters very seldom make sensible men or women ... If, however, a girl be inclined to commit poems etc to memory, let me warn the fond mother not to persuade her to display this trifling attainment in company.[16]

This attack on mothers opens up a space for a professional discourse. Professional detachment, fuelled by the energies of reason and observation, is embodied in the working/thinking/writing woman, her virtues figured as the unspoken opposites of all 'Mama's' faults. She is not 'luxuriant' or 'anxious' or 'indulgent'; having worthwhile work she has no need to make 'play-things' of children, nor spoil them; with a cultivated mind, she has objectives to achieve which require self-knowledge and discipline, those powerful hindrances to 'weeds'. The novelty here is not the attack on 'Mama' but the assertion of a positive icon of professional womanhood.

Mitzi Myers observes how such characters operate as moral fantasies of benevolent female power. She cites Hannah More's Mrs Jones: an exemplary figure who demonstrates how an entire community can be remodelled through female enterprise and influence: 'With their ticklish balance of independent behaviour and domestic advice, altruistic women characters bespeak both compensatory thinking and real attainment.'[17] While it is demonstrably the case that they serve as autobiographical projections for their writers, it is also instructive to relate these 'compensatory' figures, these realizations of what Myers suggestively terms a 'fantasy of female potency' to the social world of literary and cultural production.

These 'fantasies' of the late eighteenth century reflect more of the real than may at first seem possible. It is not only in the realm of juvenile literature that we can hear an authoritative female voice speaking confidently and unapologetically to men as well as women. From the 1770s, throughout the 1780s and into the 1790s, we can detect a distinct weakening in cultural proscription of the authoritative female. This is not to say that a commercial literary market that had long situated Woman discursively at its very heart suddenly ceased to deploy its symbols in the time-honoured way. But there was a readiness to allow prominence to women. We can see this in the reverence accorded to the great tragic actress Sarah Siddons, whose impact on literary culture and women's participation in that has yet to be fully acknowledged. It can also be seen in the contributions of women writers to the leading journals of the day, such as *The Gentleman's Magazine*, where an arbiter of taste and literary critic like Anna Seward engaged in aggressive literary wars, taking for herself the Johnsonian voice of authority in order to challenge Boswell's depiction of the great man. Female potency can also be registered in the sheer range and volume of work published by women at this time. It is significant that as well as being educators, the most prominent women who wrote for children wrote – and had reputations – in other genres too. Maria Edgeworth was, like Barbauld, a teacher and writer of educational materials: with her father Richard Lovell Edgeworth (a friend and admirer of Barbauld's) she wrote and published one of the most influential texts of the genre, *Practical Education* in 1798. But she had already gone into print with *Letters to Literary Ladies* in 1795, a plea for women's education. For over forty years Maria Edgeworth was to write prolifically and maintain a high reputation as a novelist. A very large part of her output consisted of fiction and moral tales for the young. Charlotte Smith was already vividly before the public eye as a poet and novelist when late in her career she produced moral tales and volumes of natural history for children. Hannah More, who ran a school with her sisters in Bristol, began as a playwright. Her first play, *The Search For Happiness*, was a pastoral drama intended for school use. (Similarly, one of Anna Barbauld's enthusiasms was devising theatrical productions which she put on with her pupils.) Hannah More came to London in 1774 and later lodged with Garrick and his wife, thus positioning herself at the very heart of London dramatic and literary society. Her success came in 1777 with the tragedy *Percy*. It was her concern to ameliorate the social conditions of the poor which led her to employ her gift for narrative in moral fictions, published as tracts. These had a huge impact and were a publishing phenomenon. Mary Wollstonecraft, like Hannah More, was a radical polemicist and novelist. Their political allegiances differed, but like all the other women mentioned here, they were passionately engaged with the intellectual and political ideas of the day, eager to promote the virtues of rationalism (against a cultural inscription of irrationality as quintessentially feminine), energetic and ambitious. Any notion that because they wrote for children they were out of touch with the current of the times would be very mistaken. These writers found a platform in writing books for children.

Far from removing them from the major cultural discourses of the time, a preoccupation with children whether as pupils, children or readers, put women at the centre. The immense significance of the ideas of John Locke (Hannah More had an urn in memory of Locke in the garden of her cottage at Barleywood), and later Rousseau, helped focus middle-class attention on childhood. Progressive thinkers like Thomas Day, later the author of the hugely popular children's novel, *Sandford and Merton*, endeavoured to put ideas about social and psychological development into practice by adopting two girls from the workhouse. The objective was to train them up and later marry one of them. The experiment was a miserable failure.

Others flocked to see children on the stage – Mrs Siddons was not the only actress to appear on the same bill as her young son. Indeed, child actors and actresses became so common a sight backstage in the green room that one person at least – the comic actress Dorothy Jordan – declared that she had some sympathy at last with Herod's point of view. By the turn of the century, there was a mass theatrical obsession with child prodigies. In 1804–5, Master Betty, the Young Roscius, took the stage by storm. He played a variety of parts, including Hamlet. Innocent childhood had high commercial value. As performers, children were a familiar sight at musical soirées and in the concert hall. Domestically, children were accustomed to being admired for such feats as the ability to recite the first three books of *Paradise Lost* in the drawing room – as Anna Seward could do at the age of nine. This was exactly the kind of performance Mary Wollstonecraft and others objected to. But the child prodigy was also encouraged by publishers. So compelling was the attraction of the child prodigy that such a child could serve as social cement in particular localities. The end of the eighteenth/beginning of the nineteenth century saw a transition in publishing from the old days of patronage and subscription to the new world of a fully commercialized industry. Almost the last gasp of fully-fledged patronage can be seen in relation to child prodigies. An unknown child poet, for example, like Felicia Dorothea Browne, living in rural Wales and taught by a mother able to recognize her precosity, might be brought to the attention of local aristocracy and provincial gentry by circulating her poems in manuscript. A local prodigy reflected well on a neighbourhood and everybody could bask in the cachet. With aristocratic approval and gentry interest – so long as that gentry had literary connections – a subscription list could be launched. Felicia Browne's mother had the advantage of a contact with the Liverpool philanthropist and juvenile writer, William Roscoe, who put his weight behind the plan to publish poems written between the child's eighth and fourteenth year. This was no small operation. Even the Advertisement inviting subscribers was a properly printed folded sheet. The volume which eventually appeared in 1808 lists over a thousand subscribers beginning with the Prince of Wales and it is a remarkably handsome and expensive production. Legitimated by concepts of genius, something quite other than any intrinsic quality of verse is going on here. Those thousand-plus subscribers paid their money to support a cultural product they had learned over several decades to value: the child as bearer of the word.

This is even more startlingly demonstrated by the earlier example of Elizabeth Benger. Elizabeth Benger's long and very learned poem, *The Female Geniad* was published in 1791 when she was thirteen years old.

Far from hiding this fact lest it should diminish the impact and authority of her work, Benger makes great play with it in the preface:

> Could the pen of a Young Author describe the feelings of the heart, no other apology would be requisite, as the compassion excited by timidity, must disarm of criticism the most fastidious judgement; but in what manner can I, that am yet in a state of childhood, entreat the readers to pardon my offering this imperfect production to their inspection; the presumption had been unpardonable, did not the animating subject befriend me; as zeal for the honour of my sex, and admiration of shining merit, prompted my weak attempt to celebrate the female writers, and induced me to lay this feeble effort at the public mercy, hoping, that with wonted goodness, they will pity, instead of condemning, the numberless errors discernable [sic] in a juvenile essay, and which cannot but appear conspicuous in a poem that was written, originally, at the age of thirteen.[18]

Apologizing in prefaces was, as is well known, a convention of the time, and like many prefaces this one deploys innocence with great sophistication. The unaware reader of today might suppose that the poem itself, 'this feeble effort', this 'imperfect production', would betray signs of its author's youthfulness. What follows is in fact a formidably well-informed celebration and documentation in verse of the writings of women throughout history. The voice adopted by the poet all through the three cantos and fifty-five pages of *The Female Geniad* is the voice of cultural authority. The voice of the preface, however – the commercial, persuasive part of the production – foregrounds the child.

This child had been the recipient of much earnest thought and teaching within households, in schools and between the covers of books. Foremost among those delivering this teaching were women. It is paradoxical that in so far as the writers of moral tales pitched their textual efforts at producing ideal little children – often the reason they have been so heartily condemned for inhumanity – it is precociousness they validate. Successful products of their teaching would imitate the perfect adults who teach them, lisping morally unimpeachable homilies. Yet the avowed object of the moral and didactic writers was to enable children to grow into mature and reasonable adults. Feminist polemicists like Mary Wollstonecraft sought to offer young women a model of female adulthood grounded in reason and thought that would give them a measure of control over their lives. The objective was adult agency. What actually developed in the 1790s and early 1800s was a cult of childhood. For male Romantic poets this cult was fertile soil for the exploration of the poetic psyche and the development of the ego. For women it seems to have contributed, in socio-cultural terms, to a simple denial of adulthood. In place of mature women like Anna Barbauld – still very much active in the early years of the nineteenth century, but subject to critical abuse – we find that those women writers who project childlike qualities are the ones who are most applauded. Appropriate female utterance comes to be defined as something vague, emotional and uncertain. In the hyper-feminization of ideal womanhood within gentry culture which was a feature of the early decades of the nineteenth century, femininity came to be inscribed virtually as a state of infantilism. The woman writer seeking in those years to use and promote an unapologetic adult voice based on reason, authority and precision – with all the social, political and cultural implications that brought with it – had a harder task than her sister writers in the eighteenth century.

NOTES

1 This is the title given to the relevant chapter in Percy Muir, *English Children's Books, 1600–1900* (London: Batsford, 1954).
2 Sarah Trimmer, 1741–1810; M.M. Sherwood, 1775–1851; Mary Wollstonecraft, 1759–97. The comments come from John Rowe Townsend, *Written for Children* (London: Bodley Head, 1965, revised 1974 and 1983); *The Oxford Companion to Children's Literature*, eds Humphrey Carpenter and Mari Pritchard (Oxford: Oxford University Press, 1984); and Muir, *English Children's Books, 1600–1900*.
3 F.J. Harvey Darton, *Children's Books in England: Five Centuries of Social Life*, 3rd ed: (Cambridge: Cambridge University Press, 1982).
4 Edwin W. Marrs, Jnr. (ed.), *The Letters of Charles and Mary Anne Lamb*, Vol. 2, 1801–9 (Ithaca: Cornell University Press, 1976), Letter 136, 23 October 1802, pp. 81–2.
5 Earl Leslie Griggs (ed.) *Collected Letters of Samuel Taylor Coleridge*, 6 vols (Oxford: Clarendon Press, 1956–71), Vol. 1, p. 354.
6 Maria Edgeworth, *The Parent's Assistant*, ed. Christina Edgeworth Colvin (New York: Garland, 1976), p. xi.
7 Alan Richardson, *Literature, Education and Romanticism: Reading as Social Practice 1780–1832* (Cambridge: Cambridge University Press, 1994), see Chapter 3, 'Children's Literature and the Work of Culture', pp. 109–66.
8 For Edgeworth, see Mitzi Myers, 'De-Romanticizing the Subject: Maria Edgeworth's "The Bracelets", Mythologies of Origin, and the Daughter's Coming to Writing', in Paula R. Feldman and Theresa M. Kelley (eds), *Romantic Women Writers, Voices and Countervoices* (Hanover and London: University Press of New England, 1995). Other important essays by Myers include: 'Impeccable Governesses, Rational Dames, and Moral Mothers: Mary Wollstonecraft and the Female Tradition in Georgian Children's Books', *Children's Literature* 14 (1986); 'Hannah More's Tracts for the Times: Social Fiction and Female Ideology', in Mary Anne Scholfield and Cecelia Macheski (eds), *Fetter'd or Free: British Women Novelists, 1670–1815* (Athens: Ohio University Press, 1986).
9 See the Introduction to William McCarthy and Elizabeth Kraft (eds), *The Poems of Anna Letitia Barbauld* (Athens: University of Georgia Press, 1994).
10 Ina Ferris: *The Achievement of Literary Authority: Gender, History and the Waverley Novels* (Ithaca: Cornell University Press, 1991), p. 35. Ferris points out that commentators were frowning at the way women novelists introduced

didactic materials into novels, seeking 'to render what was intended only as a refuge for the indolent, a vehicle of instruction and a means of improvement' (Ferris, p. 34, quoting from the *British Critic*).

11 See Patricia Phillips, *The Scientific Lady: A Social History of Women's Scientific Interests 1520–1918* (London: Weidenfeld and Nicolson, 1990), pp. 150–3.

12 Janet Todd and Marilyn Butler (eds), *The Works of Mary Wollstonecraft*, Vol. 4, *Original Stories* (London: William Pickering, 1989), pp. 353–450.

13 Wollstonecraft, *The Works*, Vol. 4, *Thoughts on the Education of Daughters*, p. 11, p. 9.

14 Anna Barbauld, in Wollstonecraft, *The Works*, Vol. 4, *The Female Reader*, p. 306.

15 Wollstonecraft, *The Works*, Vol. 4, *Thoughts on the Education of Daughters*, p. 9.

16 Wollstonecraft, *The Works*, Vol. 4, Preface to *The Female Reader*, p. 58.

17 Mitzi Myers, 'Hannah More's Tracts for the Times', in *Fetter'd or Free'* p. 277.

18 Elizabeth Ogilvie Benger, 'Preface', *The Female Geniad* (1791).

7

FAIRY TALES AND THEIR EARLY OPPONENTS

In defence of Mrs Trimmer

Nicholas Tucker

The various self-appointed champions of childhood innocence who once went on record as opposing fairy tales as suitable reading for children have since received an almost universally bad press. This is not simply because such figures also occasionally wrote or championed alternative didactic children's literature of the type later mocked by Lewis Carroll and many others. The whole notion of condemning fairy tales for children was something that soon came to seem wilfully wrong-headed, apparently attempting to deprive the young of imaginative material unrivalled in its richness. For nineteenth-century fairy tale enthusiasts like Coleridge or Dickens this was a crime difficult or even impossible to forgive. Twentieth-century critics have largely continued in this vein. Some have also drawn upon psychoanalytic theory, insisting that fairy tales in addition offer the best guide we have to the human psyche in all its light and shade. For those with experience of living in totalitarian regimes, fairy tales have sometimes come to represent an essential freedom of the imagination often threatened by dictators eager to impose their own propaganda on every reader, young or old.

It is not surprising therefore that an eighteenth-century fairy tale opponent like Mrs Trimmer has been treated with scant respect by those writing about her since. But as a mother of twelve children whom she also taught at home, Mrs Trimmer was an impressive figure for her own contemporaries. Author of the best-selling *The History of the Robins* in 1786, she was also a leading figure in the Sunday School movement. As founder-editor of *The Guardian of Education* in 1802, she was the first children's books reviewer to operate on a large and systematic scale. Addressed to parents and governesses, the magazine closed in 1806 when the pressure upon her of having to review so many new children's books single-handed became too much.

While other eighteenth-century figures also had serious doubts about fairy tales, in subsequent literary histories it is often Mrs Trimmer who is quoted as a typical representative of the assorted liberals, evangelists and rationalists uneasy at the time about this aspect of children's reading. It was in the pages of *The Guardian of Education* that she issued the occasional warnings against certain fairy tales which have since proved a rich source for her later critics. But these attacks upon her all come from the safer position of being wise after the event. At the time, Mrs Trimmer and others had some good reasons for writing about fairy tales in the admonitory style they adopted. Published fairy tales had yet to become a familiar part of childhood. Because fewer children read them (though many more heard them told) critics lacked the experience and knowledge of fairy tales and their likely effects upon young audiences that was beginning to build up by the middle of the nineteenth century. Once such tales became more familiar and generally acceptable, awful warnings about any of their supposed bad effects could simply be met by denial from former readers now parents themselves. Since they believed such stories never did any harm to them, it stood to reason they would cause no damage to their children either. To suggest otherwise would be to impugn the adult now protesting his or her essential soundness of mind – always a dangerous course for a critic to take.

Mrs Trimmer h▪1 also enjoyed fairy tales when young. But her conscience led her to condemn this enjoyment later, urged on by her undersanding of child psychology as it then existed. She did not have available to her the research findings that now put into question the former simple cause-and-effect generalizations about the influence of reading of the type Mrs Trimmer once used to deliver. Detailed studies of reader-response are strictly a twentieth-century phenomenon. The consensus view of what actually goes on between book and reader has become far less dramatic than most experts in the past have generally supposed, including Mrs Trimmer. It is what young readers themselves bring to their reading of a book which is now seen as the deciding factor in how they react to any text afterwards. Emphasis has therefore shifted from the text itself to the different ways it is experienced from one reader to another. What texts do to readers can no longer be separated from what readers do to texts.

This focus upon the interior world of readers and how it affects the different way they construct experience contrasts with former explanations of human psychology. Although some individual differences were always acknowledged in former times, for example by ideas about the balance of the four humours or the importance of heredity, the shaping role of external influences was also seen as important too as a plausible explanation for particular individual traits. As long ago as William of Malmesbury, there was an appreciation of the role played by particularly traumatic events in a child's life. Writing in the twelfth century about the childhood of Ethelred the Unready, William was in no doubt where blame lay for one aspect of the sovereign's sorry lack of self-confidence.

> I have read that when he was ten years of age and heard the report that his brother was killed, he so irritated his furious mother by his weeping that she, not having a whip at hand, beat the little innocent with some candles she snatched up, nor did she desist until he was drenched with tears and nearly lifeless. For that reason he dreaded candles for the rest of his life, so much so that he would never let their light be brought into his presence.[1]

Belief in the explanatory importance of past traumatic events has always been a feature of psychological explanations of the individual and remains part of psychoanalytic theory to this day. Mrs Trimmer would have been aware of this way of thinking about the roots of personality. As an educated woman she would also have known about John Locke's strongly held belief in the significance of what a child actually experiences in life. By describing the child's mind as 'white paper devoid of all characters', Locke was stating that anything he or she directly experienced would then become etched on this blank paper for the rest of their days. Thus the warnings issued by him against letting servants frighten children with 'Notions of Spirits and Goblings'. For once such 'Bug-bear Thoughts ... got into the tender Minds of Children' they sank deep and fastened themselves 'So as not easily, if ever, to be got out again.' Not only did they then haunt children with 'strange visions'; they also caused them to become 'Afraid of their Shadows and Darkness all their lives after.'[2]

Locke, with Newton, was one of the two intellectual giants of his time. For many who read him his opinions were facts not mere theories. Numbers of parents also attempted to put his ideas on education into practice with their own children. It is therefore hardly fair to blame Mrs Trimmer for the way she too was influenced by current Lockeian ideas about the importance of associationism – in this case between what children hear in fairy tales and what they may then come to believe for themselves. Thus her condemnation of *Little Red Riding Hood* and *Bluebeard* for their 'terrific images'. For her, these tales 'Usually make deep impressions, and injure the tender minds of children, by exciting unreasonable and groundless fears.'[3] In fact, *Bluebeard* is one of those fairy stories that many parents of small children today also have problems with. Walter de la Mare has written lyrically about 'A sorrowful, a tragic, even a terrifying tale, picture or poem. That too may feed the imagination, enlighten the mind, strengthen the heart, show us *ourselves*.'[4] Most parents however would still side with Mrs Trimmer over the importance of protecting infants from the most gory and misogynist of traditional fairy tales. It is not always wrong to limit children's access to strong material when they are still at a tender age.

Without recourse to today's controlled experiments, longitudinal surveys, statistical studies or any of the other scientific ways now used to validate theories that make predictions about human behaviour, it was natural for Mrs Trimmer to rely upon purely anecdotal evidence about the relationship between children and books. When her various correspondents assured her of the damaging effects they believed fairy tales to have upon children, there is no reason why she should not have believed such primitive case-studies as true at the time. Claims about the supposed negative effects of certain films or video programmes continue to be made today at a similarly anecdotal level. Few stand up to any scientific rigour, but this does not stop the continuing wide circulation of generalizations on such matters often arising from no more than personal and possibly quite atypical experiences.

But was Mrs Trimmer unfairly prejudiced against fairy tales, constantly ignoring their positive side in favour of an obsession with their darker moments? Once again, those quick to condemn her are not taking the early publishing history of fairy tales into account. Far from appearing in the tastefully bound and lovingly illustrated volumes familiar today, the first published fairy tales usually turned up in the less-respectable world of contemporary chapbooks. The contents of these publications ranged from the inoffensive to material that would be seen as objectionable for children now. Titles like *How to restore a lost Maidenhead, or solder a Crackt one*[5] could hardly be expected to have endeared themselves to evangelists like Mrs Trimmer. No wonder fairy tales were often condemned by association, given that they sometimes appeared cheek by jowl with low material such as this.

The vendors of chapbooks, like the retailers of the penny dreadfuls or horror comics still to come, did not belong to the middle-class world of the respectable bookshop stocked by safe products from educational or religious publishers. Such vendors were instead closer to wandering tinkers, often selling their goods to the servants at the back door. Introduced unwittingly into a household, it was feared such literature might then come to the attention of well-born children without the master or mistress ever being the wiser. Because books written for children have until the modern paperback revolution proved relatively expensive, parents have generally been able to keep track of most contemporary reading material for children by exerting economic control over any new purchases. But chapbooks were cheap enough for children to buy direct. They could thus more easily avoid the type of censorship parents have so often liked to impose upon their children's reading.

Mrs Trimmer and those who thought like her found this prospect deeply threatening. Instead of receiving the books so carefully filtered out in her

107

magazine *The Guardian of Education*, children might instead sometimes be getting literature of a thoroughly debased kind. Some charming little chapbooks certainly existed, but how could parents be certain that their precious children saw only these and none of the other sort? The fact that the fairy tales in chapbooks proved popular with an uneducated readership also worked against them. Mrs Trimmer was by no means the only literary critic then or since to see the world of children's books in the light of the British social class system. Middle-class children have long been expected to turn to middle-class approved literature, so establishing yet another fence between them and their less-privileged contemporaries. Many parents since the days of Mrs Trimmer have confiscated cheap romances, 'bloods' or comics from their households for fear of cultural contamination. Condemning fairy tales for the low literary company they attracted would be an unexceptionable thing for Mrs Trimmer to do in a society greatly concerned with maintaining class barriers.

Mrs Trimmer and her supporters had other reasons for disliking fairy tales unconnected with their lowly social status. She found them profoundly anti-rational: a serious charge in the century of enlightenment with its emphasis upon reason in all things. This particular line of attack upon fairy tales still finds some defenders in modern times. Earlier this century, the great educationalist Maria Montessori also condemned fairy tales for infants under seven years of age, and the schools founded in her name continue not to stock them for this age group. Distinguished psychologists like the professors John and Elizabeth Newson, who have written widely about twentieth-century parenting patterns in Britain, make a point in their work of attacking the parental practice of 'bamboozling' children with silly answers to serious questions.[6] 'The meaning of deprivation is the deprivation of meaning' became something of a slogan among British and American developmental psychologists during the 1970s.

This does not mean that modern psychologists also usually oppose fairy tales for young listeners. It is now thought that most children possess fairly good mechanisms for sorting out fact from fantasy, at least when the intention is not consciously and deliberately to mislead. Fairy tales in particular generally have enough internal clues to indicate to children that what they are hearing is not to be taken literally, from the first 'Once upon a time' to the final neat tying up where everyone lives happily ever after. Reading out aloud from books in the slightly different storyteller's voice most of us adopt is in itself a situation most infants soon come to recognize as artificial and therefore something special. But it would be unjust to condemn Mrs Trimmer for not believing the same type of thing nearly two centuries earlier. Psychologists have so much more evidence to draw upon in this and in other matters than was available to her at the time.

Nor can Mrs Trimmer fairly be attacked now for criticizing fairy tales as a means of spreading superstition. Many of her less-educated contemporaries would still have believed in the fairies and witches we now accept as purely imaginary creations. In *A Candle in the Dark: Or, A Treatise Concerning the Nature of Witches & Witchcraft*, Thomas Ady listed fifteen causes which upheld 'The damnable doctrine of Witches Power.' The fourteenth of these was 'Old Wives Fables, who sit talking, and chatting of many fake old Stories of Witches, and Fairies, and Robin Goodfellow, and Walking Spirits, and the Dead walking again: all which lying fancies people are more naturally inclined to listen after than to the Scriptures.'[7] Although this was written in 1656, some people still held similar beliefs at the time Mrs Trimmer was writing. When John Marshall, who published about seventy children's books in the 1780–90 period, declared that his publications were 'Entirely divested of that prejudicial Nonsense (to young Minds) the Tales of Hobgoblins, Witches, Fairies',[8] he would have expected applause not censure from liberal adults writing then or in the future. It was far more dubious to defend fairy stories featuring witches when those actually suspected of witchcraft were still sometimes persecuted, particularly in small outlying communities where traditions die hard.

Literal belief in fairies in the West has taken a long time to die, with W.B. Yeats and Conan Doyle this century continuing to insist upon the reality of the little people. But so long as belief in the actual existence of fairies was a major issue largely dividing the poor and uneducated from those who had the benefit of schooling, stories that treated fairies as if they were real could quite fairly be seen as continuing to foster an ignorance at times leading to disabling superstition, terror or prejudice. Today topics like the occult or Satanism are largely avoided in children's books, given that there is still just enough residual belief in such phenomena within the community to alarm educated parents should numbers of authors also start spreading such ideas around in their fiction. Fairy stories however are largely free to go their own way since few believe that their contents will ever be taken literally. But the situation was very different in 1800, and once again it is hard to maintain that Mrs Trimmer was wholly wrong for taking the stand that she did.

Two more charges made by Mrs Trimmer against fairy tales deserve more sympathy than they commonly get. Perhaps the most famous statement associated with her is the quotation she prints from one of her correspondents, condemning *Cinderella* for promoting 'envy, jealousy, a dislike to mothers-in-law and half-sisters, vanity, a love of dress, etc. etc.'[9] But with John Locke insisting that children were deeply impressionable to whatever they came across, it was reasonable to assume that exposure to stories containing suspect values might also lead to the adoption of such values in the lives of the young readers concerned. Whether the story of *Cinderella* does in fact contain false values is a matter for debate. But if Mrs Trimmer sincerely believed that it did, she would have been right to oppose their dissemination to young minds at a time when every fleeting impression from childhood was thought to carry the possibility of permanency once a child had been exposed to them.

As for Mrs Trimmer's defence of step-mothers, referred to here as mothers-in-law, this strikes a curiously contemporary note. Now there are greater numbers of step-mothers in Britain than at any other time this century, complaints about their poor literary image have recently become common from various sources. While no one is demanding that literary step-mothers or fathers should from henceforth always be seen in a good light, their almost universally bad press in children's books is seen as unfair and as such yet another burden for parents to take on when trying to move into a new family as harmoniously as possible. In partial response, modern children's authors writing stories that feature today's reconstructed families are more careful than before about creating the stereotyped step-villains of former times.

In Mrs Trimmer's time, many children would also have possessed step-parents following the death rather than the divorce of their own. Fairy stories, with their unfavourable images of step-parents, could fairly be seen as unhelpful in this situation, particularly given the Lockeian stress on the durability of children's first impressions. There is some evidence too that evil parents in the oral versions of traditional fairy tales were sometimes changed by editors or transcribers into step-parents instead. The brothers Grimm certainly used to transform wicked fairy-tale mothers, in the tales they were collecting, over to step-mothers. By doing this, they believed they were protecting the sanctity of the blood relationship between parent and child that they saw as part of the greatness of the true German soul. This celebration of an overall Teutonic culture was for the Grimms always a most important part of their work in assembling and publishing their tales in the first place.

No one would now sympathize with Mrs Trimmer's condemnation of *Cinderella* for stirring up bad family feeling. Today's attitude would be to aim at a fairer balance by making other fairy tales available where step-parents get better treatment. But once again, Mrs Trimmer had at least some justification for writing as she did about possible injustice to step-parents in the fairy-tale versions around at the time. A modern age that has enthusiastically taken up the cause of promoting positive images of groups or individuals previously stigmatized in most children's books should think twice before condemning Mrs Trimmer's own partial defence of the step-parents she felt had been unjustly persecuted in popular literature.

Mrs Trimmer finally attacked fairy tales for occasionally terrifying the young, and here it is difficult to fault her. There have been many autobiographical accounts describing the miseries of listening to stories that proved too frightening to young minds at the time. Those who inflicted such stories on infants were not always purely sadistic; sometimes the terror they caused was used to frighten infants from leaving their beds at night, so cutting down on the work for the adult in charge. One such adult and her short but horrific repertoire of fantasy stories is described by Dickens in his essay *Nurse's Stories* published in 1867. 'This female bard . . . [was] the daughter of a shipwright. Her name was Mercy, though she had none on me.'[10] The two stories she repeatedly narrated to the young Dickens are retold by him here with great gusto. But there is also strong feeling in this brilliant essay for the 6-year-old child he once was, so cruelly terrified night after night almost out of his wits.

When Dickens attacks fairy tale reformers in other essays he forgets to mention the misery terrifying stories can sometimes cause. Today only the most insensitive of parents or teachers would read *Hansel and Gretel* or *The Juniper Tree* to very small children. Mrs Trimmer was at least half right; some fairy tales are disturbing and if told to children too young could prove highly upsetting. Had more parents listened to her advice at the time, smaller children at least might have been spared some nightmares. But children cannot be endlessly protected, and Mrs Trimmer overstated her case for shielding all young readers from frightening stories. A small child's fear can always be an older child's delight at an age where being scared in the imagination becomes a more generally acceptable challenge.

Dickens's chief butt when inveighing against fairy tale reformers was the famous illustrator and born-again teetotaller George Cruickshank. Mrs Trimmer was long dead when Cruickshank produced *The Fairy Library* in 1853, but her ghost would surely have approved of the various improving messages he worked into well-known tales like *Cinderella* and *Jack and the Beanstalk*. Dickens however would have none of it. In his superb essay 'Fraud on the Fairies', published in *Household Words* later in the same year, he weighs in against his 'own beloved friend' for altering 'the text of a fairy story; and against his right to do any such thing we protest with all our might and main'. For Dickens, all fairy tale

> must be as much preserved in their simplicity, and purity, and innocent extravagance, as if they were actual fact. Whosoever alters them to suit his own opinions, whatever they are, is guilty, to our thinking, of an act of presumption, and appropriates to himself what does not belong to him.[11]

To press home his point, Dickens then presents his own version of a ludicrously improved *Cinderella*. It still reads well, while Cruickshank's own laboured efforts were soon forgotten. But although Dickens easily won this particular dispute, his own arguments were often somewhat wayward. He wrote as if fairy tales were a fixed established canon, whereas scholars today suggest they have always been in a process of change. Obscene or overly religious fairy tales were usually quietly dropped from anthologies during the nineteenth century, while other famous titles were bowdlerized when it was thought necessary. Many other fairy tales published during Dickens's lifetime or shortly before were at least partially rewritten by editors and translators in tune with current ideologies. This was particularly true of the Grimms' famous collection, first translated into English in 1823. The shaping hand of the two brothers is evident both in the selection of the tales and in the way the published versions continued to change each time their collection reprinted.

Dickens would probably not have known about these changes made to traditional fairy tales on their journey from oral versions to final publication. So he is perhaps unwittingly unfair when accusing Cruickshank of importing social messages into fairy tales while remaining oblivious to the fact that other published versions have always contained a measure of contemporary ideology. Because Dickens shared the implicit conservatism found in nineteenth century editions of fairy tales, he was unable to see that this was in its way as strong and pervasive a belief as anything found in Cruickshank's versions. For him, such conservative beliefs were so normal that any attack upon them had necessarily to be wrong-headed.

This type of attitude could help explain the particular ire Dickens shows against Cruickshank, who was in fact advocating far more than teetotalism in his improved versions. By attacking the Corn Laws and advocating free universal education in *The Fairy Library*, Cruickshank was being as openly political as Hermynia Zur Mühlen this century, whose translated *Fairy Tales for Workers' Children* appeared in 1925 under the auspices of the Daily Worker Publishing Company. While no communist himself, Cruickshank's suggestion that evil giants should be reformed rather than slaughtered also broke with a tradition that saw wickedness as a problem caused by certain individuals rather than something implicit in the way society was organized. By wresting established fairy tale versions so far from their normal stereotypes, Cruickshank was making a strongly political point. Orthodox versions of fairy tales can be political too, but in a way that is less easy to spot. As Jack Zipes has written,

> In almost all the Grimms' fairy tale, male domination and master-slave relationships are rationalised so long as the rulers are benevolent and use their power justly. If tyrants and parents are

challenged, they relent or are replaced, but the property relationships and patriarchy are not transformed.[12]

This is not an agenda that conservative critics would object to, since it confirms all their own prejudices. No wonder Dr Johnson in his own time believed children should read *Jack the Giant Killer* rather than concentrate on becoming 'prematurely wise'. Yet the eighteenth century also saw a number of other books for children that encouraged both questioning and learning about the world as it was. Such books were often dull and didactic, but the intention to inform children was not in itself bad. For old Tories like Dr Johnson, too much is 'expected of precocity, and too little performed'. He was much happier when children read fairy tales instead, featuring child characters who often play a minor and generally rather passive role in a world that is somewhere else. But desiring children to read such tales may not simply reflect an altruistic wish for them to have a good time. Fairy tales certainly feed the imagination; they also leave undisturbed any more general understanding of how society works in a way highly sympathetic to those who oppose any idea of radical change in favour of never rocking the boat.

Conservative critics also tend to be in sympathy with the way fairy stories hark back to a former feudal model of society. As Ruskin put in 1868,

All the best fairy tales have owed their birth, and the greater part of their power, to narrowness of social circumstances: they belonged properly to districts in which walled cities are surrounded by bright and unblemished country, and in which a healthy and bustling town life, not highly refined, is relieved by, and contrasted with, the calm enchantment of pastoral and woodland scenery, either under humble cultivation by peasant masters, or left in its natural solitude.[13]

An idealized image of rural Britain has always been less threatening to the established social order than the urban living of contemporary reality.

Arch-conservatives for their own time like C.S. Lewis and J.R.R. Tolkien also shared this type of vision along with a love of traditional fairy tales. Their wise and perceptive descriptions of fairy stories only fall short when they treat them as the last word on human aspirations without considering that the same tales are also products of particular times and ideologies. The offence caused by all fairy tale reformers is to highlight the existence of such ideologies by insisting so openly upon the validity of their own in the versions they sometimes produce. It is much more comforting for natural conservatives to believe that the fairy tales they are used to and the values these enshrine are in themselves immutable and eternal.

Perhaps Cruickshank's greatest offence in Dickens's eyes was to turn

Cinderella into such a sparky, energetic character – a marked contrast to the feeble young heroines Dickens created in his own novels. In his parody, Dickens makes Cinderella throw 'open the right of voting, and of being elected to public offices, and of making the laws, to the whole of her sex'. This for Dickens was self-evidently absurd; certainly the fairy tales he knew bore no hint of such female determination. Scholars since have suggested that more assertive images of femininity were systematically excised in the selection and editing of fairy tales during the nineteenth century.

Mrs Trimmer was also not looking for more generally self-assertive female characters in the fairy stories she criticized. But by attacking such tales in general, she foreshadowed the type of cultural criticism that analyses the underlying ideologies found in all the expressive arts from established classics to the most familiar popular culture. By considering fairy tales as fair game for criticism rather than unthinking worship, Mrs Trimmer is at one with scholars today who have also written critically about the ideologies found in some individual stories. Attacking fairy tales for their sexist bias is now commonplace in contemporary criticism. Those who adopt this line have more in common with Mrs Trimmer, however much they may disagree with her in detail, than they have with those defenders of fairy tales who deny all criticism from whatever source and for whatever reason.

Were Mrs Trimmer to return from the dead and inspect the current fairy tale collections in print she might in many ways be agreeably impressed. Some of the tales she most disliked have long dropped away, however popular they may once have been. The story of *Bluebeard* has lost its position in the nursery, and other shockers like the anti-Semitic ballad *Hugh of Lincoln* are found only in old collections. Racial slurs, descriptions of torture, lavatory humour – all these once popular ingredients in fairy tales no longer have a place in most modern anthologies. Other children's writers sometimes also rewrite or generally embroider traditional fairy tales, whatever Dickens had to say about this practice. Mrs Trimmer may have preferred the efforts of moralists like George Cruickshank to anything written by modern authors like Adèle Geras or Angela Carter in this respect. But the success of their books suggests there is nothing intrinsically sacrosanct about fairy tales that cannot be changed by those who think they may occasionally be on to something better. Once again, Mrs Trimmer would surely have agreed.

She may also have approved of the fact that psychoanalytic writers like Bruno Bettelheim who have argued the case for traditional fairy tales as essential to mental health are now generally believed to have overstated their case. The tales he analysed in his famous *The Uses of Enchantment*[14] owe more to the interpolations and excisions of the Grimm brothers and less to a collective unconscious than he realized. Followers of Jung who argue for the existence of eternal archetypes in fairy tales must also meet the argument that sometimes such archetypes may instead be particular, time-bound social constructs. The idea of the passive woman, for example, may be less archetypal and more the contribution of a patriarchal culture in a particular phase of history than Jung conceded in his writings. Such arguments will continue to rumble on, but at least no responsible critic now would argue that all fairy tales are necessarily inviolate from any possible criticism or modification simply by the fact of their being fairy tales. That is what Mrs Trimmer believed too, and she might well feel glad that others are coming round to her point of view.

Should Mrs Trimmer visit a modern children's library, she might enjoy and admire the many brilliantly illustrated and brightly written information books that exist today for children. Young people can get their facts straight now if they wish; the habit of bamboozling children at a time when fairy tales may sometimes have been the only literature they would regularly come across, is no longer with us. She would surely also approve of the careful reviewing of children's books that is still a feature of the quality press. Mrs Trimmer too thought it important to try to sort the wheat from the chaff in children's literature rather than simply rely upon chance or crude market forces. The fact that so many adults continue to review children's books today suggests that we agree with her over this central issue, however differently modern critics may react to the texts that Mrs Trimmer once discussed. I suspect if she was still around now she would try to relaunch the *Guardian of Education* as a useful checklist for schools and libraries. If not, the love she clearly had for much of her former reading coupled with her fear for some of its possible consequences – and the occasional contradictions these conflicting feelings sometimes led her into – might drive her instead to write for that home of all worried liberalism, the *Guardian* newspaper itself.

NOTES

1 Quoted in M. Rosen *The Penguin Book of Childhood* (London: Viking, 1994), p. 14.
2 Quoted in S.J. Pickering, *John Locke and Children's Books in Eighteenth Century England* (Knoxville: University of Tennessee Press, 1981), p. 42.
3 Ibid., p. 44.
4 W. de la Mare, *Animal Stories* (London; Faber, 1939), p. xix.
5 Quoted in Pickering, *John Locke and Children's Books*, p. 5.
6 J. Newson and E. Newson *Seven Years Old in the Home Environment* (London: Allen & Unwin, 1976).
7 Quoted in Pickering, *John Locke and Children's Books*, p. 42.
8 Ibid., p. 76
9 Quoted in F.J. Harvey Darton, *Children's Books in England: Five Centuries of Social Life*, 3rd edn (Cambridge: Cambridge University Press, 1982).

10 Quoted in N. Tucker, *Suitable for children? Controversies in Children's Literature* (Berkeley and Los Angeles: University of California Press, 1967), p. 136.
11 Ibid., p. 47–8.
12 J. Zipes, *Fairy tales and the Art of Subversion* (London: Heinemann, 1983), p. 59.
13 Fairy Stories, Quoted in L. Salway, *A Peculiar Gift, Nineteenth Century Writing on Books for Children* (London: Kestrel Books, 1976), p. 30.
14 B. Bettelheim, *The Uses of Enchantment* (New York: Knopft, 1976).

8

IN THE ABSENCE OF MRS LEICESTER

Mary Lamb's place in the development of a literature of childhood

Janet Bottoms

'It at once soothes and amuses me', wrote Coleridge on the fly-leaf of an early edition of *Mrs Leicester's School*, 'to think – nay, to know – that the Time will come when this little volume of my dear and well-nigh oldest Friend, dear Mary Lamb, will be not only enjoyed but acknowledged as a rich Jewel in the treasury of our permanent English literature.'[1] Time has not been as perceptive as he imagined, but it is still perhaps as worthy of note that a book written explicitly for children should be accorded the status of 'permanent literature', as that its author should have disappeared so completely from literary histories as seldom even to be given an entry under her own name. When *Mrs Leicester's School* appeared in 1808, however, Coleridge was not the only one to respond to it with a recognition that here was something new and exciting. This is not the place to go into why Mary Lamb and her work – except for the ubiquitous *Tales from Shakespear* – should have dropped out of sight in the latter part of the century, but the reasons for continuing to see her 'little volume' as of great importance in the history both of literature for children and the literature of childhood are the subject of this chapter.

Mrs Leicester's School, or the History of Several Young Ladies Related By Themselves consists of ten stories set in a very slight narrative frame, the explanatory 'Dedication to the Young Ladies at Amwell School', and a few semi-dramatized interjections made by 'M.B.', their supposed teacher.[2] Three of the stories were written by Charles Lamb: the remainder, and the idea for the project, were Mary's, and just as the idea of transforming Shakespeare's plays into stories for children had not been thought of before Mary Lamb undertook it, so *Mrs Leicester's School* is also radically new. The innovative nature of the work, however, has been obscured by the title, a fact which may partly account for the easy manner in which it has too often been dismissed. The publication of collections of stories loosely linked within an educational setting, whether they are

117

ostensibly told by the adult mentor or by the children themselves, was modelled, in England, on Sarah Fielding's *The Governess or, Little Female Academy* (1749), and derived more indirectly from the precepts of Fenelon who, in his *Traite de l'Education des Filles*, recommended teachers to exploit children's passion for stories by telling them instructive tales and moral fables.[3] If the title of *Mrs Leicester's School* seems to signal its descent from *The Governess*, however, the difference between the two books is more significant. Fielding's Mrs Teachum takes 'no more Scholars than she could have an Eye to herself, without the Help of other Teachers', and she keeps that 'lively and commanding Eye' on her pupils, creating in them both awe and an eagerness to gain her approval.[4] Mrs Leicester, on the other hand, is remarkable for her total absence from the book which bears her name. She engages an inexperienced helper and seems to leave the care of the girls to her, even though the school is a new one. This helper, who signs herself simply as 'M.B.', describes their arrival in the introductory Dedication. 'Every carriage that drove from the door, I knew had left a sad heart behind. – Your eyes were red with weeping, when your governess introduced me to you as the teacher she had engaged to instruct you'. Though equally sad and lonely herself, the young teacher decides that her first duty must be 'to divert the solitary young strangers', and in pursuance of this she encourages them to tell their own life stories, acting, with their approval, first as their 'amanuensis', and then their 'faithful historiographer'.

The expressed purpose behind these stories is therefore very different from the typical children's books of the period. Mrs Mason, the stern preceptress of Mary Wollstonecraft's *Original Stories from Real Life*, follows very closely the educational precepts of Fenelon, including the use of stories to 'very strongly enforce what I have been saying'.[5] Maria Edgeworth, in *The Parent's Assistant*, is equally clear about the purpose of her stories, although she concedes that 'to prevent precepts of morality from tiring the ear and the mind, it was necessary to make the stories in which they are introduced in some measure dramatic'.[6] Sarah Fielding prefaces *The Governess* by asking her readers to 'consider with me, what is the true Use of Reading', concluding that it is 'to make you wiser and better', and to prove that 'Pride, Stubbornness, Malice, Envy, and, in short, all manner of Wickedness, is the greatest Folly we can be possessed of', and though the book contains a range of different types of story each is justified by the same sternly moral purposes. Jenny Peace, the eldest of Mrs Teachum's pupils, encourages the rest to tell their own stories because there is 'nothing more likely to amend the future Part of any one's Life, than the recollecting and confessing the Faults of the past' (p. 23), while the pretext for having them recorded is that their Governess wishes to keep her eye on the girls even when she is not physically present.

*In this manner, the epitaph on my mother's tomb being
my primer and my spelling-book, I learned to read*

Figure 8.1 Mrs Leicester's School: frontispiece to the first edition (reproduced
by permission of the Syndics of Cambridge University Library)

Therefore that she might not be any Bar . . . to the Freedom of their Speech . . . she called Miss Jenny Peace in to her Parlour after Dinner, and told her, She would have her get the Lives of her Companions in Writing, and bring them to her.[7]

Mary Lamb's young teacher takes a surprisingly modern approach. Faced with a collection of unhappy girls, strangers to their new surroundings and to each other, her first reaction is not to instruct but to warm. She invites them to draw near to 'a bright fire which blazed in the chimney, and looked the only cheerful thing in the room', and for a time the 'solemn silence' of the sad little company is punctuated only by her 'repeated requests that you would make a smaller, and still smaller circle, till I saw the fireplace fairly inclosed round'. The same need to comfort and encourage is also the inspiration of her proposal that they should each tell a story about themselves. It is presented as a way of getting to know each other, and in terms of strict equality – the order in which the tales are told is decided by lot. M.B. decides to write up the stories so that the girls themselves may each be given the account of their 'own biographical conversations'. She also recognizes the problems inherent in this, pointing out, apologetically, that though her intention is to be as faithful as possible to the style and manner of the original narrators, 'what is very proper and becoming when spoken, requires to be arranged with some little difference before it can be set down in writing'; and finally she admits that her own way of thinking may 'too often intrude itself', in spite of her intentions.

Mary Lamb's own way of thinking also informs the whole book, but it is only when we compare *Mrs Leicester* with its supposed models that we can see just how radical she was in treating children's narratives as valuable in themselves. M.B. responds to her pupils' initial fear that they won't know what to say or how to begin by suggesting they talk about their first memories, or something that made a great impression on them when they were very young. After that, she says,

if you find you can connect your story till your arrival here to-day, I am sure we shall listen to you with pleasure; and if you like to break off, and only treat us with a part of your history, we will excuse you, with many thanks for the amusement you have afforded us.[8]

This is a remarkably effective formula for a convincing literary presentation of the child's-eye view of the world. The girls vary in age, self-reflectiveness, and the degree to which they consciously shape their narratives, but as each story is made up of early recollections mediated through a more advanced but not yet mature understanding, so each one can also be read on more than one level. There is the primary experience of the

120

child, the story, to use Blake's term, of 'Innocence'; there is the voice of the girl reflecting upon her younger self – the story of 'Experience'; and finally there is the shaping power of the adult author, whose subtly ironic perspective on the social world within which the children struggle to make sense of their lives informs the whole. Child readers can identify directly with the narrator heroines, while adults may be struck by the view from this novel angle. In spite of its title, *Mrs Leicester's School* is concerned with pedagogic issues only in an oblique way. Though the stories are about education of a kind, it is not always the kind intended by the adults, and the lessons they learn are not always recognized as such by the girls themselves.

Louisa Manners, 7 years old, is the youngest and the nearest to the experience she describes. Her story concerns a lengthy visit to her grandmother's farm, at the age of 4, and the London-bred child remembers every detail of her first experience of the country with great clarity. She was struck by the strange isolation of the farmhouse with 'no house to be seen at all near it'. Her shame at not having remembered her grandmother, who 'was very glad to see me, and she was very sorry that I did not remember her, though I had been so fond of her when she was in town but a few months before', has impressed itself on her memory. The delight with which she encountered the ducks, sheep, flowers, bees, and all the other sights of country and farm are expressed with such naïve enthusiam as makes the reader experience with her the new world and new freedom she enters into. Louisa's story is not consciously 'shaped'. She does not distinguish between what is trivial and what is important or, rather, might seem to an older listener to be important, and in the end M.B. interrupts her, sensing that the other girls are becoming bored with her inconsequential 'prattle'. Some of the older girls do, however, find their own meaning in it: Ann Withers, remembering 'how early I learned to disregard the face of Nature, unless she were decked in picturesque scenery', thanks her for preaching 'an useful lesson to me . . . which I shall not easily forget' (p. 290).

On another level, it is possible to see a kind of education being given to Louisa, who records, without irony, the explanations and comments by which she learns how to understand and evaluate the world. Her grandmother and sister Sarah are her chief teachers. 'Grandmamma says a hen is not esteemed a very wise bird', recalls the eager pupil, along with many other examples of folklore, whimsy, and practical advice, all received with equal conviction. 'Birds' nests we might not look for', she explains, because her grandmother had said 'the little birds would not sing any more, if their eggs were taken away from them', but a hen 'was a hospitable bird, and always laid more eggs than she wanted, on purpose to give her mistress to make puddings and custards with'. As for the flowers, at first Louisa valued them all equally, but Sarah soon taught her which she should prefer, and though occasionally she would pick even a daisy, in spite of knowing that 'it was the very worst flower of all', she was 'very careful to love best the flowers which Sarah praised most'.

Other stories show children teaching or learning less innocent lessons. In 'A Visit to the Cousins', young Emily Barton describes how she was sent to live with some relations for a year, without explanation and without any visit from her parents in all that time, 'though', as she insists, 'they were remarkably fond of me'. Her first pleasure at having other children to play with soon changed to feelings of loneliness and injustice. All the toys seemed to belong to one or other of her cousins, who guarded their property jealously, and whenever they quarrelled with her would complain to their mother who 'always took Sophia's part because she was so young; and ... never suffered me to oppose Mary, or Elizabeth, because they were older than me'.

> Nobody could help, I think, being a little out of humour if they were always served so: but if I shewed any signs of discontent, my aunt always told my uncle I was a little peevish fretful thing, and gave her more trouble than all her own children put together. My aunt would often say, what a happy thing it was, to have such affectionate children as hers were. She was always praising my cousins because they were affectionate; that was sure to be her word. She said I had not one atom of affection in my disposition, for that no kindness ever made the least impression on me. And she would say all this with Sophia seated on her lap, and the two eldest perhaps hanging round their papa, while I was so dull to see them taken so much notice of, and so sorry that I was not affectionate, that I did not know what to do with myself (p. 312).

This is the authentic voice of confused and emotionally abused childhood, and calls to mind young Jane Eyre or David Copperfield, though the sequel for Emily is not so desperate. Instead, retrieved by her own parents with as little explanation as when she was abandoned, she finds herself showered with toys, books and other indulgences, with the natural result that she becomes extremely possessive in her turn. When another child and her mother are invited to tea, she quickly makes it clear that her toys are to be played with only on her terms.

> Then presently I took occasion to begin a little quarrel with her, and said, 'I have got a mamma now, miss Frederica, as well as you, and I will go and tell her, and she will not let you play with my doll any longer than I please, because it is my own doll.' And I very well remember I imitated as nearly as I could, the haughty tone in which my cousins used to speak to me (p. 316).

Emily does point the moral of this herself. She recalls her mother's reproach, which makes her see 'as plain as could be, what a naughty girl I was, and I promised not to do so any more'. The language is that of the tutored child, but it is not the idea of Emily's 'naughtiness' which the reader carries away from her story.

*

The narratives in *Mrs Leicester's School* are concerned both with the development of the child, and with the child's-eye view of the adult world around her. They are also placed just at that point in the child's life when she becomes conscious of being on her own, a 'solitary stranger' in a world of strangers. In his essay on 'Children's Literature and Literature's Children', Victor Watson describes the history of children's books as having to do with 'the struggle to find a voice to express an absence, a loss, a distance between parents and children', and he sees the publication of *Jane Eyre* as an occasion of great significance in this history.

> The opening chapters of *Jane Eyre* provided the imaginative ante-cedent of what was subsequently to be referred to as 'children's literature'. It was not those legions of hack writers who had been producing didactic books for children since the Puritans; it was not even John Newbery . . .; it was certainly not Hannah More and the writers of the Religious Tract Society . . . Childhood was born into articulate meaning when Jane Eyre climbed into her window-seat – but it was born *dispossessed and parentless*.[9]

An equally significant, though now largely forgotten, moment occurred that day nearly forty years earlier when ten girls, their eyes still 'red with weeping', gathered round the fire in Mrs Leicester's School to comfort and strengthen each other.

Ironically, the girls in *Mrs Leicester's School* are frequently 'orphaned' or dispossessed not so much by death or malice as by the good intentions of adults. As children, they are often shown finding their own way of coping with the literal deaths of parents. In the story of 'The Sailor Uncle', Elizabeth Villiers recalls that her first memory is of her curate father teaching her the alphabet from the letters on her mother's tomb. To the child there was nothing morbid or sentimental about this. Whereas in the house her father 'would often be weary of my prattle, and send me from him', he would always leave his books and accompany her when she said she wanted to 'go and see mamma'.

> Here he was all my own. I might say anything, and be as frolicsome as I pleased here; all was chearfulness and good humour in our visits to mamma, as we called it.

The loss of the living mother was not consciously felt, because her grave had been made to fill her place, a place where the child could play, learn, and feel secure. Her father would talk about how one day they would all three sleep together in the same grave, and when the child went to bed she would often wish she was 'sleeping in the grave with my papa and mamma'.

> In my childish dreams I used to fancy myself there; and it was a place within the ground, all smooth, and soft, and green. I never made out any figure of mamma, but still it was the tombstone, and papa, and the smooth green grass, and my head resting upon the elbow of my father (p. 277).

The little girl's dispossession begins with the arrival, after long absence, of her mother's sailor brother, for as he weeps over the grave Elizabeth is made to feel uneasy for the first time. 'At last he took me in his arms and held me so tight, that I began to cry, and ran home to my father, and told him, that a gentleman was crying about mamma's pretty letters.' The meeting between the two men is still more disturbing for the child, who resists the well-meant efforts of the servant to keep her in the kitchen 'that I might not disturb the conversation', but when her uncle tries to take her in his arms she turns away and clings more closely to her father, 'having conceived a dislike to my uncle because he had made my father cry. Now I first learned that my mother's death was a heavy affliction.'

In 'The Father's Wedding Day' another motherless child is similarly shown finding her own way of dealing with loss. Her story begins with the day when her father set her on his knee, called her his 'dear little orphaned Elinor', and told her that a Miss Saville 'was going to be so kind as to be married to him', to live with them, and be her mamma. 'My father told me this with such pleasure in his looks,' says Elinor, 'that I thought it must be a very fine thing indeed to have a new mamma' (pp. 302–3). In both stories, the degree to which the child's understanding of the world is shaped by her perception of the adult's feelings is subtly contrasted with adult imperception of the child's. Elinor is excited by the general excitement, but when the housekeeper shakes her head over 'how soon children forget everything', she is puzzled, 'for I instantly recollected poor mamma used to say I had an excellent memory'. Elinor has not forgotten her mother, for 'when I was drest in my new frock, I wished poor mamma was alive to see how fine I was on papa's wedding day'. However, she does not understand death in the way that adults do, and while those around her never speak to her about her dead mother, the child, by means of a habit 'which perhaps had not been observed', has developed her own way of coping with the mysterious nature of the world. Taking her doll and her mother's footstool, she regularly goes to the door of the room in which her mother had spent her last, long illness. There, after trying to open it, and peeping through the keyhole, from whence I could just see a glimpse of the crimson curtains, I used to sit down on the stool before the door, and play with my doll, and sometimes sing to it mamma's pretty song, of 'Balow my babe'; imitating as well as I could, the weak voice in which she used to sing it to me. My mamma had a very sweet voice. I remember now the gentle tone in which she used to say my prattle did not disturb her (p. 303).

In both these stories the child is made, by the well-meaning intervention of adults, to construct a new way of visualizing the mother and the mother's loss. The sailor uncle of Elizabeth Villiers decides that the grave-yard visits are bad for both child and father and must be stopped. At first this creates great resentment in the little girl, who senses a criticism of her father in his attitude, but as her uncle buys her books and teaches her to read them, plays with her and tells her stories of his travels, she learns to shape her attitudes by his, and becomes 'a little woman in understanding'. She no longer plays around her mother's grave but regards it with 'awe and reverence'. The figure of her mother 'which before seemed an ideal something, no way connected with life', becomes a 'real mamma' – though perhaps no less of an 'ideal something' since she is represented as the image of feminine grace, elegance, and modesty.

If ever in my life I shall have a proper sense of what is excellent or becoming in the womanly character, I owe it to these lessons of my rough unpolished uncle; for, in telling me what my mother would have made me, he taught me what to wish to be (p. 281).

To a twentieth-century reader this picture of the 'rough' male educating a little girl into the masculine ideal of femininity is deeply ironic. How far Mary Lamb felt this is difficult to tell, though it is worth noting that she herself never laid any claim to having 'nice maidenly manners', and told her friend Sarah Stoddart that she had observed 'many a demure Lady who passes muster admirable well' whom they could easily learn to imitate if required. Elizabeth Villiers, the girl narrator, certainly intends no irony. She wants to please, and is herself pleased when she hears her father commended on how well she has been brought up. Psychologically, the development of the motherless child yearning for her father's atten-tion, into the good daughter lacking in self-esteem, is entirely convincing.

Elinor Forrester's image of her mother is also displaced in favour of one created by an adult. When her father told her that Miss Saville was to become her 'new mamma' she interpreted this to mean that 'miss Saville was to be changed into something like my own mother, whose pale and delicate appearance in her last illness was all that I retained of her remembrance'. This mistake, understandable in the child but equally understandably unsuspected by the adult, is followed by the shock of the visual contrast when her father brings home her 'new mamma'.

> I said, 'Miss Saville shall not be my mamma', and I cried till I was sent away in disgrace. Every time I saw her for several days, the same notion came into my head, that she was not a bit more like mamma than when she was miss Saville (p. 304).

Her father is angered by what he sees as his daughter's 'sullen' resistance, but the new wife, perceiving as nobody else had done the importance to the child of her mother's room, has it opened up.

> I was so pleased to be taken into mamma's room! I pointed out to her all the things that I remembered to have belonged to mamma, and she encouraged me to tell her all the little incidents which had dwelt in my memory concerning her.

However, Miss Saville had also been her mother's school friend, and promises to tell her 'stories of mamma when she was a little girl no bigger than me'. As the child is enabled to take possession of her mother's memory and her mother's room, so also her mother's image begins gradually to be reconstructed as that of a child, while the 'new mamma' takes over the maternal role, teaches her to read, and rewards her 'with some pretty story of my mother's childhood', generally containing 'some little hints that were instructive to me, and which I stood greatly in want of; for between improper indulgence and neglect, I had many faulty ways'.

If the two surrogate parents in these stories are recognized by the girls as helping them to grow up, however, they are also responsible for 'orphaning' them afresh. Her 'new mamma', says Elinor, 'would have continued to teach me, but she has not time, for she has a little baby of her own now, and that is the reason I came to school'. In the bare statement, the abrupt conclusion to her story, we may perhaps read a new sense of loss of a kind that had not been experienced before. Elizabeth's sailor uncle goes away again, leaving her not only to grieve over his departure but also to feel guilt for her first rejection of him. 'All my little quarrels with my uncle came into my mind, now that I could never play with him again, and it almost broke my heart. I was forced to run into the house to Susan for that consolation I had just before despised.' As befits the curate's daughter, she concludes her narrative on a more positive note with her father's kindly moral advice. It is noticeable, however, that hers is the only story which does so.

Another child who is more literally 'dispossessed' is Ann Withers, the 'changeling', who begins her story:

> My name you know is Withers, but as I once thought I was the daughter of sir Edward and lady Harriot Lesley, I shall speak of

myself as miss Lesley, and call sir Edward and lady Harriot my father and mother during the period I supposed them entitled to those beloved names.

The reader who pauses to consider this sentence may find something briefly disturbing in this linking of love to the name, the abstract concept 'father and mother'. Ann does not pause. On the level on which she consciously chooses to tell it, her story is to be seen as a 'moral tale' in which pride comes before a fall and modesty and affection receive their due reward. Yet it is not this formal moral, but the hint that love belongs to names, and names may be changed, which underpins the emotional structure of the story.

'The Changeling' is a simple enough story in essence. When Lady Harriot becomes seriously ill, following the birth of her daughter, the mother of Ann Withers is engaged as a wet-nurse. One day, grieving over the very different fortunes of the 'little lady-babe' and her own child, she switches the two children. Nobody notices the exchange, but later, filled with guilt, she confesses it to her 'daughter'. Meanwhile the two girls, socially divided, have become regular companions and one day the supposed Ann confides the story to the supposed Miss Lesley, under a vow of confidentiality. To the older girl this is a romantic story, and when Sir Edward suggests she compose a play for performance by herself and some visiting children, to entertain the houseparty, it occurs to her that her friend's story would make a highly effective drama:

> the costly attire of the lady-babe, – the homely garb of the cottage infant, – the affecting address of the fond mother to her own offspring; – then the charming équivoque in the change of the children: it all looked so dramatic: – it was a play ready made to my hands (p. 294).

Unfortunately Mrs Withers, the former nurse, has been invited to watch the show among the humbler servants, and she collapses in hysterics and confesses the truth before the whole company. Uproar naturally follows. The audience, in a dramatic reversal of roles, become the actors, with Lady Harriot near to fainting, Mrs Withers in tears of remorse and terror, Sir Edward roaring for her arrest, while her 'daughter', the newly recognized baronet's heir, falls on her knees, begging the other children around to help her ask forgiveness for her 'mother'.

In the days of her pride, Ann had dwelt complacently upon the idea of restoring the other girl to the rights of her birth, but, as she says, 'I thought only of becoming her patroness, and raising her to her proper rank; it never occurred to me that my own degradation must necessarily follow.' Now the reversal of the two girls' fortunes is swiftly made clear.

The company withdraws to another room, ignoring or forgetting the deposed child, who is left weeping behind a chair.

> Ann too went with them, and was conducted by her whom I had always considered my own particular friend. Lady Elizabeth took hold of her hand, and said, 'Miss Lesley, will you permit me to conduct you to the drawing room?' (p. 297).

It is only the youngest child, not yet perhaps imbued with an understanding of the importance of 'birth', who protests 'She is not miss Lesley.' Though Lady Harriot kisses and promises Ann that 'she would never forget how long she had loved me as her child', the social and legal importance of inheritance rights, and ideological assumptions about blood and rank, make it impossible for Ann's condition not to be irrevocably altered.

Ann Withers is no ill-treated Jane Eyre or David Copperfield; she does not suffer physically, but what is shown through her story is a deeply hurt and confused child struggling to comprehend and come to terms with her changed circumstances. Naturally, she is unable consciously to criticize or challenge the moral and social assumptions of her upbringing. In retailing her catastrophe and the period that followed, she makes no criticism of her former parents, who are depicted as doing everything within their power and the constraints of the social system to treat their erstwhile 'daughter' with affectionate care for her feelings. 'Circumstanced as I was,' she says, 'surely I had nothing justly to complain of.' That 'surely', however, hints, subtly, at a suppressed resentment, while 'every fresh instance even of kindness or attention I experienced went to my heart, that I should be forced to feel thankful for it'. She wrestles with her natural jealousy and resentment of the new 'Miss Lesley', who 'had been so highly praised for her filial tenderness, I thought at last she seemed to make a parade about it'. She prays and struggles 'earnestly' to be able to love her real mother, feeling that 'she was now my only parent'.

> Yet ever when I looked in her face, she would seem to me to be the very identical person whom I should have once thought sufficiently honoured by a slight inclination of the head, and a civil How do you do, Mrs Withers? (p. 298).

Meanwhile, the new Miss Lesley, learning with modest gratitude to fill the role she was born for, engages the affection of her new mother without losing that of her old, and Ann discovers that 'nothing makes the heart ache with such a hopeless, heavy pain, as envy... To have in a manner two mothers, and Miss Lesley to engross them both, was too much indeed.' At last, in spite of all the excellent intentions and earnest endeavours of everybody involved, the tensions of the situation become too great, and Ann is told that it has been decided 'it would conduce to [her] happiness to pass a year or two at school'.

Mary Lamb's interest in – and sceptical or ironic attitude towards – the social distinctions based on birth may have been partly inspired by her childhood visits to Blakesware, the Jacobean mansion where her maternal grandmother, Mary Field, was housekeeper. Mrs Field lived on for fourteen years after the death of her mistress, ruling the house 'in a manner as if it had been her own', and visited by both Mary and Charles, who wandered through the deserted rooms and took imaginative possession of them. 'Mine was that gallery of good old family portraits,' wrote Charles later. 'Mine too ... [the] noble Marble Hall', for 'the claims of birth are ideal merely, and what herald shall go about to strip me of an idea'.[10] Mary Lamb shows that ideas as well as things and people can be stripped away. The thought-worlds in which her children live are constantly being broken into or taken from them by the actions of the adult world. Sometimes these are damaging, sometimes the change is for the better. Always they are outside the child's comprehension and control.

Blakesware is certainly the setting for the story of 'Margaret Green, The Young Mahometan'. Margaret's widowed mother is housekeeper-companion to Mrs Beresford, a rich old lady who lives in a 'large family mansion' but keeps no company and confines herself almost totally to three rooms. Margaret is an only child, and because she is also Mrs Beresford's goddaughter her mother is 'very kindly permitted' to have her live with her, but this note of distant toleration is the keynote of her life.

> Every morning when she first saw me, she used to nod her head very kindly and say, 'How do you do, little Margaret?' But I do not recollect she ever spoke to me during the remainder of the day (p. 306).

Mrs Beresford's obsession is needlework, but as her eyesight no longer allows her to undertake any more herself Margaret's mother becomes her surrogate, and needlework comes to engross both women, while Margaret, bored and lonely, is left to amuse herself by solitary ramblings through the large house.

In a way this is yet another story about a deprived and lonely child, who makes for herself a world of her own to compensate for what is taken away. Margaret does not lose her mother by death, but she does lose her to the silence and isolation apparently endemic in the house, for 'my mother, following the example of her patroness, had almost wholly discontinued talking to me'. From morning to night hardly a word is spoken to her. In this situation, the figures in the pictures, the family portraits and the tapestry hangings become her imaginary companions, and it is in talking to these, or dwelling on their stories, that she largely amuses herself until one day she finds a previously locked room open to her, giving access to a large library. This opens to her the world of books, but it is an adult world, entered without guide or compass, and one which seems at first as resistant and dumb towards her as the world she leaves behind.

> If you never spent whole mornings alone in a large library, you cannot conceive the pleasure of taking down books in the constant hope of finding an entertaining book among them; yet, after many days, meeting with nothing but disappointment, it becomes less pleasant (p. 308).

Just when she is on the point of giving up, however, she discovers a familiar face. In an obscure corner of the room, she sees a book with a 'charming print', large letters and, best of all, 'in the first page I looked into I saw the name of my favourite Ishmael, whose face I knew so well from the tapestry, and whose history I had often read in the Bible. I sate myself down to read this book with the greatest eagerness'.

Again, in Margaret's narration we are given a glimpse both of the initial experience of the young child and the reflection of her older self, for the book, as she immediately goes on to explain, 'was a very improper book' – not, that is, in any obvious way which might immediately have made her uncomfortable, but because 'it contained a false history of Abraham and his descendents'. The book was *Mahometism Explained*, a 'history of what the Turks, who are a very ignorant people, believe concerning the impostor Mahomet, who feigned himself to be a descendent of Ishmael', but one which to the child was simultaneously 'as entertaining as a fairytale' and guaranteed by its association with her familiar world. She 'used to read the history of Ishmael, and then go and look at him in the tapestry, and then read his history again', but Ishmael led on to Mahomet, and 'if Ishmael had engaged so much of my thoughts, how much more so must Mahomet? His history was full of nothing but wonders from the beginning to the end.' Having little experience of books other than the Family Bible, Margaret naturally accepts this wonderful new book in the same way, and when she reads that those who believe the stories of Mahomet are called 'Mahometans and true believers' she concludes that she 'must be a Mahometan, for I believed every word I read'.

Both Mary and Charles Lamb believed strongly in the importance of reading as food for children's imaginations, but they also knew from their own childhood experience how it could disturb. Margaret's first delight in *Mahometism Explained* is succeeded by fear as she reads of a bridge 'no wider than a silken thread' which must be crossed after death, and from which all who are not true believers will slip into the bottomless gulf below. She becomes terrified for Mrs Beresford and for her mother, torn between an anxiety to convert them for their own safety and a fear

130

of confessing to her illicit reading, while 'the habit of never speaking, or being spoken to, considerably increased the difficulty'. The stress makes her ill, and when one night she wakes from a feverish sleep to beg her mother 'that she would be so kind as to be a Mahometan', she is thought to be delirious and a doctor is sent for. It does not take the doctor long to perceive the effect on the child of her isolated life. He takes her to his own house for a month and puts her into the care of his wife who takes her to the fair, invites other children to visit her, clears a room so that they can play blindman's buff, and puts up a swing in the garden. She also talks to Margaret about *Mahometism Explained*, making it clear that there is nothing secret about its contents, but equally that 'the author of it did not mean to give the fabulous stories here related as true'. The difference between this treatment and the silence to which she had been subjected before is clear enough to the reader, though Margaret, as the narrator, cannot blame her mother except obliquely, suggesting that this might have been the reason for her own 'strange forgetfulness' that 'it is very wrong to read any book without permission to do so'. At the conclusion of the month, she is taken home 'perfectly cured', and 'very much ashamed of having believed so many absurdities'; but whether her mother has also learned anything is left open. All the narratives in *Mrs Leicester's School* have only temporary or provisional endings, for while the children who tell them may consciously seek for a moral or a secure position within them, the situations in which they described themselves as placed are larger than they are able to comprehend. Their arrival at school cannot be more than a punctuation mark in a longer story, but it is for the reader to imagine what that story might be.

*

A shrewd understanding and sympathy for the confusions and pain of youth seems to have been a marked feature of Mary Lamb's character. Mary Cowden Clarke, one of the children she befriended and taught in later years, recalled that if she 'thought she perceived symptoms of an unexplained dejection in her young friend'; she would seek out the cause, 'more as if mutually discussing and consulting than as if questioning', and her advice was always gentle, practical and appropriate.

> She had a most tender sympathy with the young... She threw herself so entirely into *their* way of thinking, and contrived to take an estimate of things so entirely from *their* point of view, that she made them rejoice to have her for their co-mate in affairs that interested them.[11]

This capacity for empathizing with the young may have been born of Mary Lamb's own slightly isolated and insecure position, a position which may also have contributed to her quietly sceptical attitude towards the orthodoxies of education for girls.[12] Though she was no obvious radical any more than she was an obvious moralist – her suggestions, said Mary Cowden Clarke, were 'dropped in with the air of agreed propositions, as if they grew out of the subject in question, and presented themselves as matters of course' – the lessons which emerge 'as matters of course' in *Mrs Leicester's School* concern the needs of children for love and companionship, games and stories, teaching and understanding. Above all, they concern the need to be heard – to be able to tell their own stories. This last point alone serves to show the difference between the usual run of 'school' stories, and those told in the absence of the 'governess', Mrs Leicester.

NOTES

1 Autograph note by Samuel Taylor Coleridge, quoted in Reginald L. Hine, *Charles Lamb and His Hertfordshire*, (London, 1949), p. 135.
2 *Mrs Leicester's School* was published anonymously by J.M. Godwin, for Godwin's Juvenile Library, at the end of 1808, though dated 1809. It went through at least eleven editions before the middle of the century. E.V. Lucas used the 2nd edition, 1809, in volume III, *Books for Children*, of the collected *Works of Charles and Mary Lamb* (London, 1903–5). This is the edition to which any page numbers in the body of the text refer. For Mary's responsibility for the book's conception see Edwin W. Marrs (ed.) *The Letters of Charles and Mary Lamb*, Vol. II (Ithaca and London, 1976), pp. 235, 247.
3 H.C. Barnard, *Fenelon on Education* (Cambridge, 1966), pp. 33–4.
4 Sarah Fielding, *The Governess or, Little Female Academy*, ed. Jill E. Grey (London, 1968), pp. 3–4.
5 Mary Wollstonecraft *Original Stories from Real Life; with Conversations Calculated to Regulate the Affections and Form the Mind to Truth and Goodness*, 1791, p. 42.
6 Maria Edgeworth, *The Parent's Assistant; or Stories for Children*, 1796.
7 Fielding, *The Governess*, pp. 78–9.
8 Lucas, *Works*, III, p. 275.
9 Victor Watson, 'Children's Literature's and Literature's Children', in M. Styles, E. Bearne, and V. and Watson (eds) *The Prose and the Passion: Children and Their Reading*, (London, 1994), pp. 169, 174.
10 Charles Lamb, 'Blakesmoor in H-shire', in Lucas *Works* II, pp. 156–7.
11 Mary Cowden Clarke, 'Recollections of Mary Lamb by One Who Knew Her', *National Magazine* 3 (1858), 360–5.
12 Mary Lamb's views on the moral emphasis placed on needlework in the lives and education of women and girls are clearly set out in her anonymously published essay 'On Needlework', which appeared in the *New British Lady's Magazine* in 1814 (see Lucas, *Works*, I, pp. 176–80). They can also be guessed as underlying her letter to a young friend, Barbara Betham, describing her pleasure in watching her at her book, and the day when, 'conscience-struck at having wasted so much' time reading, and feeling herself to be 'quite useless', Barbara had insisted on hunting out some of Mary Lamb's unhemmed handkerchiefs, 'and by no means could I prevail upon you to resume your story-books till you had hemmed them all' (*Letters*, II, 116).

9

FROM THE FRONT LINE

Jan Mark

Without belittling either it can be noted that the more memorable and influential nineteenth-century children's authors were polarized into two specialisms. The great fantasists were men – George Macdonald, Lewis Carroll, Charles Kingsley, Frank Stockton, Frank Baum. The great realists were women, writers operating in the front line of domestic discord.

'All happy families resemble each other. Each unhappy family is unhappy is its own way.' Leo Tolstoy's opening dictum in *Anna Karenina* (1873–6) has become a kind of paradigm of simplistic generalization. Nevertheless, he was not merely seeking an arresting start for his novel, and his assertion is essentially accurate. Happy families resemble each other in their happiness. The members of the family are happy with each other; the gestalt is happy. It is in the fact of circumstances enabling amicable coexistence that the resemblance lies. By chance these individuals' individuality is subsumed into the whole; the happy family.

In unhappy families the individual characteristics of each member are irrepressible. It is the internal, incompatible differences that cause the unhappiness, the friction that in its turn engenders fiction.

Early children's fiction, as a vehicle for moral instruction, was soon found wanting as a form of entertainment since it relied heavily on the presentation of a serene and stable environment in which parents and elders functioned as exemplars. Clearly this was necessary. Not only charity begins at home, *everything* begins at home. A writer would make a poor case for little boys accepting instruction from father and striving to imitate him, if father were to be found roaring about the house inflamed by drink and violating the kitchenmaids. What was learned at mother's knee had to be sound and virtuous. Parents were shown always in agreement or occasionally in cahoots; they did not argue or throw things and storm out of the house. Mamma did not entertain gentlemen callers.

On the other hand, these things did happen and were known to happen. They happened in bad families, unhappy families; they reminded the good children of good parents how fortunate they were. A grisly portrait of such a family is painted in 'The Punishment of Wilfulness' collected by Jane Trimmer in 1840 but evidently of earlier date. William and Eliza Darnley, against their mother's considered advice, wish to visit the Thorntons. Nowadays we would call the Thorntons dysfunctional.

'the scramble between them was a violent one, and in the midst of it they both fell over me and tore my new India muslin dress in such a terrible way that I could not appear in the street in it and was compelled to send for a carriage to ride home.'

'Dear me,' said William and Eliza, 'what a pity! why, where was their mother all that time?'

'In the room, talking to me about the difficulty of keeping servants in order, and managing unruly children, and occasionally screaming out, "James, put down Mrs Darnley's parasol, you will certainly break it." . . . In the midst of the quarrel for it, master Henry Thornton came in. "Mama," said he, "do you see how James and Mary are treating Mrs Darnley's *umbrella*?" "Yes," said she, "I see the naughty creatures, but how can I help it? They are so headstrong that I cannot manage them for my life."

' "If you cannot," said he, "I will".

' "Do let them alone, Henry," said his mother, "they will only make the more noise if you meddle with them."

' "Come, you sirs," said he, "give up the parasol this minute." Not being accustomed to obey, they held on the faster; and in trying to get it away from them he knocked their heads together, and set them screaming in the most violent manner . . .'

'In the midst of it Mr Thornton entered.

' "Mercy on me," said he, "what is the cause of all this disturbance? Why, you must be beside yourselves! I shall surely be obliged to punish you severely for this unruly conduct of yours, which I am always sure to witness on entering the house."

'They were dumb the moment their father spoke; who, on account of their mother's excessive weakness and indulgence, was compelled to rule them with a rod of iron when at home . . .'

Mr Thornton glumly describes his domestic arrangements as 'a private madhouse', but Mrs Darnley observes: 'I could not take Mr Thornton's part against his wife; he married her for her fortune, without inquiring whether she had any mind or not . . .'

There is no doubt, however, that this frightful menage is far more stimulating to write – and read – about than the ideal home of the Darnleys. The writer finds herself in danger of being actually funny; there is no comparable comedy to be found *chez* Darnley. The Thorntons exist as an awful warning, but it is their very cantankerousness that makes them interesting.

As the pleasures of creating fiction began to override the urge to instruct in these early authors, so the knowledge that a perfect family is a dull one began to influence their scenarios. As yet unable to engage with the notion of severely dysfunctional parents at centre stage they could, all the same, see that one cause of instability might be the *absence* of a parent. In 1809 Mary Lamb (see Chapter 8), contributing seven of the ten stories that she and her brother Charles published as *Mrs Leicester's School*, wrote 'The Father's Wedding Day' in which Elinor Forrester, a very small girl who has lost her mother, is delighted to learn that her father intends to marry Miss Saville who will live with them and be her mother. Under the impression that Miss Saville will be somehow miraculously transformed into her lost mamma, Elinor is desolated when she continues to be the same Miss Saville, and refuses to call her Mother, or even to speak to her. The father, bewildered and thwarted, is at a loss to deal with the situation and leaves the young stepmother to solve the problem, which she does by encouraging the little girl to grieve properly. Hitherto she has been regarded as too young to understand her loss.

Catherine Sinclair, writing in *Holiday House* (1839), described a household in which three children who have lost their mother are quartered with their grandmother and uncle while father, on doctor's orders, travels abroad to recuperate from the death of his wife. Sinclair aimed to portray 'normally naughty children' in Harry and Laura (big brother Frank is a paragon, rewarded by an early death) but their upbringing is woefully abnormal, as their conduct is variously dealt with by indulgence and savagery. It is never suggested that the children's naughtiness is the result of neglect, but neglected they are, by permissive Uncle David, ailing ineffectual Lady Harriet, sadistic Mrs Crabtree and, primarily, by their father who appears only at the very end to witness the death of his elder son. It is impossible, however, not to suspect that in a stable, two-parent family, Harry and Laura would never have had the opportunity to do anything worth writing about.

The Brinker family (*The Silver Skates*, Mary Mapes Dodge, 1865) is at the other end of the social scale, belonging to the deserving poor and, moreover, seeming faintly quaint, being Dutch. This is virtually a one-parent household since Raff Brinker met with an accident ten years previously, suffering brain damage that has left him incapable and intermittently violent. Structurally, the novel is a mess, the narrative pointlessly interrupted by travelogues and disquisitions upon Old Dutch Christmas customs. Few of the characters develop as people, they remain puppets; virtuous Hilda, noble Hans, dear little Gretel, coquettish Katrinka. Even so, Dodge gives us a convincing picture of the appalling burden inflicted upon the mother and children by the father's illness.

The pre-eminent family-under-a-microscope are Louisa May Alcott's Marches. When first encountered in *Little Women* (1868) they are functionally a one-parent family, Mr March having unnecessarily decamped to join the Union army as a chaplain, leaving his wife and daughters to survive on the home front. Even after he is invalided home, this most shadowy paterfamilias rarely manages to capture his author's attention for more than a few lines. At the beginning of the sequel (*Good Wives* 1869) she makes a tepid attempt to re-establish him in what the reading public might suppose to be his rightful place:

> To outsiders the five energetic women seemed to rule the house, and so they did in many things; but the quiet man sitting among his books was still the head of the family, the household conscience, anchor and comforter; for to him the busy, anxious women always turned in troublous times, finding him, in the truest sense of those sacred words, husband and father.

That the five women might have been less busy and anxious had the quiet man emerged from among his books more often is a question not overtly addressed. Adversity is what drives the stories along, and a clue to the true state of affairs may be deduced earlier, in *Little Women*, during a discussion between Mrs March and her second daughter Jo on the dangerous consequences of uncontrolled rage:

> 'You think your temper is the worst in the world; but mine used to be just like it.'
> 'Yours, mother? Why, you are never angry!' and for the moment, Jo forgot her remorse in surprise.
> 'I've been trying to cure it for forty years, and have only succeeded in controlling it. I am angry nearly every day of my life, Jo; but I have learned not to show it.'

To a child reader, accustomed to incurring maternal wrath, this probably passes unremarked – it did not, for instance, surprise me as a 10-year-old – but the immediate adult response is: angry every day of her life? *Why*? A glancing acquaintance with the autobiographical facts that underlie Alcott's fiction makes it only too clear why, and resentful, combative Jo must, like her creator, fight in order to be. In *Jo's Boys* (1886), finally attended by fame and success won by her own efforts, she discovers, paradoxically, that fame and success bring no more rest to her perturbed spirit than did poverty and disappointment. In contrast Rose, the heroine of *Eight Cousins* (1875) and *Rose in Bloom* (1876), orphaned but cushioned by wealth and an adoring family, drifts on the narrative current like a water hyacinth, beautiful but unrooted.

Jo's middle years are occupied in running a school with her husband. When she first mentions the project at the end of *Good Wives*, she makes it clear that in setting up this small boarding establishment she wants to create a family for herself and for the pupils. Having only two sons of her own she sets about collecting the neglected, mistreated, unloved and abandoned offspring of other people, who avail themselves of the opportunity to offload children who are in some way damaged by ill health, mental and physical handicap or their own parental shortcomings, thus ensuring for the duration of two books a succession of interesting personality clashes.

It is instructive too to read between the lines of the work of Alcott's contemporary Sarah Chauncey Woolsey, who wrote as Susan Coolidge. Her novels about the Carr family, *What Katy Did*, *What Katy Did at School* and *What Katy Did Next* (1872, 1873, 1886), open with a picture of the six motherless children of an overworked doctor, who are being raised by their Aunt Izzie, a conscientious but irascible woman of whom Coolidge remarks, 'The children . . . called her "Aunt Izzie" always, never "Aunty". Children will know what *that* meant.' Fortunately the little Carrs discover her hidden reserves of warmth before she is carried off by sudden death, that convenient but not unrealistic standby of nineteenth-century writers (Alcott similarly rubbed out Jo's brother-in-law in a single night). The Carr children are vaguely resentful of their aunt. Naturally it does not occur to them that this is a woman who has given up her own chance of a family to raise her widowed brother's thankless brood, an instant family of six, undisciplined, often at loggerheads. Mamma is 'but a sad, sweet name, spoken on Sunday and at prayer-times' and therefore safely out of the ruck.

Edith Nesbit (1858–1924) allowed her star creation, Oswald Bastable, to make fun of the Coolidge ethos in the second book about the Bastable family, *The Wouldbegoods* (1901). Dora, the eldest, is confined to bed by a foot injury. Alice reports on a friend's suggestion:

> 'we should all go to her with our little joys and sorrows and things, and about the sweet influence from a sick bed that can be felt all over the house, like in *What Katy Did*, and Dora said she hoped she might prove a blessing to us all while she's laid up.'
>
> Oswald said he hoped so, but he was not pleased, because this sort of jaw was exactly the sort of thing that he and Dicky didn't want to have happen.

In spite of this knee-jerk contempt for an earlier writer (a failing to which many successive children's authors are prone) the Bastables are the spiritual heirs of the Carrs. Again there are six of them, the eldest being, like Katy, about twelve, motherless and left in the care of a preoccupied father. Mamma is not even a sad sweet name spoken on Sundays, but her absence is a physical void in the lives of her children. As Oswald declares belligerently, on the first page of the first book, *The Story of the Treasure Seekers* (1899), 'Our mother is dead, and if you think we don't care because I don't tell you much about her you only show that you do not understand people at all.'

It becomes apparent, from later references, that her death is fairly recent, a matter of months. For the children there is no unsatisfactory but reliable Aunt Izzie, only a succession of generally indifferent servants. Father, cheated by his business partner after his wife's death, lives in fear of bills and bailiffs, pawns his few valuables and tries to protect the children from fully understanding the extreme precariousness of their financial position. In this he is only partly successful, for it is the children's bewilderment and insecurity, as such as their loss, that create the situations in each story. Owing to their departed affluence, much like that of the March family, they cannot perceive themselves as poor. The Poor are a distinct class; they are not of it. Rather than attend a free Board School, they do not go to school at all; they live in a shabby-genteel neighbour-hood – where the people next door hide behind shutters for a week rather than admit that they cannot afford a holiday – and range hopefully over South London seeking, officially, treasure, actually the attention and warmth that have suddenly gone out of their lives.

After one potentially disastrous adventure in which they attempt to borrow business capital from a moneylender – of whom, unknown to them, their father is already a client – there is a rare family gathering:

That evening Father had a letter by the seven o'clock post. And when he had read it he came up into the nursery. He did not look quite so unhappy as usual, but he looked grave.

'You've been to Mr Rosenbaum's,' he said.

So we told him all about it. It took a long time, and Father sat in the armchair. It was jolly. He doesn't often come and talk to us now. He has to spend all his time thinking about his business . . .

Father said, 'I haven't much time to be with you, for my business takes most of my time. It is an anxious business – but I can't bear to think of your being left all alone like this.'

He looked so sad we all said we liked being left alone. And then he looked sadder than ever.

Then Alice said, 'We don't mean that exactly, Father. It *is* rather lonely sometimes, since Mother died.'

Then we were all quiet a little while.

The children's thoughtless bullying of Albert-next-door is credibly unat-tractive, but they are without malice and it is their equally artless generosity which finally wins them their treasure in the shape of a benev-olent uncle. As with the Carrs and the Marches, familial affection overcomes internal divisions, the need to pull together against the slings and arrows of outrageous fortune. Two American clans, each missing a father, also lived by the code United we stand, divided we fall; the Wiggs family and the Peppers.

The Five Little Peppers (Margaret Sidney) Ben, Polly, Joel, Dave and Phronsie, live in The Little Brown House with their mother Mamsie who raises them single-handed after the death of their father, on the proceeds of her sewing and tailoring. ' "Poor things," she would say to herself, "they haven't had any bringing up; they've just scrambled up." ' Her fear is that, as breadwinner, she has had no time for conventional mothering, but the children's efforts to help her and look after each other testify to her nurturing influence. Unlike the Carrs, the Marches and the Bastables, the five little Peppers are never motivated by self-interest, never quarrel, never succumb to baser instincts. Significantly they have never followed the Carrs and the Marches to England although their wholesome influence still seems to pervade certain American family television shows such as *The Waltons* and *The Cosby Show*, which the British enjoy but watch with disbelief suspended at a great height.

Mrs Wiggs of the Cabbage Patch (Alice Caldwell Hegan 1901), who survives with her family in an industrial wasteland, was not created for children, but she too has a large and fatherless brood, Jim, Billy, Asia, Australia and Europena. Mrs Wiggs herself breathes a deathless optimism in the Pollyanna mode, but this is a generally gritty tale of a grim life as evinced in the account of her husband's death: 'Mr Wiggs travelled to Eternity by the alcohol route . . .'

Thus the size of a family was both its handicap and its saving grace. Numbers rarely fell below five. In *Pat* (1874) Stella Austin, a little-remembered British writer, recounted the adventures of a semi-orphaned family of eight, the Vanes. Their father the Colonel has died at Gibraltar, disappointingly of a fever. His seven elder offspring, who regard themselves as 'The Army Children', rather regret that he did not die a hero's death in battle. So military-minded are they that they refer to their youngest brother, born posthumously, as 'only a civilian', and the unfortunate child grows up thinking that 'civilian' is some pejorative term condemning him to a lifetime's inferiority.

Pat has all the ingredients and promise of a good family story; differentiated characters, sibling rivalry, involving not a little humour, but it never achieves lift-off. This is possibly a stylistic fault since the book is written in the present historic tense and the author maintains her introductory device of describing the family and their house as if she were conducting a guided tour. However, its chief disadvantage is that nothing seriously affects the Vanes. We never see them develop, which is one area where there can be a distinct difference between adult and juvenile fiction. Child characters in adult books are plot devices. Adults appear in children's books because they are inescapable. Adults cause things to happen because of their hierarchical position. Children change because of the things that happen to them. Austin describes various crises in the Vane household and assures us that character development has occurred, but we have to take her word for it. Pat himself is shaken by the death of his hero, the young French Prince Imperial, cut down in the Zulu wars, but this takes place in the penultimate chapter; there is only the briefest of summings-up at the end to indicate that Pat has been profoundly altered by his experience.

A book which has survived against expectation – perhaps because it was the first of its kind in its own country – is Ethel Turner's *Seven Little Australians* (1894). There is little evidence in nineteenth-century children's fiction to support the myth of the stern Victorian father. Fathers, on the whole, might be inadequate but they were rarely tyrannical, and then, at the end of the century, on the other side of the world, appeared Turner's Captain Woolcot, one of the least attractive parents in fiction, remote, arbitrary, violently punitive. One can only gape at his short-sighted self-indulgence in replacing his recently dead wife with a girl of 20. The new Mrs Woolcot, only four years older than her eldest step-daughter and with a new baby of her own, is thus expected to assume responsibility for a family of seven.

Catherine Sinclair's declaration in 1839 that she was going to write about 'normally naughty children' in *Holiday House*, echoes eerily over half a century in Turner's preface to her book:

> Before you fairly start this story I would like to give you just a word of warning . . .
>
> If you imagine you are going to read of model children, with perhaps a naughtily inclined one to point a moral, you had better lay down the book immediately and betake yourself to *Sandford and Merton*, or similar standard juvenile works. Not one of the seven is really good, for the very excellent reason that Australian children never are.
>
> In England and America and Africa and Asia the little folks may be paragons of virtue. I know little about them.

This is sadly evident. The defiant colonial assertion betrays severely circumscribed reading habits. She adds, subsequently, 'Nursery tea is more an English institution than an Australian one; there is a kind of *bon cameraderie* feeling between parents and young folks here, and an utter absence of veneration on the part of the latter.'

Bon cameraderie is signally lacking in the Woolcot home; Esther, the step-mother, is less the children's comrade than fellow-sufferer. They certainly do not venerate their father, they fear him. The name of the house, Misrule, is rather more apposite than the author may have cared to acknowledge.

One of the most peculiar families ever to grace the pages of fiction was the Peterkins who first appeared in the *St Nicholas* magazine in 1868, the stories later to be published as a book in 1880. Their creator, Lucretia Peabody Hale, settled them in her home town of Boston, Massachusetts, where for a decade or so they pursued a course of insanely pedantic logic-chopping in the face of minor everyday problems that were usually solved at a stroke by the commonsense intervention of 'the Lady from Philadelphia'. Even the family names had a presciently satirical ring, considering the fanciful handles later endured by the Wiggses and Peppers; Elizabeth Eliza, Agamemnon, Solomon John and 'the little boys', a nameless conglomerate. The Peterkins were remorselessly stupid, but really they have no place in this survey. They were also, in their witless way, perfectly happy.

NOVELS REFERRED TO IN TEXT

Louisa May Alcott, *Little Women* (1868).
Louisa May Alcott, *Good Wives* (1869).
Louisa May Alcott, *Eight Cousins* (1875).
Louisa May Alcott, *A Rose in Bloom* (1876).
Louisa May Alcott, *Jo's Boys* (1886).
Stella Austin, *Pat* (1874).
Susan Coolidge (Sarah Chauncey Woolsey), *What Katy Did* (1872), *What Katy Did at School* (1873), *What Katy Did Next* (1886).
Mary Mapes Dodge, *Hans Brinker, or The Silver Skates* (1865).
Lucretia Peabody Hale, *The Peterkin Papers* (1880), *The Last of the Peterkins with Others of their Kin* (1886).
Alice Caldwell Hegan, *Mrs Wiggs of the Cabbage Patch* (1901, USA; 1902, UK).
Charles and Mary Lamb, *Mrs Leicester's School* (1809).
Edith Nesbit, *The Story of the Treasure Seekers* (1899).
Edith Nesbit, *The Wouldbegoods* (1901).
Margaret Sidney, *The Five Little Peppers and How They Grew* (1881).
Catherine Sinclair, *Holiday House* (1839).
Jane Trimmer (ed.), 'The Punishment of Wilfulness', in *Stories for Children* (c. 1840).
Ethel Turner, *Seven Little Australians* (1894).

10

'OF THE SPONTANEOUS KIND'?

Women writing poetry for children – from
Jane Johnson to Christina Rossetti

Morag Styles

> I'll nurse you on my knee, my knee,
> My own little son;
> I'll rock you, rock you, in my arms,
> My least little one.[1]

> Rock on, rock on
> My pretty boy.
> And you shall be
> Your mother's joy.[2]

The first of these extracts is by Christina Rossetti (1830–94), the second
by Jane Johnson (1706–1759). Unless you happen to know Rossetti's
poem, I doubt whether you can tell which is by one of the finest poets
of all time and which is a little rhyme a mother used to amuse her
children. Christina Rossetti was one of the greatest poets of the Victorian
period; Jane Johnson, writing more than a hundred years earlier, was an
obscure middle-class woman who produced stories and poems for her
own children with no thought of publication. The fact that it is easy to
find similarities in the writing for children by two such different women
living at different times raises some interesting questions about gender,
literacy and childhood. I want to suggest, for example, that if we explored
some of that neglected literature of the eighteenth and nineteenth centuries – namely, what women, often mothers, were writing for and reading
to their children – there might be quite a few alternatives to the received
canon of children's literature of that period.

Roger Lonsdale[3] tells us that only two collections of poetry by women
were published in the first decade of the eighteenth century (I assume he
means poetry *for adults only*); in the 1790s the total reached was over
thirty. Although there was some improvement over a hundred years, it
was still the case that women were poorly represented in published poetry
up to and including the nineteenth century. But women *were* writing
poetry: 'There were in fact dozens of women at all social levels who, with

variable ambition and competence, experienced the mysterious urge to express themselves in verse and, by one means or another, found their way into print.'[4] It is important to remember how hard it was for women with the income, time, inclination and opportunity to take up a successful literary career in this period, let alone the majority of working women struggling with their menfolk to earn enough to feed and clothe the family. For many women with literary or educational aspirations, writing for children was the *only* way to get published at all. It is no surprise then that so many women took to writing for children with a passion and worked so hard at it.

But writing for children offered more than an outlet for literary women. Victor Watson[5] suggests that children's literature provided a space where affection between adults and children could be openly addressed and that this option was mainly taken up by women. I want to explore this notion in the light of Rossetti's *Sing-Song*. I also want to look at how women's voices might be different from those of men and how readers might have to learn to appreciate these qualities. We certainly need to find out more about what women might have written in the private domain in the nineteenth century and before, some of it for their children. Exciting new information about this area has come to light through Jane Johnson's Nursery Library,[6] providing evidence that at least one woman was writing delightful, low key, child-centred texts before Newbery started publishing his little books in the middle of the eighteenth century. How many more Janes were there?

The first quotation above comes from Christina Rossetti's only collection of poetry for children, *Sing-Song*,[7] although her better-known *Goblin Market* has been marketed and illustrated for the young, as well as for adults. By examining some of the poems in *Sing-Song* and considering possible precursors, I want to make a case for viewing this outstanding collection as the culmination of work by a long line of women, demonstrating how children could be the subject matter and audience for poetry. *Sing-Song*, despite its great appeal, has been more often out of print than in it: even in Rossetti's centenary year (1995), it was hard to find a copy. Only generations of editors of anthologies for children have kept the poetry of *Sing-Song* in the public eye since her death.

It is worth remembering that Christina Rossetti is one of the few women poets of the nineteenth century to make it into the children's canon. My research into eighteenth- and nineteenth-century poetry for children shows that women were predominant in that sphere, despite the difficulties of getting into print.[8] If there was no lack of good poetry written by women, what then was the reason for their apparent exclusion from poetry anthologies? Coventry Patmore's influential *A Children's Garland*[9] of 1862 is subtitled 'from the best poets', and *Poems Every Child Should Know*,[10] 1904, is a selection from 'the best poems of all time' – both contain only a handful of poems by women; Andrew Lang's *The Blue Poetry Book*,[11] 1892, had three poems by women out of a hundred. Patmore is quite explicit about excluding 'nearly all verse written expressly for children, and most of the poetry about children for grown people'.[12] By making that choice Patmore, and so many like him, excluded a large proportion of writing by women. He also makes a precedent of marginalizing poetry written specifically for children, as if it were somehow of lesser value. Could it also be the case that literary men like Patmore and Lang, and many who followed in their footsteps, have failed to recognize some of the best poetry for children – poems that ring like bells, but are apparently light on the surface, like most of the poems in *Sing-Song*?

> The dog lies in his kennel,
>   And Puss purrs on the rug,
> And baby perches on my knee
>   For me to kiss and hug.
>
> Pat the dog and stroke the cat,
>   Each in its degree;
> And cuddle and kiss my baby,
>   And baby kiss me.[13]

Geoffrey Grigson's *The Cherry Tree*,[14] sixty years later, had six poems by women out of a possible 170. That is quite common. Although there are half a dozen poetry anthologies exclusively by women for children currently on the market, the representation of women in most poetry books is minimal. Christina Rossetti is often the token woman for anthologists who don't think balance of gender is an issue in compiling poetry – unfortunately,   that   is   *most*   editors   of   the   past   and present!

I will begin with Christina Rossetti's poetry for children and trace my way back to Jane Johnson. Rossetti is the success story, yet her work has been marginalized too. William Rossetti,[15] her beloved brother, has a lot to answer for:

> I have said elsewhere, but may as well repeat it here, that her habits of composition were entirely of the casual and spontaneous kind, from her earliest to her latest years. If something came into her head which she found suggestive of verse, she put it into verse. It came to her (I take it) very easily, without meditating a possible subject, and without her making any great difference in the first from the latest form of the verses which embodied it; . . . I question her having ever once deliberated with herself whether or not she

144

would write something or other ... something impelled her feelings, or came into her head, and her hand obeyed her dictation.

But he wasn't sure ...

Jan Marsh,[16] in her recent biography, tracks the genesis of several poems, showing that several days at least were spent on their composition. So William Rossetti was not entirely correct in his supposition. And if her composition was largely spontaneous, is that a real weakness when the resulting poems are so strong? Many writers describe first drafts as coming from they know not where – the unconscious part of the writing process. William was aware that Christina revised her work: 'but *some* difference, with a view to right and fine detail of execution, she did of course make when needful'.[17] No doubt Christina Rossetti's modesty and well-known self-disparagement colluded with William's version of her craft, but how easily he slips into that role.

His description of Christina's writing process has influenced many subsequent scholars. Walter de la Mare[18] edited a book of her poetry in 1930 where he is both appreciative and patronizing: after all, he described Rossetti as 'that still rarer thing, a woman of genius' ... it is said that every man of genius shares the hospitality of his heart with a woman and a child. Christina Rossetti was that still rarer thing, a woman of genius'. J.D. Symon[19] in a preface to a beautiful edition of her *Verses*, 1906, says this:

> She sang the moment's emotion with a diffuse and amiable facility ... questions of form never seem to have hindered her spontaneity ... her first fresh moment of inspiration gives a vision of an unearthly world that was granted in fuller measure to the poet's brother, Dante Gabriel'.

How wrong he proved to be. Notice the condescension of words like 'amiable' and 'spontaneity'.

In his preface to *The Poetical Works of Christina Rossetti*, William Rossetti[20] considers her poetic stature: 'within the range of her subject and thought, and the limits of her executive endeavour, a good one ... fully conscious as I am of their limitations ...' Though astute, kindly and loyal, there is still a sense of William Rossetti's reluctance to recognize his sister's talent in full measure. His view of the capacities of women is depressing; here is his assessment of Felicia Hemans, a popular nineteenth-century poet, writing a generation before his sister: 'certainly the peculiar tone and tint of Mrs Heman's faculty were not such as to supply the deficiency which she, merely as a woman, was almost certain to evince'.[21] The difficulties facing women hoping for a fair critical response to their writing are evident when one remembers that William Rossetti was an enlightened, intellectual, fairly liberal man.

Let us return to his sister as a young girl, already religious, with a literary bent, and claiming Felicia Hemans as the 'most obvious influence on her juvenile work'.[22] William's present for her fourteenth Christmas was *The Sacred Harp*[23] containing many poems by Hemans which Christina described as beautiful. There seems to me some resemblance between the poem Christina wrote for her mother, aged 11 and Hemans's birthday poem for her son,

> Where sucks the bee now? Summer is flying,
> Leaves round the elm-tree faded are lying;
> Violets are gone from their grassy dell,
> With the cowslip cups, where the fairies dwell;
> The rose from the garden hath passed away –
> Yet happy, fair boy, is thy natal day! (Hemans[24])

To my Mother on her Birthday

> Today's your natal day
>   Sweet flowers I bring;
> Mother accept I pray,
>   My offering.
>
> And may you happy live,
>   And long us bless
> Receiving as you give
>   Great happiness. (Rossetti[25])

Hemans, like Rossetti, showed early promise and had a collection of poetry published when she was only 13. If she is recognized at all these days, it tends to be as the author of 'Casabianca[26]' which has been parodied so often that it is hard to do the poem justice and read it seriously. The regular 'sing-song' quality of the metre, the passionate voice, the tendency towards melodrama make it an easy poem to parody; many poems for children come into this category. But I believe it is as good a heroic poem as Kipling ever wrote and rather moving. As the single mother of five boys herself, Hemans is likely to have empathized with the sad tale, based on a true story of her day. If it sounds a little sentimental today, it also does that unusual thing – treats a child like a hero.

> The boy stood on the burning deck
>   Whence all but he had fled;
> The flame that lit the battle's wreck
>   Shone round him o'er the dead.
>
> Yet beautiful and bright he stood,
>   As born to rule the storm –

146

A creature of heroic blood,
  A proud, though child-like form.
      [...]
There came a burst of thunder-sound –
  The boy – oh! where was he?
Ask of the winds that far around
  With fragments strewed the sea! –

With mast, and helm, and pennon fair,
  That well had borne their part;
But the noblest thing which perished there
  Was that young faithful heart!

 Another inspiration for the 'sweet flowers' might have been Charlotte Smith whose *Elegaic Sonnets* and other poetry and prose were highly valued at the end of the eighteenth century and early in the nineteenth century. If Christina Rossetti did not know Charlotte Smith's poetry for adults, she could have come across *Conversations Introducing Poetry To Children*[27] which was first published in 1804. This contains nature poetry both sensuous and lush, yet full of sadness and disappointment, hallmarks of Rossetti's poetry, too.

Queen of fragrance, lovely rose,
Thy soft and silken leaves disclose.
The winter's past, the tempests fly.
Soft gales breathe gently through the sky
The silver dews and genial showers
Call forth a blooming waste of flowers;
And lo! thy beauties now unclose
Queen of fragrance, lovely rose!
Yet, ah! how soon that bloom is flown!
How soon thy blushing charms are gone!
Today thy crimson buds unveil,
Tomorrow scattered in the gale.
Ah! human bliss as swiftly goes,
And fades like thee, thou lovely rose.

Jane and Ann Taylor's *Original Poems for Infant Minds*[28] almost certainly influenced Christina Rossetti with their observations of childhood and, particularly, their gentle poems of motherly love. Certainly, Rossetti was familiar with Charlotte Yonge's series of articles for *Macmillan's Magazine* about children's literature which appeared around the time *Sing-Song* was published, where Yonge gave credit to the Taylor sisters 'for their astonishing simplicity without puerility'.[29] Indeed, this may be one of the hallmarks of women's voices for the young – simplicity without stupidity. Nursery rhymes share that distinction.

Original Poems was published in 1804, but continued to be in print in one form or another until the first decade of this century. Until the Taylors' seminal collection, most published poetry for children was harsh, didactic and certainly uninterested in exploring loving relationships between mothers and children. Harvey Darton[30] describes *Original Poems* as awaking the nurseries of England: the Taylors were extremely influential in their period and beyond, sparking off a flurry of publishing by other writers in the same genre and many different illustrated versions of the poems.

If Christina Rossetti was to make the cradle song her own, it was the Taylor sisters in 1804 who had opened the nursery door. At last, affection between mother and baby was being openly and tenderly expressed in poetry written specifically for children. Another noticeable feature of the Taylors' work, which Rossetti also employed to advantage, was the use of loving, inconsequential language – the sort of affectionate, rhythmic talk, often quite close to nonsense, that adults tend to use with babies.

The Baby's Dance
Dance, little baby, dance up high,
Never mind baby, mother is by;
Crow and caper, caper and crow,
There little baby, there you go:
Up to the ceiling, down to the ground,
Backwards and forwards, round and round.
Then dance, little baby, and mother shall sing,
With the merry gay coral, ding, ding, a-ling, ding. (Ann Taylor[31])

Such a poem looks absolutely commonplace to sympathetic readers. But it must have felt like a breath of fresh air to children used to being bossed about by adult authors telling them how to behave. The Kind Mamma is another such example.

> Come, dear, and sit upon my knee,
> And give me kisses, one, two, three,
> And tell me whether you love me,
> My baby.[32]

There is a direct line to Rossetti, I think, particularly in the concreteness and physicality of the poems.

> I'll nurse you on my knee, my knee,
> My own little son;
> I'll rock you, rock you, in my arms,
> My least little one.[33]

Certainly, in Rossetti's *Sing-Song* the mother's eyes are always on the baby and she offers unconditional love. In the next poem, she directs our attention to the baby in the mother's arms, looking up into her eyes, as she murmurs sweet nothings. It is very simple, melodious and exquisitely tender.

> Love me, – I love you,
>   Love me, my baby;
> Sing it high, sing it low,
>   Sing it as it may be.
> Mother's arms under you,
>   Her eyes above you
> Sing it high, sing it low,
>   Love me, – I love you.[34]

Jan Marsh[35] suggests that this empathy for mothers and babies sprang from Rossetti's own childhood: 'As the youngest, she was cradled at the breast while the older children played, with that sense of utter security later invoked in her children's verses...' Certainly her early childhood was a very loving and secure one with Italian parents who were, perhaps, more attentive, demonstrative and affectionate than many English parents of the period.

> You are my one, and I have not another;
>   Sleep soft, my darling, my trouble and treasure;
> Sleep warm and soft in the arms of your mother,
>   Dreaming of pretty things, dreaming of pleasure.[36]

Original Poems provoked a great number of imitators in the first decade of the nineteenth century, including Charles and Mary Lamb who produced their *Poetry For Children*[37] in 1809. One of the most appealing poems in their collection, and one of the most popular at the time, is 'Chusing a Name'. It is written as if in the voice of a child, something rather rare before this date and no mama in sight!

> I have got a new-born sister;
> I was nigh the first that kiss'd her.
> When the nursing woman brought her
> To Papa, his infant daughter,
> How Papa's dear eyes did glisten –
> She will shortly be to christen:
> And Papa has made the offer,
> I shall have the naming of her.

As we know from Charles's letters that Mary wrote two-thirds of the poetry (although we don't know which two-thirds was hers) we can claim her as one of the, now forgotten, women poets writing for children. The lively tone of 'Chusing a Name' recalls one of Rossetti's:

What does the bee do?
– Bring home honey.
And what does Father do?
– Bring home money.
And what does Mother do?
– Lay out the money.
And what does baby do?
– Eat up the honey.[38]

William Rossetti recorded that the baby Christina often sat on her father's knee while he played clapping rhymes with her. It seems likely she drew on her own babyhood when writing *Sing-Song* and the confidence and authenticity came from her own experience of adults sharing a homely experience with a toddler, like the example which follows:

Mix a pancake,
Stir a pancake,
  Pop it in the pan;
Fry the pancake,
Toss the pancake, –
  Catch it if you can.[39]

Christina Rossetti is one of the few poets of the nineteenth century to write as if a mother was softly addressing a small child, holding it very close and whispering in its ear. It is sad that such sensuous poetry should be written by someone who never had a baby of her own, reminding us of Dorothy Wordsworth (1771–1855) who also wrote tender poems to someone else's child.

The days are cold, the nights are long,
The north wind sings a doleful song;
Then hush again upon my breast;
All merry things are now at rest,
  Save thee, my pretty love!

The kitten sleeps upon the hearth,
The crickets long have ceased their mirth;
There's nothing stirring in the house
Save one wee, hungry, nibbling mouse,
  Then why so busy thou?

Nay! start not at that sparkling light;
'Tis but the moon that shines so bright
On the window pane bedropped with rain:
Then little darling, sleep again,
  And wake when it is day![40]

This poem is entitled, 'The Cottager to her Infant', one of Dorothy Wordsworth's acute and moving observations of the real life of the poor. Her domestic, informal writing is typical of many women then – modest, unpretentious, honest and, perhaps, spontaneous. This is a body of work Christina Rossetti could not have known as Dorothy Wordsworth never published any of her writing. A recent editor of her journal describes her thus: 'Dorothy Wordsworth was one of those sweet characters whose only life lies in their complete dedication to a man of genius.'[41] Rubbish! Dorothy Wordsworth was devoted to her brother, but her journal makes plain that she had other interests: her love of nature, her pleasure in reading, her joy in physical exercise, her garden, her satisfaction in domestic pursuits (notwithstanding the hard work involved). Her humanity, particularly for the poor, and her empathy for children is also well documented.

Rossetti probably knew Sara Coleridge's *Pretty Lessons In Verse For All Good Children*,[42] a rather didactic title for a Romantic poet's daughter in 1834. The most memorable poem in it, 'The Months of the Year', is still popular in anthologies.

> January brings the sleet and snow,
> Makes our feet and fingers glow.
> February brings the rain,
> Thaws the frozen lake again.

Rossetti does her own version:

> January cold desolate;
> February all dripping wet;
> March wind ranges;
> April changes.[43]

Rossetti is, perhaps, the first and best 'green' poet. Her attachment to the less glamorous inhabitants of the animal kingdom was well known in her family.

> Hurt no living thing:
> Ladybird, nor butterfly,
> Nor moth with dusky wing,
> Nor cricket chirping cheerily,
> Nor grasshopper so light of leap,
> Nor dancing gnat, nor beetle fat,
> Nor harmless worms that creep.[44]

There are a number of pattern poems in *Sing-Song* which have an educational intention as well as a nice sense of fun, reminding us of Jane Johnson who, a hundred years earlier, must have spent hours and hours of her time planning as well as making her educational artefacts. Christina

Rossetti's mother used 'learning rhymes' with her as a child, so there may be echoes from her own nursery days. The fact that she was bilingual probably gave her an edge playing language games.

Here's a puzzle poem:

> A pin has a head, but has no hair;
> A clock has a face, but no mouth there;

a counting poem:

> 1 and 1 are 2 –
> That's for me and you.
> 2 and 2 are 4 –
> That's a couple more;

a sort of riddle:

> No dandelions tell the time,
> Although they turn to clocks;
> Cat's-cradle does not hold the cat,
> Nor foxglove fit the fox.[45]

But she was no crude didact. The best riddle is moving and unforgettable:

> What are heavy? sea-sand and sorrow:
> What are brief? today and tomorrow:
> What are frail? Spring blossoms and youth:
> What are deep? the ocean and truth.[46]

During her childhood, Christina Rossetti became familiar with Mary Howitt's poetry and translations of Hans Andersens's fairy tales. Howitt was a prolific writer for children and one of the most eminent women poets in the 1840s. As a little girl, Rossetti may have been read 'The Spider and the Fly', included in *Sketches from Natural History*,[47] 1834. The poem is still enjoyed today, but how many people know the author's name is Mary Howitt?

> 'Will you walk into my parlour?' said the Spider to the Fly,
> ' 'Tis the prettiest little parlour that ever you did spy;
> The way into my parlour is up a winding stair,
> And I have many curious things to shew when you are there.'
>
> [...]
>
> With buzzing wings she hung aloft, then near and nearer drew.
> Thinking only of her brilliant eyes, and green and purple hue –
> Thinking only of her crested head – poor foolish thing! At last,
> Up jumped the cunning Spider, and fiercely held her fast.

He dragged her up his winding stair, into his dismal den,
Within his little parlour – but she ne'er came out again!

I must mention one poem not included in *Sing-Song*, Christina Rossetti's famous carol, 'In the Bleak Midwinter', one of the most beautiful and painful ever written, which was published shortly after the poems. It is likely that Rossetti would have read *Hymns For Little Children*[48] published in 1848 by the devout and popular poet, Cecil Frances Alexander, which included hymns such as 'All Things Bright And Beautiful', 'There Is A Green Hill Far Away' and 'Once In Royal David's City'. She would also have been familiar with Anna Barbauld's writing, as she was one of the most distinguished authors of the eighteenth century, particularly her *Hymns In Prose For Children*,[49] 1781.

The golden orb of the sun is sunk behind the hills, the colours fade away from the western sky, and the shades of evening fall fast around me . . .

Rossetti would also have been aware of the Taylors' *Hymns For Infant Minds*,[50] 1810.

Kind angels guard me every night,
As round my bed they stay:
Nor am I absent from thy sight
In darkness or by day.

Good as they were, none of them could match the exquisite tenderness and yearning of 'In the Bleak Midwinter'[51] which seemed to draw on all Rossetti's passionate Christian devotion and compassion for the best in human nature. Some commentators have suggested that the poem is about being barren and childless; it is certainly a hymn that dwells on harsh, stark, cold images. It opens with a bleak universe all right for that first Christmas.

In the bleak mid-winter,
Frosty wind made moan,
Earth stood hard as iron,
Water like a stone;
Snow has fallen, snow on snow,
Snow on snow,
In the bleak mid-winter
Long ago.

But it does warm up when we get to the stable, the loving mother and those who want to give the special baby a present. You might argue that serenity, for Rossetti, comes with religion; the cold place is the real world.

Angels and archangels
May have gathered there,
Cherubim and seraphim
Throng'd the air,
But only his mother
In her maiden bliss
Worshipped the Beloved
With a kiss.

All God's angels 'Throng'd the air' and the landscape is hard as iron, but the baby's mother recognized that what he needed was the human touch or 'a kiss'. It takes a woman, a mother, and poor people to bring warmth to the frozen stable in the bleak mid-winter by giving all they have. If this is what women write 'of the spontaneous kind', we certainly have something to be thankful for.

What can I give Him,
Poor as I am?
If I were a shepherd
I would give a lamb,
If I were a wise man
I would do my part –
Yet what can I give him,
Give my heart.

I will end Rossetti's story here. Although Isobel Armstrong[52] states firmly in *Victorian Poetry* that 'in the depth and range of their projects, and in the beauty and boldness of their experiments with language, Tennyson, Browning and Rossetti stand pre-eminent', Rossetti has not been accorded the same critical respect and attention as her fellow male poets. As for the other women who may have influenced her, their work is hardly known at all today.

Which brings us back to Jane Johnson and the England of the 1740s. What good luck kept so many of her books for children together and in good condition, I do not know. Jane Johnson's work uncovers for us some of that secret history of the domestic literacy of women and children in the eighteenth century. Although Jane Johnson was artistically gifted and the little books and artefacts are ingenious and delightful, I suspect she represents an outstanding example of what many women of her period were doing: expressing affection between mothers and children in writing, promoting literacy in an informal setting and in the process giving some scope for their own creativity. If this is typical of what women were privately engaged in with no thought of publication, there is a lot more work to be done on opening up the nursery.

Jane Johnson's verse[53] does not exhibit what have come to be regarded

as qualities of literary distinction, but these poems seem to me to chime
like nursery rhymes.

> As John with his rake went out to make hay,
> He met with his sweetheart, and stopped on his way.

> At a house by a steeple,
> Did live many people,
> Who all did love pudding and pie.
> And good bread, and good meat,
> Which they each day did eat,
> And drank small beer when they were dry.

> A duck and a drake
> jumped into the water.
> And all the young ducks
> did paddle in after.

> An eagle flies high,
> But can't touch the sky.

And the link with Rossetti?

> Rock on, rock on
> My pretty boy.
> And you shall be
> Your mother's joy.

Here are two extracts from poems Jane Johnson wrote to her daughter,
Barbara. The first is from 'An Invitation to Miss B.J. to Come into the
Country'[54] (a new ballad by her Mama, May 1st 1747):

> How Fine and Sweet it is to see
> The Flowers grow on every tree,
> To hear the pretty Cuckoo sing,
> And welcome in the joyous spring;
> The Gold Finch, Linnet, and the Thrush,
> Now Charm our Ears from every bush;
> The shrill larks soaring to the sky,
> Most sweetly singing as they fly.
> The Nightingale with tuneful song,
> Enchanting Warbles all night long;

> [. . .]

> Then come Miss Johnson come away,
> No longer in Dull London stay.

But let the Country be your choice.
We'll welcome you with heart and voice.

This piece of writing is full of personal references and delightful detail of the natural world which is specifically tailored to the desires of her little girl. It is truly child-centred. The second is more formal in language and tone; it is a eulogy on the merits of her young daughter entitled, 'On Miss Barbara Johnson, March 16th 1752'.[55] How many poets have written so seriously of children?

> All sweet and soft of every charm possest
> What can adorn or grace the human breast
> That soul capacious large extensive wise
> Without one thought that needs the least disguise
> Such worth on earth will never more be found
> When her sweet form is buried underground.

Finally, remembering my theme is the opportunity women took to write affectionately to their children, here is one of Jane Johnson's letters to her son, Robert, just one of many affectionate letters she wrote to all four of her children.

My Dear Robert,
    I am sorry you have had such bad weather ... I heartily wish you a good journey home with your father and I shall be glad to see and hear the pretty account you will give of all you have seen since you left Olney ... I would have you teach little Benny to be very good and tell him he should pray to God a good many times in a day as you do and say God Bless me and make me a good man. I have sent him and you a few more nuts and raisins, I have nothing else to send you, or I would send it, for I love you dearly and think you one of the most sensible children of your age in the world. Pray give pretty Miss Purvey a kiss for me and tell her she is much in my favour. I have not time to write any more, so I wish you a good night. Past seven o'clock July 30th 1755.

> On earth who hopes true happiness to see
> Hopes for what never was, nor ne'er will be.
> In heaven, are joys and pleasures ever new,
> And blessings thicker than the morning dew.
> (Learn these by heart before you come home.)

And then, tacked on as an afterthought, the sentiment every mother can recognize:

Oh! Robert, live for ever.[56]

NOTES

1 Christina Rossetti, *Sing-Song* (originally London, 1872; facsimile edition, London: Dover, 1968).
2 Jane Johnson, unpublished handmade materials for her own children held in the Lilly Library, University of Indiana, USA.
3 Roger Lonsdale, *Eighteenth Century Women Poets* (Oxford: Oxford University Press, 1990), p. xxi.
4 Ibid.
5 Victor Watson, *The Prose and the Passion* (London: Cassell, 1994).
6 Johnson Collection op. cit. The Bodleian Library also obtained some manuscripts in 1996 which had previously been in private hands – these are letters, a commonplace book, jottings, a story and other printed matter by Jane Johnson.
7 Rossetti, *Sing-Song*.
8 See Morag Styles, *From the Garden to the Street: An Introduction to Three Hundred Years of Poetry for Children* (London: Cassell, 1997).
9 Coventry Patmore (ed.), *The Children's Garland* (London: Macmillan, 1862).
10 Mary E. Burt, *Poems Every Child Should Know* (London: Doubleday, 1904).
11 Andrew Lang (ed.), *The Blue Poetry Book* (London: Longmans, Green & Co., 1892).
12 Patmore, *The Children's Garland*.
13 Rossetti, *Sing-Song*, p. 67.
14 Geoffrey Grigson (ed.), *The Cherry Tree* (London: Phoenix House, 1959).
15 William Rossetti, *The Poetical Works of Christina Rossetti* (London: Macmillan, 1904), p. lxviii.
16 Jan Marsh, *Christina Rossetti: A Literary Biography* (London: Jonattan Cape, 1995).
17 Rossetti, *Works of Christina Rossetti*.
18 Walter de la Mare (ed.), *Christina Rossetti Poems* (Newton, Montgomeryshire: Gregynog Press 1930).
19 J.D. Symon (ed.), *Christina Rossetti Verses*, (London: Eragny Press, 1906).
20 Rossetti, *Works of Christina Rossetti*, p. lxxi.
21 William Rossetti (ed.), *The Poetical Works of Mrs Hemans* (London: Ward Lock & Co., 1880), p. xxvii.
22 Rossetti, *Works of Christina Rossetti*, p. lxxi.
23 Anon; *The Sacred Harp* (London: Routledge).
24 Felicia Hemans, in Rossetti (ed.), *Works of Mrs Hemans*.
25 Christina Rossetti, *Verses*, published privately by G. Polidon (London, 1847).
26 Rossetti, *Works of Mrs Hemans*.
27 Charlotte Smith, *Conversations Introducing Poetry to Children* (London: Harris, 1804).
28 Ann and Jane Taylor, *Original Poems for Infant Minds* (London: Darton, 1804).
29 Charlotte Yonge, 'Aunt Charlotte's evenings at home', *Macmillan's Magazine* (London: Marcus Ward & Co, 1881).
30 F.J. Harvey Darton, *Children's Books in England* (Cambridge: Cambridge University Press, 1982).
31 Ann and Jane Taylor, *Rhymes for the Nursery* (London: Darton, 1806).
32 Ibid.
33 Rossetti, *Sing-Song*, p. 13.
34 Ibid., p. 2.
35 Marsh, *Christina Rossetti*.

36 Rossetti, *Sing-Song*, p. 19.
37 Charles and Mary Lamb, *Poetry for Children* (London: Godwin, 1809).
38 Rossetti, *Sing-Song*, p. 108.
39 Ibid, p. 78.
40 I. Opie and P. Opie (eds), *Oxford Book of Children's Verse* (Oxford, 1973).
41 Dorothy Wordsworth, *Home at Grasmere*, ed. Colette Clark, (Harmondsworth: Penguin, 1960).
42 Sara Coleridge, *Pretty Lessons in Verse for all Good Children* (London: George Routledge & Son, 1872)
43 Rossetti, *Sing-Song*, p. 49.
44 Rossetti, *Sing-Song*, p. 100.
45 Ibid., pp. 54, 44, 65.
46 Ibid., p. 34.
47 Mary Howitt, *Sketches from Natural History* (London: Effingham Wilson, 1834).
48 Cecil Frances Alexander, *Hymns for Little Children* (London: Joseph Masters, 1848).
49 Anna Barbauld, *Hymns in Prose for Children* (London: Johnson, 1781).
50 Ann and Jane Taylor, *Hymns for Infant Minds* (London: Darton, 1810).
51 Christina Rossetti, 'In the Bleak Midwinter', written in 1871.
52 Isobel Armstrong, *Victorian Poetry*, (London: Routledge, 1993).
53 Jane Johnson Collection at Lilly Library, Indiana University, USA.
54 Jane Johnson, manuscripts in The Bodleian Library.
55 Ibid.
56 Ibid.

Part IV

LEARNING TO READ IN SCHOOL

11

THE DOMESTIC AND THE OFFICIAL CURRICULUM IN NINETEENTH-CENTURY ENGLAND

David Vincent

Opening the Nursery Door is concerned with a double trajectory of change. On the one hand there are the radical developments in the form, content and volume of the printed word which was read to or by children. On the other there are the children themselves, making and remaking their identities through contact with a variety of shaping forces, amongst which books and the skills required to decode them were becoming increasingly important. In this sense, the study of children's literature represents a particularly complex branch of literary history. To describe the endlessly shifting interaction between the two processes of change requires a breadth of approach, both theoretical and empirical, which is far from easy to establish or apply. The traditional historiography of children's learning in the nineteenth century has rarely risen to this challenge. Explicitly or implicity it has set out to account for the origins of the post-war systems of instruction. It is of course necessary to place the series of reforms from the 1944 Education Act to the imposition of the National Curriculum in a longer temporal context, but such an enterprise encourages a dangerously restricted programme of study. The preoccupation with official policies, official schooling and official curricula directs attention away from the crucial processes by which mass literacy was achieved. An understanding of the changing engagement of children with the printed word requires first of all a breach in the walls between the inspected classroom and the world of learning and living beyond it.

For this reason, a welcome should be given to a new attempt to present a genuinely broad history of nineteenth-century children. Eric Hopkins's *Childhood Transformed*[1] lays no claim to be a major work of research, neither does it impose a challenging theoretical framework on existing material in the way of Wally Seccombe's recent *Weathering the Storm*.[2] However, it makes a real effort to come to terms with both the range and the scale of the changes to which children were exposed during the period of the Industrial Revolution. Long sections on the history of education, and shorter passages on recreational reading, are set in the context of transitions in the fields of child labour, the family economy, domestic life, juvenile crime and various forms of welfare provision. There is no doubt that down this broad path we must all of us go, even if our individual interests and skills keep us more to one side of it than another. In this respect, Hopkins has made a modest but useful contribution, especially for those who have to teach the history of teaching.

Yet in the end, the subject of childhood, and the particular topics which are of concern to Hopkins's collection of essays, remains obstinately untransformed. The book's capacity creatively to explore the articulation of the different aspects of children's lives is confined by its one-dimensional analytical framework. At the heart of the difficulties are the linked issues of sources and causation. Apart from a handful of memoirs, the bulk of the material in the study is from official surveys and commentaries. In turn the conception of the forces of change is entirely top-down. 'The key to understanding the transformation of children's lives in the nineteenth century', Hopkins writes, 'is really provided very largely by middle-class action, especially in the fields of working conditions and of education.'[3] The notion that working-class children and their parents could have any shaping influence over how they became literate and what they did with their skills is nowhere entertained. In the field of schooling, for instance, the complex and extensive history of private adventure schools, well established by the work of Phil Gardner,[4] is either ignored or dismissed by citing the critical comments of HMIs. At the same time, the possibility that evidence can be located which might give an extensive insight into the perspective of the children themselves is largely discounted.

This is a familiar problem. The most recent major monograph on the nineteenth-century education of the poor in Britain, Neil Smelser's 500-page *Social Paralysis and Social Change* of 1991,[5] presents a loving analysis of the official actions of official men recorded in official documents with barely a backward glance at the world beyond the school inspectors' reports. It represents at best a coping stone, at worst a tombstone, on a tradition of educational history which has run its course. We are still faced with the task of breaking what Harold Silver has recently called the 'silence of historians' in the field of teaching working-class children their letters. Surveying the historiography of both British and American education, Silver complains that

A historical view of policy as expressed in the complexities of intellectual as well as political processes, as stimulated or confronted by popular constituencies as well as the major power players, as distorted in implementation by experience, as requiring historical as well as other social science and political explanations, has not emerged in any scale in either country.[6]

His complaint is that in their attempt to break out of the ghetto of narrative educational history, historians and social scientists have become over-engaged with the broader political, economic and social systems within which schools are embedded, and have lost sight of the classroom, the schoolchild and the schoolchild's family. Reviewing seventeen years of the main British journal, *History of Education*, he finds that over this period, 'only three articles . . . can be said to be seriously about children in school'.[7] Too often a claim to context takes the analysis away from rather than towards the curriculums of the classroom and the home.

. What I want to argue here is that the efforts to escape the traditional constraints of educational history have generated a sense of thickness which is at best partial and at worst wholly illusory, and that a proper understanding of learning to read in nineteenth-century elementary schools requires a different kind of breadth in the approach to both evidence and agency.

*

In the first instance it is a matter of sources. Smelser, like Hopkins, reviews accounts produced by the working class, and observes, quite properly, that these documents are themselves 'skewed' in various ways, and that is the last we hear of them.[8] Official records must always form a part of any study, but it is far more difficult than Hopkins and Smelser realize to generate a radical approach to the subject on the basis of so conservative a search for evidence. There is now not only a broad, if often fragmentary and awkward, body of material outside the Parliamentary Papers, but also a growing range of methodological guides to their use.

These are not all confined to what might be regarded as the wilder shores of printed and oral evidence. An example of what may be contributed by a relatively mainstream but still largely underexploited source, is Ian Michael's recent bibliographical exercise published by the newly formed Colloquium on Textbooks, Schools and Society.[9] *Early textbooks on English*, which is derived from Michael's authoritative 1987 monograph, *The teaching of English*,[10] sets the publication history of aids to reading in the context of the wider history of print and its dissemination, and in doing so identifies important new avenues of research.

Michael finds, for instance, that, 'In most subjects, from the middle of the eighteenth century, there are many prose works written for children which are instructional but designed for use at home by a mother or governess.'[11] The explosion of school textbooks which takes place after 1830 only doubles the production of new English textbook titles – from an average of seventeen to one of thirty-five a year. As he realizes, this raises the matter of the relationship between books bought and used in the home and those supplied in the schools:

> Underlying it is the question whether, and how, literature was taught before it was institutionalised by public examinations, and especially during the second half of the eighteenth century when the interpretative aspects of traditional rhetoric had been flattened into *belles lettres*. Much was written for children at that time. Did it get into the classroom?[12]

We still need more work on price, print-runs and market, but there is evidence of a relatively broad diffusion. Alongside the traditional practice of adapting books, tracts or newspapers written initially for adults, there are indications that by the early nineteenth century primers and spelling books were being used in working-class homes. In 1805 Darton and Harvey, a leading publisher and distributor of children's literature, listed a wide range of teaching aids for parents, including twelve separate types of spelling books at prices from 6d to 1/6d, 'Alphabet Cards with Picture, 6d per pack coloured', and 'Battledores for Children 1d, 2d, 3d each'.[13] *Cobbett's Grammar,* first published in 1818, had sold 100,000 copies by 1834, by which time it had been joined by his *Spelling Book with Appropriate Lessons in Reading*.[14] Many of the primers were originally intended for a middle-class market, which began to expand rapidly in the middle decades of the eighteenth century, but they were so cheap and published in such numbers that it was not difficult for a working-class parent to get hold of something like William Mavor's *English Spelling Book* which was into its 322nd edition by 1826.[15] Michael himself quotes Crabbe writing of elementary textbooks, 'Soil'd, tatter'd, worn and thrown in various heaps.'[16] The widespread foraging on these heaps may help to explain how two-thirds of grooms could write their names before the state spent a farthing on public education.[17]

Here we begin to approach the central theme of this chapter, that there existed curriculums of learning both at home and in the classroom, and that the complex and evolving relation between them was crucial to the identity of each. Textbooks teach us to be less preoccupied with the work of schools and their teachers and the bureaucratic structures in which they were embodied. Adults from a wide range of backgrounds had for centuries accepted a responsibility for instruction in basic literacy, and continued to play a role alongside the growth of state-funded and controlled education. At the same time they instruct us to think much more sharply about the meaning of the physical context of teaching. Whereas teachers were influenced by their teaching materials, those materials themselves changed their function and eventually their content during their transition from the home to the classroom. In the field of textbooks, as more generally, the major turning points which have dominated the nineteenth-century histories, the series of reports and bills and acts, dissolve into a long-term interaction between the private and public domains of childhood.

If we stay with the reading materials, for instance, the initial impression of the first years of the British and National Schools Societies is the sheer antiquity of their basic classroom literature. They inherited a method of teaching children their letters which predated printing.[18] The system embodied in the first primer published in 1538 had been in use for several centuries and was in turn based on what were thought to be classical techniques of instruction. There were pedagogic disputes and occasional innovations over the centuries, but the pace of change was scarcely electric.

During the period which witnessed the American, French and Industrial Revolutions, the lists of syllables with which primers began evolved from 'ba be bi bo bu' in lesson one in Thomas Dyche's primer of 1710,[19] to 'ba ab ca ac' in the first lesson of Henry Innes's 'Plain, Pleasing, Progressive System' of 1835.[20] The combination of longevity and dispersal meant that the sixteenth-century schoolboy would have been quickly at home in the early nineteenth-century classroom, just as the schooled poor man's son could have swopped primers with the home-educated heir of a landed gentleman.[21] Yet the experience of learning letters in the monitorial systems employed in the first modern elementary schools was significantly different from either contemporary or past home instruction, and that difference in the end forced the most significant change in teaching literacy for half a millennium.

Traditional teaching methods were founded on two principles. First, that spelling should be mastered alongside rather than subsequent to reading[22]; second, that learning proceeded from the particular to the whole. The pupil was to begin with the alphabet, then combine letters into syllables which were succeeded by simple monosyllabic words.[23] In the more ambitious primers of the early nineteenth century, the subsequent word lists were carefully arranged in ascending length, with the curriculum ending with seven-syllable tongue-twisters which the child might never again encounter in any passage of prose or poetry.[24] The decomposition and reconstitution of language was at the heart of the great majority of teaching books, despite their authors' ritual claims to originality. It was believed that a child's learning processes naturally operated by combining fragments of knowledge into larger wholes, and it seemed logical to begin with the smallest units of language and work upwards.[25] Furthermore, the task of selecting and arranging the syllables and the word-lists justified the need for specialist pedagogic literature, and, increasingly, specialist teachers.[26]

As the eighteenth century advanced, the commercial market for teaching materials began to display a greater plurality. Alongside the traditional alphabets and primers, anthologies of leading writers were compiled to entice the young reader forwards, and entrepreneurs such as John Newberry introduced a range of games to ease the pain of instruction. The Jane Johnson collection, which is the inspiration of this book, contains a variety of aids to learning, including both conventional alphabets and carefully fashioned flash cards. We still know very little about how pupils and their teachers used these materials in their journey to literacy. In the absence of further research, it is unclear how far and in what way domestic tutors moved between commercial products, homemade aids to learning, and other forms of print in the household. Whilst methods were prescribed in the primers, their users were free to adapt and combine them with other specialist and non-specialist media as availability and aptitude dictated. In the home, the pace, direction and means of progress were open to continual adjustment and variation.

It was otherwise in the monitorial system which was at the heart of the National and the British and Foreign Schools Societies (BFSS) of the early decades of the nineteenth century. Here the deconstruction of language was embraced as a theory of organization rather than knowledge.[27] The sequence of rebuilding words in the primers provided a ready-made solution to the problem of mass instruction. There were eight classes in the early BFSS schools. The first four progressed from the alphabet to four-letter syllables; the next two mastered one and two-syllable words; the final two encountered simple religious passages and then some anthologies carefully vetted for their improving content.[28] The primers, which once had served only to prepare children for continuous prose, now became exclusive and self-sufficient courses of learning. Only the most advanced children were introduced to consecutive sentences, which did not include any of the comparatively rich literary anthologies of the late eighteenth century.

The changing function of the primers severely aggravated the long-standing problem of context. It had never been very clear how the child was to connect the syllables and word-lists either to its oral vocabulary or to the tasks of reading and writing joined-up paragraphs. But where domestic tutors might improvise and muddle through, the new generation of trained schoolteachers ran on a narrow, prescribed track. In their hands, the artificiality of this technique of instruction was exposed with forbidding clarity. As the teaching methods became more intense, learning to read became increasingly divorced from the child's encounters with language in the home. The fragments of words and sentences which it faced in the classroom bore no visible relation to the complex linguistic skills which had been mastered in infancy and early childhood. At no stage in the domestic learning process had the child spoken in disconnected syllables, or been expected to memorize columns of words which

166

had in common only their length. The inevitable strangeness of print had become unnecessarily absolute.

By the time the state started to subsidize and then inspect the work of the church schools, doubts were surfacing about the value of the tables of syllables and unmeaning combinations'.[29] The growing body of reports and the continuing process of revising textbooks and teachers' guides was forcing critical attention on the limitations of the analytical method of teaching basic literacy. The professionals themselves began to ask questions about the connection between the lessons and the linguistic abilities the child had acquired before ever it encountered the written word, and about the relation between polysyllabic mastery and a genuine competence in independent reading.[30] The outcome was the emergence of the 'Look and Say' method, which was under discussion in the late 1840s and received official sanction in the 1852 Minutes.[31] As with almost every other innovation of this and later periods, it is possible to trace a lineage for this approach back down the centuries; Jane Johnson certainly seems to have included it in her array of home-made devices. But it remained on the margins of pedagogic theory until the limitations of the particularistic method were exposed by its use to structure the first generation of elementary schools. Under the new approach the pupil was to be introduced to complete, monosyllabic words, preferably in the context of short sentences. The way in which the words were spelled would be taught after, not before the pupil had learned to recognize them.[32]

The speed and scale of the transformation is difficult to gauge. The better inspectors recommended some combination of the holist and particularist routes. The alphabet still needed to be learned, and the syllabic method retained a superficial logic and simplicity. However the shift in emphasis was of genuine importance. The new approach required the teacher to make an accommodation with the knowledge and skills that pupils acquired before or outside their schooling. Where a young child learned to talk by imitation, only later becoming conscious of the rules which controlled spoken language, now for the first time it was permitted by the schoolmaster to use guesswork as it began to read. And where the oral vocabulary had been discounted, it was now recommended that, 'The first lessons should consist entirely of words with which the ear of children is familiar.'[33] The point of departure was to be the language the pupil already possessed. 'It is most important', insisted J.S. Laurie in his *First Steps to Reading* of 1862, that the early lessons should 'contain matters which shall be interesting to him, and that the words that occur in them should be within the compass of his vocabulary.'[34]

In 1862, the apparently regressive Revised Code was introduced. I will return to the significance of this reform later in the chapter but here it should be noted that in the field of reading the newly defined standards brought forth a generation of textbooks which represented a clear advance over their immediate predecessors.[35] The tradition of literary anthologies which had flourished in the later eighteenth century was revived in publications such as J.S. Laurie's *Graduated Series of Reading Lesson Books*, which confirmed the progress of the later years of the pre-revised system and anticipated the more ambitious materials of the last quarter of the century. In the reader for the First Standard, the child travelled straight from the alphabet to complete sentences and thence to self-contained passages of prose before moving up to the next Standard.[36] Moral lessons remained, but in a more secular form; *Aesop's Fables* replaced the Bible as the most common source of precept. For the first time for more than half a century, material was included for no other purpose than the entertainment of the pupil.[37] The pattern was extended by later series, most notably Nelson's *Royal Readers* of 1872, which presented the advanced pupil with a cornucopia of prose, poetry and drama, interspersed with travellers' tales and natural history. 'There was plenty there to enthral any child' recalled Flora Thompson, ' "The Skater Chased by Wolves"; "the Siege of Torquilstone", from Ivanhoe, Fenimore Cooper's, Prairie on Fire; and Washington Irving's Capture of Wild Horses.'[38]

*

The case of the reading primers is an instance of the larger issue of the interaction of the domestic and school curriculum, and their relevance to the overall history of elementary schooling. Hopkins is good on the intersection between the regulation of child labour and the growth of compulsory schooling, which together he sees as the key to the transformation of nineteenth-century childhood. Smelser seeks, in his own words, 'to explain the structural outcomes in the primary education system by referring to the structural processes (class, religious, economic, and political) transpiring in the larger society'.[39] What I want to stress here is that not only are key topics excluded from these analytical structures, but that the explanations which are provided will not operate without them. It is not enough merely to acknowledge, as Hopkins does, that, 'it is difficult to generalise about working-class parents' attitudes to education ... [and] it is equally difficult to describe children's attitudes to the schooling they received',[40] or ritually to observe, as Smelser does, that 'a great deal of education occurred outside those special social structures known as schools'.[41] Unless we venture into these mostly uncharted areas to learn something of the outlook of all the participants and the nature of all the alternative forms of learning, we can measure neither the impact of institutional education, nor can we fully understand the process of reform which gave rise to it.

The remainder of this chapter briefly surveys the basic elements of the domestic curriculum, and then returns to the moment when the official curriculum was forced to begin to come to terms with it. However harsh and brief the experience, childhood was always a time of learning. It is possible to identify four components of the *cursus honorum*: skills, information, imagination and morality. The growing girl or boy had to learn how to live and work, how the family and neighbourhood operated, how fantasy could be developed and expressed, and how to negotiate the prevailing expectations of right and wrong. The curriculum varied from period to period, from community to community, and from child to child within a family. It was never theorized, never inspected, never completed. Yet it was no less inevitable than elementary education was to become later in the nineteenth century, and far more extensive.

The curriculum began with walking and talking. However confined the child's physical and cultural background, he or she would have made immense progress in skills of locomotion and communication by the time of entering the door of the classroom.[42] By imitation, experiment and casual instruction from everyone they met, children's faculties were enlarged and capacities were discovered. In this context, the task of gaining command over the tools of written communication was merely one amongst many, and it was far from being the most difficult. Some working-class autobiographers of the period had acquired a basic facility in reading at an age when they possessed few other skills which would be recognized or valued by their families.[43] Given adequate attendance, a school might expect to teach an average child its letters by its ninth or tenth year, when he or she would still be deemed unfit for mastering any but the most routine manual tasks. In many cases, the children went to school not because they were old enough to be taught, but because they were still too young to begin the serious business of learning and needed something to do to fill in the time. It was several years beyond the most extensive elementary schooling before a boy was thought ready even to commence the serious business of an apprenticeship, which would end at the same age as a conventional university education. Put side by side, the craftsman had a far wider range of skills and information to impart to his apprentice than the schoolteacher had to his pupil.[44] Alfred Ireson, a stonemason's son brought up near Oundle learned as he grew up how to swim and fight, to play the fife, to make potato nets and peel osiers, to work gainfully in a bookbinder's, an iron foundry, and a carpenter's before his father, 'having charge of building new schools at Warmington decided that I should go with him to learn the stone-mason's trade'.[45] Ireson had absorbed almost nothing from his intermittent attendance at two elementary schools but was now to begin his serious course of learning by constructing them.

At one level, skills were merely applied knowledge. Children spent all their days finding out the people, places and events which constituted their community. The sources of this information embraced both 'the education of circumstances',[46] and the conversation of those who were further ahead in the curriculum. A recent survey of teaching literacy has concluded that, 'parents with very little or no educational background ... would be unable to use the spoken word as a means of precise communication, or as a vehicle for interesting conversation'.[47] This was not the experience of 'William Bowyer', the son of a Battersea ironmonger, who had a proper respect for his grandfather, then in his late eighties: 'In a small boy's eyes he was a man of immense learning, with an astonishing memory and a vast fund of information on every subject I could mention, and I do not doubt that actually he was a well-informed man, of penetrating and balanced judgment, though he had had no opportunity whatever of formal education.'[48] However well-trained, no schoolmaster had as much to impart, however well-written, no textbook contained as many interesting facts. The fruits of formal learning were confined to a subordinate role. However, literacy was gradually increasing its function for storing and transmitting information within the communities of the labouring poor. Knowledge of the past had long been reinforced by lists of names in the family Bible, and knowledge of the world beyond the locality was now being extended by literature encountered inside or outside the classroom.

Tales of exploration were particularly welcomed by inquisitive children. Captain Cook and his successors transported the young reader across the physical boundaries of the neighbourhood, supplying lessons in geography, anthropology and history, and stimulating the imagination as voyages of exploration were mounted into the fields and woods which were still within reach of the relatively compact new urban communities. Reading fed into play which in turn increased the appetite for fantastic stories. The source of most of these had always been the memories of the older generation. Jack Lawson's mental development owed a great deal to his father who was a merchant seaman: 'Although he was almost illiterate, he told wonderful stories in choice English – never using a word of dialect ... All unconsciously he was playing the schoolmaster to me, for he was quickening the mind and touching the imagination.'[49] Just as play merged the real and the imaginary, so the tales and songs which stimulated it elided the literary with the oral. The young John Clare, for instance, heard stories and ballads from the old women in his village which he later discovered had been embodied in chapbooks and broadsheet ballads at various stages in their journey down the centuries.[50]

In childhood, as in later life, the greatest appetite for the printed word was in the realm of imagination, which was why the inspected schools at first resisted literary anthologies on the grounds of distraction and over-stimulation, and then allowed them back into the classroom in the middle decades of the nineteenth century when they began to try positively to attract the attendance and attention of pupils. By contrast, the area in which the early schools placed all their emphasis, the spiritual education of the rising generation, was in practice least influenced by the printed word. In the domestic curriculum, moral education was largely a matter of people rather than books, example rather than moral instruction. For most children, ethics were a family concern. It was not Christ but their parents, and especially their mothers, who had most obviously suffered that they might live. The 'exemplary and heroic character' of those who had sacrificed food, comfort and rest for their growing children provided the most powerful lessons.[51] James Saunders, a butcher's son who became a miller, traced his principles back to their source:

> I believe my mother was one of the most absolutely unselfish women who ever breathed, but at the same time I never met any one with a more clear and emphatic sense of right or wrong, or with so accurate and instantaneous an insight into character . . . She instilled into my mind a firm belief in the certain victory of integrity and perseverance.[52]

There was no necessary conflict between this practical instruction and the prolonged encounters with the Bible and other sacred texts in the reading lessons of the first generation of elementary schools. At the very least, the religious literature provided a language for the numerous auto-biographers who wrote about their moral development. None the less it is noticeable how infrequently the substance of the accounts accorded a significant role to the work in the classroom. On the few occasions when they did, the relevant influence was not the curriculum but the personality of the individuals who ran the sparsely staffed schools. In spite of the contemptuous official reports, there were gifted teachers amongst the army of untrained proprietors of dame and proprietary establishments. And in spite of the damaging rigidity of the training and methods, there were men and women in the state-subsidized schools whose vocation and humanity survived the system in which they were employed. Such individuals could make a major impact on the lives of children whose parents were losing the struggle to protect their family from the pressures of the outside world. In the rare instances where a teacher possessed both the personal qualities and the opportunity to exercise such care, it was not forgotten.[53] In most children's lives there were too few adults able or willing to treat them as children.

The domestic curriculum was a rich and complex and at the same time a limited and incomplete programme of learning. Growing children never exhausted the body of information, skills, imagination and values which resided in the memories and behaviour of those with whom they lived and worked, but increasingly were aware that there were additional sources of instruction and entertainment contained in the printed word. Literacy was one amongst many tools for living that might be mastered inside or outside the classroom, and in its capacity to record and create knowledge, wisdom and especially fantasy it had a role to play in the remainder of the domestic curriculum. If they led to the acquisition of practical communication skills, the lessons taught in school were not necessarily irrelevant to the broader programme of discovery, but they were not essential and neither did they constitute any sort of replacement. To a boy or girl, an adult could be learned, wise and endlessly entertaining yet functionally illiterate, and in turn a child could graduate with honours from its course of learning without once encountering the written word.

*

'In Great Britain and Ireland', wrote the founder of the National Schools Society, 'at least 1,750,000 of the population of the country at an age to be instructed, grow up to an adult state without any instruction at all, in the grossest ignorance.'[54] The early church schools were founded on a total dismissal of the programme of learning in the private domain. 'The education of the children of the poor', wrote Sarah Trimmer in 1801, ' . . . should not be left to their ignorant and corrupted parents; it is a public concern, and should be regarded as public business.'[55] The inspectors later appointed to oversee the education of such children accepted that, as one put it, 'It is indeed a sad and evil necessity, if the first lesson which they learn at school is to beware of their own parents and to look with disgust, if not horror at the filthiness and abominations of their own homes.'[56] The education which took place in the public domain was to supplant rather than supplement the work of the home. It was a large ambition. The teacher, acting *in loco parentis*, would have to take responsibility for every aspect of the child's development. Attendance at church or at Sunday school, even if either could be secured, was no longer thought sufficient to compensate for the damage caused by the domestic curriculum, especially in the realm of moral training.[57] Joseph Fletcher summarized the challenge in 1846: 'Distrusting, and with reason, the education which is given to the poor by the "world" – by the unregulated influences which bear upon them in the scenes of their daily life – their conception of a school for the children of the poor, is, that it should be a little artificial world of virtuous exertion.'[58]

By this time, however, the little artificial world was becoming difficult to sustain. We have seen how methods of teaching literacy began to be adapted to meet the language the child learned in the home. This was accompanied by a more general secularization of the public curriculum, partly as a result of the growing specialization of teaching methods, which rendered the Bible less and less satisfactory as a medium of instruction, and partly as a consequence of growing fears that, as the inquiry into the Battle of Bossenden Wood of 1839 put it, 'a course of exclusive religious reading, has . . . a tendency to narrow the mind, and instill fallacious ideas'.[59] Serious attention began to be paid to the demands of teachers that the religious content of instruction be leavened by secular knowledge which would broaden the outlook and anchor the judgement of the newly literate. The Bible was displaced from the centre of the curriculum in an effort to bring the moral instruction, which remained the principal concern of education, closer to the real world of the pupils and their parents.[60]

The most dramatic shift in the relationship between the learning processes of the home and school was the product of a crisis in official funding. The church societies managed to persuade the state in 1833 that their work was critical to the survival of the industrializing society, but in time the subsidy exposed them to both systematic inspection and intermittent Parliamentary inquiry. With public expenditure rising at a rate of £100,000 a year by the mid-1850s increasing concern was voiced about the issue of value in education.[61] On closer enquiry, it finally became evident that value was a matter of perspective. A crucial section of the subsequent Newcastle Commission Report of 1861 set out for the first time the conflicting requirements of the suppliers of education and those who were still at liberty not to send their children to inspected schools or indeed to any form of specialized education at all:

> The general principle upon which almost every one who for the last half century has endeavoured to promote popular education has proceeded, has been that a large portion of the poorer classes of the population were in a condition injurious to their own interests, and dangerous and discreditable to the rest of the community; that it was the duty and the interest of the nation at large to raise them to a higher level, and that religious education was the most powerful instrument for the promotion of this object. The parents, on the other hand, cannot be expected to entertain the same view of the moral and social condition of their own class, or to have its general elevation in view. They act individually for the advantage of their respective children; and though they wish them to be imbued with religious principles, and taught to behave well, they perhaps attach a higher importance than the promoters and managers of schools to the specific knowledge which will be profitable to the child in life. It is of some importance in estimating the conduct of the parents to keep this difference of sentiment in view.[62]

This difference will have come as no surprise to many teachers struggling to maintain the presence and interest of their pupils. The state was now discovering its importance because of the urgent need to justify the escalating costs of elementary education. Whilst attendance was voluntary, further investment would be pointless without increased parental support. And without the cooperation of the great majority of families, compulsion would be politically, socially and financially ruinous. It remained only to identify the substance of parental ambition. The answer was provided by one of the Commissioners:

> I have been asked whether the poor have a preference for one system of education over another, whether they neglect the education of their children because of religious indifference, and whether in short there is anything in the present schools which indisposes parents to send their children to school. I made the most diligent inquiry into these matters, and found no difference of opinion. Schoolmasters, clergymen, ministers, city missionaries, all told me that the poor in selecting a school, looked entirely to whether the school supplied good reading, writing and arithmetic.[63]

Out of this discovery emerged the Revised Code of 1862. Where the teaching of basic literacy had been the subordinate concern of the schoolmaster, a means to a much larger and more important end, it was now placed at the centre of the curriculum. The Bishops protested at the acceleration in the decline of religious instruction, and the professional educationalists were appalled at the reversal of the trend towards a wider range of secular subjects. 'The reclamation of these children from barbarism', protested Kay-Shuttleworth, 'is a good greater far than mere technical instruction in the three lowest elements.'[64] But contemporary critics missed the crucial element of compromise in the new system, as have most later historians. A major justification of the reform was the inescapable fact that working-class parents were for the time being only interested in 'mere technical instruction in the three lowest elements'.[65] The concession to the demands of the consumers was the sole means of realizing the increasingly urgent goal of universal elementary education without incurring on the one hand unmanageable expenditure and on the other unmanageable hostility from the working-class community. Alongside the contraction and rigidity of the Revised Code was to be found the first real attempt to negotiate with the domestic curriculum. Where the subordinate status of reading and writing in the early church schools had reflected the more general dismissal of home instruction so the prominence now given to literacy was a consequence of the respect which the government had been forced to pay to the requirements of the working-class family. Although the concept of a partnership between teachers and parents would not be formally articulated until the end of the century,[66] it is possible to detect the beginnings of a working relationship between the private and public domains of instruction. Henceforth inspected schools would do more to extend than dismember the learning which took place in the home.

*

174

The Revised Code represented a double structural change within the school system, fundamentally altering both the content of the official curriculum and the way it was funded. However, both the causes and the consequences of the reform can only be understood if we step back from the classroom and consider all the components of childhood learning and the changing articulation between them. We still need to know a great deal more about how parents and children experienced the evolving relationship between the two curriculums in this period. There is some evidence that the task was more complex for girls than for boys. Although there was formal equality of access to elementary education, and the literacy rates of girls were improving from a lower base at a faster rate than boys,[67] there were significant differences in the interaction between the courses of instruction. On the one hand, the tendency of girls to be treated as deputy mothers in the home made their attendance at school much more vulnerable to household crises, even after the imposition of compulsion in 1880. On the other, their requirement to learn domestic skills such as needlework in the classroom reinforced gender roles and confined career expectations.[68] Girls will have found it even harder than boys to use their formal schooling as a means of challenging or escaping from the restrictions of their domestic curriculum, the more so when a narrow ladder to secondary and university education was set up following the 1902 Education Act.

My concern about the tradition of education history which is still being written is that its engagement with processes beyond the education system is fatally partial. It is of course necessary to understand the complexities of the political and religious conflicts of the period, and the general changes in the patterns of child labour, but if no notice is taken of the classroom and the changing relation with the programme of domestic instruction, accounts are produced which fail properly to explain what Smelser terms the 'decisive moments of change and truce points in the nineteenth century' – the Acts of 1833 and 1870 and 1880, the Revised Code – around which they are organized.[69]

The general histories of childhood and the intervention of social scientists like Smelser are of some value, but they also reveal the need to engage with a more varied range of sources and disciplines. What is needed now is a more rigorous and theoretically informed treatment of issues such as cognitive development, social psychology, orality and literacy, the economics of supply and demand. As an admirable example of the last of these, I might cite David Mitch's recent *The Rise of Popular Literacy in Victorian England* (1992), which makes the first systematic attempt to investigate the relative roles of parents and official providers. Of particular interest is his concluding section, which reinforces Grace Belfiore's finding that the implementation of compulsory education after 1870 demanded further negotiation with the domestic curriculum. 'Effective compulsory schooling laws', he writes, 'appear to have required not just a natural consensus for Parliament to enact them but also widespread local support for local authority to enforce them.'[70] Which fact, he properly observes, 'raises the question of whether the resources devoted to establishing and enforcing compulsory schooling and other restrictions on child labour would have been better devoted to improving the quality of the public schooling that was offered.'[71]

Reluctantly the politicians had to begin to enlarge their frame of reference to include the customers as well as the suppliers of education, and sooner or later historians will have to follow suit.

NOTES

1 E. Hopkins, *Childhood Transformed. Working-Class Children in Nineteenth-Century England* (London, 1994).
2 W. Seccombe, *Weathering the Storm. Working-Class Families from the Industrial Revolution to the Fertility Decline* (London, 1993).
3 Hopkins, *Childhood Transformed*, p. 5.
4 P. Gardner, *The Lost Elementary Schools of Victorian England* (London, 1985).
5 N. Smelser, *Social Paralysis and Social Change. British Working-Class Education in the Nineteenth Century* (Berkeley, 1991).
6 H. Silver, 'Knowing and Not Knowing in the History of Education', *History of Education* 21, 1, (1992), p. 101.
7 Silver, 'Knowing and Not Knowing', p. 106.
8 Smelser, *Social Paralysis*, p. 6.
9 I. Michael, *Early Textbooks of English* (Reading, 1993).
10 I. Michael, *The Teaching of English* (Cambridge, 1987).
11 Michael, *Early Textbooks*, p. 2.
12 Ibid., p. 3.
13 Darton and Harvey, *Books for Youth* (London, 1805).
14 M.L. Pearl, *William Cobbett. A Bibliographical Account of his Life and Times* (Oxford, 1953), p. 68; G. Spater, *William Cobbett, The Poor Man's Friend* (Cambridge, 1982), vol. II, p. 372.
15 For the wide availability of Mavor and other cheap primers on mid-nineteenth-century bookstalls, see, C.M. Smith, 'The Press of the Seven Dials', in, *Little World of London* (London, 1987), p. 261.
16 Michael, *Early Textbooks*, p. 7.
17 For a fuller account of schooling and the advent of mass literacy in this period, see, D. Vincent, *Literacy and Popular Culture. England 1750–1914* (Cambridge, 1989), chs 2 and 3.
18 For the antiquity of teaching methods embodied in printed materials see I. Michael, *The Teaching of English, passim*; H. Graff, *The Legacies of Literacy* (Bloomington, 1987), p. 72.
19 T. Dyche, *A Guide to the English Tongue*, 2nd edn (London, 1710). Also, W. Markham, *An Introduction to Spelling and Reading English*, 5th edn (London, 1738).
20 H. Innes, *The British Child's Spelling Book* (London, 1835). Also, C.W. Johnson, *The English Rural Spelling-Book* (London, 1846).
21 E.M. Field, *The Child and his Book*, 2nd edn (London, 1892), pp. 113–225;

M.F. Thwaite, *From Primer to Pleasure in Reading*, 2nd edn, (London, 1972), pp. 4–7; A. Ellis, *Educating our Masters* (Aldershot, 1985), pp. 87–102.

22 Michael, *The Teaching of English*, p. 14.

23 W.B. Hodgson, 'Exaggerated Estimates of Reading and Writing', *Transactions of the National Association for the Promotion of Social Science* (1867), p. 400.

24 M. Matthews, *Teaching to Read, Historically Considered* (Chicago 1966), pp. 19–74.

25 Michael, *The Teaching of English*, p. 56, 91, 117.

26 Gardner, *Lost Elementary Schools*, pp. 107–8.

27 Michael, *The Teaching of English*, pp. 124.

28 *Manual of the System of Primary Instruction Pursued in the Model Schools of the British and Foreign Schools Society* (London, 1831), p. 15.

29 *Manual of the System of Primary Instruction Pursued in the Model Schools of the British and Foreign Schools Society* (London, 1831); H. Dunn, *Popular Education; or, The Normal School Manual* (London, 1837), p. 69.

30 See the evidence of Henry Dunn to the 1834 *Select Committee on Education*, PP 1834, IX, p. 25.

31 *Minutes of the Committee of Council on Education, 1851–2* (London, 1852), II, p. 48. See also, C.W. Connon, *A First Spelling Book* (1851), p. 4.

32 W.F. Richards, *Manual of Method for the Use of Teachers in Elementary Schools* (London, 1854), p. 66. For the parallel development of this theory in the United States, see, Matthews, *Teaching to Read*, pp. 75–101; and in Russia, J. Brooks, *When Russian Learned to Read.* (Princeton, 1985), p. 50.

33 J. Gill, *Introductory Text-Book to School Management*, 2nd edn (London, 1857).

34 J.S. Laurie, *First Steps to Reading* (London, 1862).

35 For a survey of the expansion of this literature, see A. Ellis, *Books in Victorian Elementary Schools* (London, 1971), pp. 21–32.

36 J.S. Laurie, *Laurie's Graduated Series of Reading Lesson Books* (London, 1866). See also, E.T. Stevens and Rev. C. Hole, *The Grade Lesson Books in Six Standards* (London, 1871).

37 On the arrival of a new generation of secular readers in the schools, see, J.M. Goldstrom, *The Social Content of Education, 1808–1870* (Shannon, 1972), pp. 94–151.

38 F. Thompson, *Lark Rise to Candleford*, 1982 edn (Harmondsworth), p. 180.

39 Smelser, *Social Paralysis*, p. 4.

40 Hopkins, *Childhood Transformed*, p. 142.

41 Smelser, *Social Paralysis*, p. 19.

42 For a survey of this process, see, H. Bee, *The Developing Child*, 3rd edn (New York, 1981), pp. 170–220.

43 See, for instance, Thomas Cooper's account of his education in, T. Cooper, *The Life of Thomas Cooper* (London, 1872), p. 5.

44 C. More, *Skill and the English Working Class, 1870–1914* (London, 1980), esp. pp. 181–94.

45 Ireson, 'Reminiscences', p. 87.

46 F. Place, *The Autobiography of Francis Place*, ed. M. Thale (Cambridge, 1972), p. 61.

47 A. Ellis, *Educating our Masters*, p. 170.

48 'William Bowyer' [William Bowyer Honey], *Brought out in Evidence: An Autobiographical Summing-Up* (London, 1941). Also H. Snell, *Men, Movements and Myself* (London, 1936), pp. 63–4; J. Saunders, *The Reflections and Rhymes of an Old Miller* (London, 1938), p. 86.

49 J. Lawson, *A Man's Life* (London, 1932), p. 11.
50 G. Deacon, *John Clare and the Folk Tradition* (London, 1983), p. 24. For a fuller discussion of the movement between the oral and the printed record see, R. Elbourne, *Music and Tradition in Early Industrial Lancashire 1780–1840* (Woodbridge, 1980), pp. 55–6; Vincent, *Literacy and Popular Culture*, pp. 197–210.
51 D. Barr, *Climbing the Ladder: the Struggles and Successes of a Village Lad* (London, 1910), p. 16. Also W. Adams, *Social Atom* vol. I, p. 35; J. Sexton, *Sir James Sexton Agitator* (London, 1936), p. 229; W. Citrine, *Men and Work* (London, 1964), pp. 12–13; G.N. Barnes, *From Workshop to War Cabinet* (London, 1923), p. 2.
52 Saunders, *Reflections and Rhymes*, pp. 12–13. Also G. Haw, *Workhouse to Westminster. The Life Story of Will Crooks M.P.* (London, 1911), pp. 6, 18.
53 See the accounts in C. Shaw, *When I Was a Child* (London, 1903), p. 139; A. Rushton, *My Life as a Farmer's Boy, Factory Lad, Teacher and Preacher* (Manchester, 1909), p. 32; F. Hodges, *My Adventures as a Labour Leader* (London, 1925), pp. 5–6.
54 A. Bell, *Extract from a Sermon on the Education of the Poor*, 2nd edn (London, 1807), p. 10.
55 S. Trimmer, *Oeconomy of Charity* (London, 1801), vol. I, p. 12.
56 *Minutes of the Committee of Council* (1847), cited in A. Digby and P. Searby, *Children, School and Society in Nineteenth-Century England* (London, 1981), p. 120. Also R. Colls, ' "Oh Happy English Children": Coal, Class and Education in the North-East', *Past and Present* 73 (1976), pp. 86–91, 96.
57 Dunn, *Popular Education*, p. 14.
58 J. Fletcher, *Minutes of the Committee of Council* (1846), p. 287, cited in Digby and Searby, *Children, School and Society*, pp. 77–8.
59 F. Liardet, 'State of the Peasantry in the County of Kent', in Central Society of Education, *Third Publication* (London, 1839), p. 128.
60 J.A. St John, *The Education of the People* (London, 1858), pp. 50, 93–107.
61 For the growing crisis, see M. Sturt, *The Education of the People* (London, 1967), pp. 238–58; A.J. Marcham, 'The Revised Code of Education 1862: Reinterpretations and Misinterpretations', *History of Education* 10, 2 (1981), pp. 87–90; Ellis, *Educating Our Masters*, p. 93.
62 *Report of the Commissioners Appointed to Inquire into the State of Popular Education in England*, PP 1861, XXI, I, p. 34.
63 Ibid., p. 35.
64 J. Kay-Shuttleworth, *Four Periods of Public Education* (London, 1862), p. 590. Also M. Arnold, *The Twice-Revised Code* (London, 1862).
65 J.S. Hurt, *Elementary Schooling and the Working Classes 1860–1918* (London, 1979), pp. 30–4.
66 See for instance, G. Collar and C.W. Crook, *School Management and Methods of Instruction* (London, 1900), pp. 1–4.
67 Vincent, *Literacy and Popular Culture*, pp. 24–6.
68 J. Purvis, *Hard Lessons. The Lives and Education of Working-class Women in Nineteenth-century England* (Cambridge, 1989), pp. 76–94; M. Gomershall, 'Ideals and Realities: The Education of Working-class Girls, 1800–1870', *History of Education* 17, 1 (1988).
69 Smelser, *Social Paralysis*, pp. 23–6.
70 D. Mitch, *The Rise of Popular Literacy in Victorian England* (Philadelphia, 1992), p. 195. For Belfiore's detailed research on the implementation of the legislation, see her unpublished 1987 Oxford D. Phil. thesis, 'Family Strategies

in Essex Textile Towns 1860–1895: The Challenge of Compulsory Elementary Education'.

71 Mitch, *The Rise of Popular Literacy*, p. 198.

12

'I KNEW A DUCK'

Reading and learning in Derby's poor schools

Hilary Minns

The young readers who are the subjects of this chapter are Irish-born children I have been studying who lived in the urban, industrialized town of Derby in the English Midlands between 1841 and 1861. Their parents were attracted to Derby by the prospect of employment for themselves and their children in the town's silk mills, and the children were encouraged to enter a world of schooled literacy in the workhouse or Roman Catholic schools in Derby. Some Irish families went on to America, and many formed part of a migrant population who moved between Britain's towns and cities in search of work. Others settled in Derby, and their descendants are still there today.[1]

Two intertwining themes underpin this chapter. The first concerns the move from the position of 'young worker' to that of 'child', a complex psychological shift that was experienced by many Irish-born children in Derby who had previously worked on the land in Ireland alongside their parents, collecting turf, cultivating flax and growing potatoes. The move towards becoming a full-time scholar was a crucial factor in the institutionalization of childhood experience for the children of the Irish poor, because it set them apart from the adult world and defined them as 'learners from books', in many cases showing them *what* to learn and *how* to learn. The second theme, arising from the first, discusses the literacy development of these children. I will argue that certain non-fiction texts that formed part of their reading lives opened up new learning possibilities, and encouraged these children to develop a capacity for conceptual thought, thus putting them at one remove from their families, and inserting them into a childhood world of ideas.

In 1848 140 Irish children attended the Roman Catholic day school in Derby, and more than one hundred working girls went to the night school for two and half hours every evening. By 1849 the Sisters of Mercy had opened their schools to 300 poor children in Derby, all receiving 'gratuitous education', eighty-five boys and seventy girls, taught separately, the girls by the nuns and the boys by a Roman Catholic schoolmaster. The Irish *Lesson Books*, which I shall discuss later, formed the basis of their curriculum, and lessons in poetry, natural history, geography, history, religious studies and natural philosophy (science) were taught from this series of texts.

The mothers of Irish children in Derby were poor working women. Many brought up children alone because their husbands were away seeking work, or in prison, or else dead. It is easy to suppose that these women had no access to literacy, and no interest in the written word, except when they were required to give details of family circumstances to the Relieving Officer in the Workhouse, or to the enumerator who collected details for the census return. Irish women living in back-to-back houses, with one or two rooms for the entire family, probably had little time or opportunity for reading and writing. Their lives were spent cooking, washing, cleaning and looking after children. Some also worked outside the home in the town's silk mills, or as hawkers; others took in washing or fetched work home from the mills to finish on piece-rates. But it would be wrong to suppose that they had no interest in the written word nor in promoting learning. Tom Barclay, born in Leicester to Irish parents in the 1840s, recalled his County Mayo-born mother's life of drudgery, and praised the inner strength that helped her to face hardship and poverty with what amounted to a series of coping strategies, self-sufficiency and toughness. 'Mother was the grey mare of our family,' her son wrote many years later, 'untiring energy, unfailing health and hope and faith, and never a new dress, never a holiday, never any leisure or amusement, never I fear even a generous meal of victuals'. Barclay's mother never learnt to write, but she could read, and she taught her own children, reading Irish sermons aloud to them. She also told them the stories of Oisen, Fin, and Cuchullan, and the Gobawn Sayre, as well as singing and reciting 'a goodly number of old Irish songs and poems'. This was the same woman who spent hours sorting dusty rags and rotting bones on the brick floor of their two-roomed house, transferring a life of rural poverty to one of urban survival. And yet Mrs Barclay probably taught her own children to read by doing intuitively what good reading teachers like Jane Johnson have always done – by sharing her deep enthusiasm and using a range of strategies and texts to support her children's reading development.[2]

THE TEACHING OF READING IN THE POOR SCHOOLS

From 1846 to 1848 the Irish pupils in the Schools of the Holy Child Jesus in Derby were taught to read by a method described by Mother Cornelia Connelly in her Book of Studies.[3] The teaching of reading was introduced to young children by encouraging them to look at individual words, 'without spelling, alphabet or preparatory'. Then they 'read from the tablets' before progressing to reading books in six months. At this stage Connelly advocated the use of alphabets, letters and reading cards 'with which the teacher makes familiar words and easy sentences, sketching objects on the board, telling stories about them and not wasting time, etc.'. At this point the teacher introduced new words before each lesson. 'All exercises', she said, 'should consist of sentences, not mere strings of words. The teacher should point to and read each word, then the children repeat it simultaneously, followed by a simple explanation with questions from the mistress' and – with an intuitive knowledge of the role of the supportive teacher – 'should accept the answers of the children, however simple.'[4] Connelly showed insights into the learning process that are perhaps surprising to modern educators and historians. She set the teaching of reading in a context, encouraged teachers to develop shared meanings with child learners, and showed an interest in the child as a learner. Her method of teaching reading placed the child at the centre of the learning process, and gave a high priority to understanding the meaning of words and sentences, in a way that made sense to the young child. Irish children who were taught this way by the Sisters of the Holy Child Jesus were educated by women who had thought carefully about the learning process. In this way they were surely privileged.

The Sisters of Mercy used both alphabetical and synthesizing methods to teach reading, holding up individual letters for children to recognize, and teaching words and phrases of increasing complexity from the Irish *Lesson Books*. Insights into the use of these *Lesson Books* and the teaching of reading at the schools of the Sisters of Mercy in Derby can be gleaned from the inspectorial reports of William Marshall. In 1851 he wrote that:

> the lesson books are employed as texts, out of which a complete and systematic course of instruction is constructed by the intelligence and skill of the teachers. The minute analysis of the reading-lesson is the prominent feature of the instruction; and it may be said that bees do not more thoroughly extract from the flower its hidden treasure than these teachers each particle of knowledge which the lesson contains or suggests.[5]

It seems likely that the Sisters were using a catechetical method to help children to respond to the text, questioning them with care. In the light of later discussion I want to draw attention to Marshall's interesting comments on the children's grasp of natural history. He observed that the children had 'a considerable acquaintance with natural history, and could also explain with precision natural phenomena, such as the rainbow, the tides, etc. and readily give their information in another form when required to do so'.[6]

LEARNING IN THE WORKHOUSE SCHOOL

While most Irish children received their education in the Catholic schools in Derby, others lived temporarily or permanently in the Derby Union Workhouse, and attended its school. Pauper children were taught reading, writing and arithmetic, and the principles of Christian religion. They also had lessons in geography, history and natural history, in addition to intermittent industrial training in shoemaking, tailoring and gardening for boys, or domestic duties for girls. The overall aim of the New Poor Law of 1834 was to produce an obedient workforce who knew their place, were able to make their own way in the world, and could read, write and calculate as necessary for their work.

Irish families in Derby without any work, and no money to pay for food and lodgings, had little alternative but to apply to the Board of Guardians for relief. The Derby Poor Law records from 1837 to 1847 show that 213 Irish families or individuals – often the same people over and over again – were relieved. Between 1837 and 1847 fifty-seven Irish boys and forty-one Irish girls were taken in the workhouse, mostly on a temporary basis, often with their parent or parents. Most were likely to have stayed there for some time, attending school and, when they were old enough, being placed in suitable employment by the Guardians.

Irish children were subjected to the rules and routines of the work-house, just as all other children were, and the institutionalized practices became part of their childhood experience. On their arrival they gave their name and age and were asked to state their religion. They were told they were not allowed to leave the workhouse and that if they did they would be brought back. They surrendered their clothes, they were searched, washed, their hair was cropped and they were put into work-house dress, stiffened with size probably made from animal glue, smelly and uncomfortable. Children got up at six o'clock in the morning in the summer, and at seven o'clock in the winter months, washed, dressed, answered their names at role call, ate breakfast, all in an orderly manner, superintended by their teachers. On Sundays they put on clean clothes, and made sure their dirty clothes were put out for washing on Monday.[7]

Reports by the Education Committee of the Board of Guardians in Derby give insights into the content of the basic and somewhat gendered workhouse curriculum, taught separately to boys and girls by the master and mistress. In 1839 the boys in the first class were examined for reading, spelling, grammar, writing and accounts,[8] while girls were examined for reading, knitting and sewing. In the same year the boys were examined in reading and scripture questions 'in which they appear to have improved', although they were seen to be 'deficient in their multiplication tables'.[9]

The choice of books and maps ordered in 1855 reflects some aspects of the curriculum offered to the children in the workhouse school: geography, history and natural history were now taught alongside the subjects which were inspected in 1839 and 1841. In 1855 the schoolmaster in Derby ordered:

10 dozen Copy Books
1 copy Longman's last edition of Watts' Scripture History
Map of Africa
Map of North America
Map of South America
Map of Palestine
Half dozen Bibles
Half dozen Testaments
A few Prayer and Hymn Books
1 copy of Goldsmith's Natural History with a number of Card Boards
Two copies of Manual of Method.[10]

Workhouse children were taught their various subjects using the catechetical method, and Isaac Watts's Scripture History, ordered in 1855, illustrates this method of teaching and learning well. This typical question from page 11 of the text shows how the format of the book and the pedagogical practice used to teach its contents went hand in hand:

Q. Who were the first man and woman that God made?
A. Adam and Eve, Gen. v. 1.2; Cor. xv.45: Gen.iii.20.[11]

Only a single copy of the Scripture History appears to have been ordered in 1855, but it was standard practice to purchase only one copy of some books. W.F. Richards, in his *Manual of Method*, refers to 'two classes of book, those for the special and exclusive use of the teacher' and 'those which are to be used by the children'.[12] With only a single copy, the teacher had to read aloud from selected passages, and encourage children to learn the answers by heart. In 1844 the boys in the workhouse school seem to have succeeded in this task, because the Visiting Committee reported that they 'had examined the Boys [who] answer[ed] the Questions for Scripture very well'.[13]

THE IRISH LESSON BOOKS

The main teaching texts used in the Roman Catholic Schools and the workhouse school in Derby were the *Lesson Books* produced by the Commissioners of National Education in Ireland. The seven Irish Commissioners who had responsibility for producing these books were chosen with care by the government, so that both Protestant and Roman Catholics were represented. The Commissioners approved all texts before they went to print, and worked with eminent educationalists and churchmen on the style and content of each. Roman Catholic authorities in England urged their own schools to purchase these books since they had no set of reading texts of their own (and were not to have until the 1860s), and the Irish Commissioners agreed to supply English workhouse schools and poor schools with their texts.[14] By 1850 the Commissioners had published forty-one books, including ten lesson books, four anthologies of verse, an agricultural class book, lessons on Christianity, and manuals of needlework and accounting.[15] Many of the books remained in print from the 1830s to the 1860s, and were therefore popular for over thirty years.

By 1851 over 100,000 *Lesson Books* had been sold to English poor schools.[16] And there was a financial reason for their success too – they were sold in England far more cheaply than books published by larger publishers like Longman and Murray, who complained bitterly to the government that the Irish *Lesson Books* were 'sold in England at prices below those for which such books [could] be sold by booksellers in this country'.[17] Inevitably, as demand for the books grew, printing costs fell, and larger publishers like Longman and Murray found they could no longer compete.

There were originally five main *Lesson Books* in the series. Their reading philosophy was based on the synthesizing approach, and consisted of graduated texts of one-syllable and two-syllable words, extending to more difficult texts, then texts for the fluent reader using specialized language, and reflecting some difficult subject matter. Each book had supplementary texts published alongside it so that, just as in modern reading classrooms, children could read more books at the same level of reading ability. These supplementary books were clearly needed, since the level of complexity in the five main texts increased dramatically, and the Commissioners soon recognized that the 'advance' from one book to another was 'not sufficiently gradual'.[18] For example, the preface to the *Fifth Book of Lessons* (first published in 1846) explains that the book was intended for 'the instruction of more advanced Pupils'. The book contains highly technical lessons in specialized fields such as Vegetable and Animal Hydrostatics, the Mechanical Properties of Fluids, Specific Gravity, Pneumatics and the Mechanical Properties of Air. In contrast, the *First Book of Lessons* (first published in 1831) is made up of sentences of one syllable only and describes situations that would have been familiar to many nineteenth-century children of the poor: 'Snap bit a rat; its leg bled; it is in a trap; do not let it snap' (p. 11) and 'A flail is used to part the grain from the straw' (p. 28). And there were early moral lessons for young readers too: 'A good boy will not tell a lie.'[19] The *Lesson Books* were small and could be handled easily by small children. Closed, they measure about three inches across and five inches

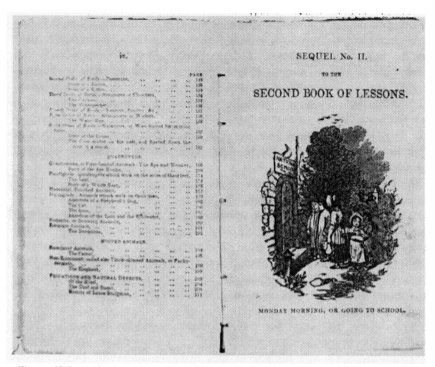

Figure 12.1 A nineteenth-century *Lesson Book* (reproduced with the permission of Leicester University Education Library)

down, yet were thick enough to offer the satisfaction of holding a 'real' book (see Figure 12.1).

The moralizing tone of much of the literature written for children in the eighteenth century found its way into the contents of the Irish *Lesson Books* and is a feature of the writing. There is no magic in these books, no fairies, witches, wolves or wizards. The stories are set in the real world, and are mostly about everyday incidents for the teacher and the reader to make moral judgements about. In the first passage of the *Second Book of Lessons* (pp. 5–6) children are addressed by an anonymous narrator in words of one syllable. They are reminded first of all of the importance of cleanliness, a difficult proposition perhaps for Irish children living in squalid Derby courts with no running water:

Lesson 1

Boys and Girls

boy stand hair
girl wrong noise
comb school learnt

hand home good
know wash class

Boys and girls must not play all day. So comb your hair, and wash your hands, and come to school. Stand up in your class; you can read words now. So you will know things which you did not know when you could not read.

The voices of the Irish Commissioners run through this text, and they impart a moral code to their child readers, showing them a way of behaving, and preparing them for adulthood. The next sentence is a celebration of the ability to read, and underlying the message is a strong didactic voice. It is clear that the working-class child was expected to understand that reading was a worthwhile thing to do:

You will be glad when you grow old that you were taught to read. But some boys and girls do not love to read, for they say it is so hard, and they do not try.

It then becomes clear through a cautionary tale what might happen to the child who does not try to learn to read. The writer has chosen a familiar everyday incident on which to make a moral judgement:

Tom Byrne took no pains to learn; he did not look at his book; so when his turn came to read out, he said the wrong words, and lost his place in the class. When school was done he was dull, for he had not been good. The girls and boys went out to play, and the sun shone, and the soft air blew, and the birds sang; but he was not so gay as they were, though he made more noise, for he had not been good. And when he went home, he had not learnt one new word, or one new thing at all.

Learning to read is equated with teacher approval and its benefits go hand in hand with conforming. The ability to read is overlaid with the moral imperative of discipline in the face of hard work; compliance and obedience are equated with reading success. There is even a kind of conspiracy by the narrator to set the child reader against Tom, the non-reader, who is to be pitied for his idleness and dullness. This text was produced by Commissioners who had a clear understanding of what learning to read meant in their terms. They conveyed their own system of values and beliefs to child readers, who were taught what to believe about reading, about themselves as readers, about how to behave and, perhaps above all, how to be good. How interesting it would be to know how Irish children in Derby reacted when they read about an *Irish* boy character in the text and one, moreover, who was seen to be a failure.

Much of the text of *Sequel No. II to the Second Book of Lessons* (first published in 1844) was also underpinned by this moral justification for learning to read, in the unquestioned authority of the narrator's voice. The book was compiled by Richard Whately, who repeated the message of the previous book on pp. 8–10:

> The next things you learn are for your own use and advantage. You learn to read. I wish I could make you perceive what an advantage you gain by knowing how to read.

But there is a shift here, and what is revealing is that some of Whately's advice to the reader is sound pedagogical practice, because it helps children to become conscious of the processes involved in making sense of text. Though modern books show illustrations of children reading in a variety of situations, I know of no child's reading book in use today where the author focuses explicitly on helping child readers to see that *understanding* is the key to successful reading and that having, as it were, a dialogue with the author, is part of this process:

> Mind, I do not, by *reading*, mean merely repeating aloud the words and sentences in your book, but understanding the meaning of them, as you understand the conversation of any one who speaks to you.

Whately then discusses the practice of reading *silently*, and describes what the process feels like for the benefit of the inexperienced child reader:

> When you read (words and sentences) by yourselves, they are to you a silent language, which your mind takes in from your eye instead of your ear.

This process is rather neatly described in visual imagery as the mind 'taking from the eye', and is evidence of the author's own learned cultural 'way of taking' from books. The cultural norm of some other social groups (including perhaps those of nineteenth-century Irish labourers and their families, where only one person in the family might have been able to read) was – and still is – for reading to be public and shared.[20] Whately assumes that his child readers will develop into silent readers. He then cautions his readers that only certain books are good ones to read:

> Of course, you may make a bad use of reading, for there are bad books in the world, as well as good ones, which you may read; but so you may make a bad use of any of God's gifts – of speaking especially, as I fear many people do.

Whately, in the role of wise parent, then justifies the effort involved in learning to read by reflecting on the knowledge young readers have available to them with their new-found skills:

> Before you learned to read, you knew very little about things and places, and people beyond the place where your own friends lived,

and not much even about that. The face of nature was a blank to you; for you had never learned to think about what you saw.

These are serious lessons indeed. Whately is in fact telling his child readers that part of learning to read is learning to choose what to read so they can learn more about the world. Contemporary writers of reading texts for children never address their child readers explicitly about the reading process in this way, nor invite them to contemplate what their skill might offer them.

An untaught reading lesson in the *Lesson Books* is the exposure to a range of typefaces which diminish in size as the books get more difficult. There are capital letters, lower-case letters, italicized words and letters used for different purposes. Children were also given the experience of reading a variety of genres within the same book – stories, poems, factual prose, including biography, as well as contents lists, lists of words, titles, sub-titles, and a variety of punctuation marks to guide their understanding and increase their ability to read aloud with expression. Another untaught skill offered by the books was the 'reading' of illustrations for various purposes. These reading lessons would not have been explicitly discussed within the pages of nineteenth-century reading manuals because knowledge of the reading process was still developing. Good teachers like Jane Johnson and Cornelia Connolly probably knew intuitively that these things were important, even though the specialized vocabulary of reading teachers was not there to support their intuitions.

Embedded in many of the stories and tracts is the belief in an ordered society, intent on increasing literacy among the poorer classes, but in a way which instructs its poor children into ways of behaving. The stories and didactic passages teach children how to live by the rules, because they are founded on a particular system of values and beliefs. This made them ideally suited for instructing the workhouse child, because through these texts the child not only achieved literacy but at the same time learnt how to behave in order to win the approbation of the ruling classes and, most importantly, of God. The tale of Martha Dunne, from the *Second Book of Lessons*, shows child readers how the social world is organized, and gives them not only a model of childhood but a preparation for adulthood of a quite particular kind, of selflessness and service to others, suited to their station in life. Here is the beginning of Martha's story on p. 158:

When Martha Dunne lost her parents, she was put under the care of an old woman, named Molly Flint, who, though not unkind, was rather cross to children. When Martha first came to live with her, she had a great deal to bear, for Molly did not like being plagued with the care of so young a child. But Martha was a very good, obedient little girl, and tried to help old Molly in every way, till at last the old woman became very fond of her.

Some critiques of these books argue that there was nothing in them which set out to change the hierarchical nature of society.[21] The nature and organization of the teaching of reading in schools in the nineteenth century was – and of course still is – controlled by the social groups who have influence in this area of learning – politicians, clergy, employers, publishers, editors, writers, inspectors and teachers: people that Harold Rosen today calls the 'writing police'.[22] In these texts conversations are between adults and children, or animals masquerading as sensible adults. They represent the adult world of reasonableness and order, as this retelling of Aesop's fable from the *Second Book of Lessons*, pp. 14–15, shows:

The Boys and the Frogs

Lesson IX

pond hurt full
play stones true
frog death head

Some boys went one day to play by a pond, and they threw stones in it for fun. Now this pond was full of frogs, and when the boys threw in a stone, it hit them. Then one of the frogs put up its head out of the pond, and said, 'Pray, do not pelt us so.' 'We are but at play,' said one of the boys. 'True,' said the frog, 'but the stones you throw hurt us all the same. What is play to you is death to us.' We should take care when we play that our fun hurts no one.

This short moral tale tells its readers – and perhaps especially its boy readers – how they should behave. But it is also the kind of tale that supports children who are learning to 'reconstruct, remake, extend and understand their experience of living in a social context with each other', according to Margaret Meek. She is commenting here on a modern children's tale, but her message is equally valid when applied to this nineteenth-century text, as is her next comment: 'When we want to make new meanings we need metaphor.'[23] In other words, this fable offers its child readers an important reading lesson which takes them beyond the literal, into the construction of 'possible worlds', giving them opportunities to enter the world of cognitive ideas, and thus increasing their powers of intelligence and symbolic thought.[24]

The Irish Commissioners were innovators in their decision to include a great deal of geographical information in books which were intended for the children of the poor, and workhouse teachers probably drew children's attention to the geography lessons embedded in some of the texts, perhaps using the maps bought in 1855 as visual aids, thereby introducing children to another form of literate behaviour – the reading of maps. Children who graduated to the *Fourth Book of Lessons* (first published in 1834) found eighty pages dedicated to geographical issues, as well as lessons in natural history, political economy, poetry and moral and religious lessons.

THE NATURAL HISTORY ACCOUNTS IN THE IRISH *LESSON BOOKS*

Many of the examples given above show that the tone and content of much of the Irish *Lesson Books* is moralistic, and perhaps I expected to find little else in these primers.[25] But to my surprise I came across a different kind of writing that had somehow found its way into these books. It appears in the *natural history* accounts, and in the *Second Book of Lessons* and *Sequel No. II to the Second Book of Lessons* in particular, the lessons contain the kind of writing that shows how authors can enlist their child readers' curiosity by drawing on observations from everyday life. It is evident that the writers of these natural history texts knew that the elements of wonder and delight are part of the learning process. Look at this extract of 'The Ant' from pp. 35–7 of the *Second Book of Lessons*:

> When you are at play on the common, or in the fields, I dare say you have often seen small heaps of earth, thrown up on all sides, and swarming with busy little insects, running to and fro. These little insects are called ants, and it is quite worth while to stop and watch how they build their houses.

Though there is perhaps a sense of the 'worthiness' of this task, I hear an experienced teacher's voice running through this text, setting the scene by introducing children to the subject matter in a familiar context. There is very much more going on here than the requirement to memorize factual information. 'When you are at play on the common, or in the fields', is a direct invitation to children to enter a familiar situation, showing them how to look afresh at an insect they might already be familiar with, building on what they know in order to teach them something new and, at the same time, inviting them to enter the world of their imagination. The lesson continues by offering a description of the insect's behaviour. Some of the language is biblical; phrases such as 'come laden', 'seek their food', 'till the time of need', were probably familiar to children schooled on the Bible:

> You will see them come laden with leaves, bits of wood, sand, earth, and the gum of trees; with these they form their little hills. When

191

their houses are built, these busy ants go out and seek their food, which they lodge in their little store houses till the time of need.

The narrator then sets out to tell a story which asks the child reader to imagine one of nature's battles. The prose is vivid, and the narrative element is embedded inside the text, making it easier for readers to use their imaginations to construct this scenario:

In one distant and very hot country, where there are numbers of these ants, the houses swarm with all kinds of nasty vermin also, such as rats, mice and clocks [?cockroaches]. From time to time, immense bodies of ants may be seen marching up to a house, and soon the walls, ceilings, and floors are alive with them, and they get into all the drawers and chests. Now begins a fierce battle, between the ants and the rats, and other vermin; it goes on for some hours; after which, you may see the ants dragging off their prey, quite dead, and feasting on their bodies outside the house. Then the people, who have been waiting out of doors, gladly return to their houses, which they find quite cleared from all vermin.

While I have not so far been able to trace the direct source of this story, there are enough examples of this kind of detailed nineteenth-century observational writing to persuade me that 'The Ant' was possibly drawn directly from the work of one of the nineteenth-century naturalists who were in the forefront of discovery and classification of insect life – see, for example, the work of J.G. Wood, who writes so eloquently about Driver Ants, telling his readers that 'they pass through houses, and at their approach all the human inhabitants vacate the premises, none daring to oppose so redoubtable a foe' and adding that 'the visits of the ants are greatly beneficial, for in a very short time the column will have passed fairly through the house, and left no living creature within its walls . . . even the rats and mice, being torn to pieces by their powerful jaws.[26] The writer of 'The Ant' possibly drew on information provided by an acknowledged expert in the field, rather than gaining his information from a range of secondary sources, as I suspect many writers of children's information texts are tempted to do today. M.F. Thwaite tells us that in the nineteenth century 'much was still to be done by the devoted amateur',[27] and it is perhaps the voice of that 'devoted amateur' that children met when they read the natural history accounts in the Irish Commissioners' *Lesson Books*.

The use of the personal narrative voice was common in nineteenth-century natural history writing, and in a lesson about birds on pp. 131–2 of *Sequel No. II to the Second Book of Lessons* we hear that same direct voice. It is almost as though the writer is in conversation with the reader, and expects an imaginative response. Yet the voice does not hesitate to introduce young readers to complex scientific language. 'We will begin with birds', the writer tells the readers. 'The knowledge of birds is called Ornithology, from two words meaning birds and knowledge.' This writer appears to have enormous respect for young learners, showing them how to observe birds in a way that teaches them to become young scientists by getting out and *doing* it for themselves. 'This knowledge', the author writes, 'requires observation, that is, looking about you, and taking notice, rather than learning.' The narrator is clearly aware that child readers might live either in the country or the town, and writes for children who can observe birds in the wild, and those who are perhaps more familiar with domesticated or caged birds:

> The appearance and habits of birds are most easily studied by those who live in the country. Yet there are several kinds of birds which have no objection to a town life, and which may be tamed so as to be quite familiar with the family they belong to.

Then the writer addresses the readers directly, in a first-person narrative voice, telling them the story of a particular bird that made an impression on her/him: 'I knew a duck which lived in the house, and was so attached to the children of the family, that it would follow them about, and walk up stairs into the room where they slept.'

The information about birds of prey in the same book includes the dramatic story of an eagle who carried off a child. The illustration of the woman and the eagle depicts a scene from this story, designed to excite but also to teach about the habits of birds of prey (see Figure 12.2).

In 1840 the ornithologist William MacGillivray related a story about a golden eagle which was reputed to have 'taken up a child from behind some reapers, in the Parish of Orphir, and carried it to her nest in Hoy; but by the assiduity of the people, who immediately followed her, the child was rescued'.[28] There are many such tales of eagles snatching up young children, and the reading lesson on birds of prey could have been taken directly from either this or from a similar piece. Within the same lesson there are illustrations of the beak and talons of a bird of prey, with the textual inclusion of the adjectives 'hooked', 'sharp' and 'strong'. These precise words are used by the ornithologist Thomas Bewick to describe the attributes of this family of birds, suggesting again that information in this lesson could have been drawn directly from the work of an expert (see Figure 12.3).[29]

Information that appears in modern primary classrooms, whether in book form or in multi-media format, is not infrequently made up of small chunks of information, such as: 'Starlings change colour as they grow older' and 'Some starlings come to visit Britain in the winter.'[30] Nineteenth-century pauper children in Derby, who had access to Oliver

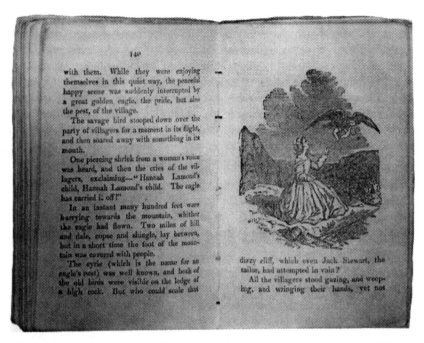

Figure 12.2 An informative illustration from *Sequel No. II to the Second Book of Lessons*

Figure 12.3 Beak and talons: 'strong and hooked for tearing flesh'

Goldsmith's *History of the Earth and Animated Nature* in the Workhouse School, were treated to a *whole page* of information about the starling, lovingly and carefully observed.[31] It is an uncomfortable notion that these children might have had a better deal in the matter of their non-fiction texts than modern children, but one we perhaps need to consider seriously.

In 1861 The Newcastle Commission singled out the *Lesson Books* for particular criticism. In spite of being 'the most popular [book] of all', teachers complained that they 'abound[ed] with words, needlessly introduced, which [were] quite incomprehensible to a child'. The Commission heavily criticized the Irish texts for their 'dry outlines of grammar and geography' and the *Fifth Book of Lessons* came in for particular criticism for its presentation of science in 'a form too technical for the purpose'.[32] The Commission was probably correct in its critical appraisal of the tone and content of much of the Irish Commissioners' *Lesson Books*, and I certainly have no wish to defend the *Fifth Book of Lessons*, which the teachers of the day found virtually unusable. But the natural history accounts in the *Second Book of Lessons* and its sequel probably met many of the criticisms raised by the Commission, and I suspect that the writers and editors of these two texts perhaps unwittingly allowed a different kind of discourse into the Irish *Lesson Books*. It is a discourse which could have given a particular intellectual freedom to its child readers by taking them on as apprentice learners at a time when it was almost impossible for them to take up apprenticeships in trades any more. Perhaps there is a subtle link between the vanishing learning world of work and the new learning world of books, with authors becoming teachers at a distance.

There is a great deal of evidence that the *Lesson Books* offered a variety of reading experiences to working-class children which gave them some control of written information in an increasingly literate society, and an introduction to approved forms of childhood behaviour, which included the knowledge of how to behave as a reader. In 1963 M.F. Thwaite commented that 'the whole field [of nineteenth-century information books] for children needs much further exploration'.[33] Over thirty years later there is still a great deal of work to be done. This chapter is offered as a small contribution to our knowledge and thinking in this area, where the production of special texts for the teaching of reading, specifically written for child learners, was a precise indicator of the entrance into a world of childhood and literacy.

I want to suggest that some of these texts were equal to the best available in today's classrooms, and offered more learning opportunities than many modern non-fiction texts. Children today have access to exquisitely produced books, and some of these do indeed echo the best of nineteenth-century material. But many do not; though superficially attrac-

Figure 12.4 'Ralph not only visited him, but brought him bones, and attended him with peculiar marks of kindness'

tive, their impoverished textual world presents children with no opportunity to go out and look, smell, touch, and feel, and to take their own emotional and practical worlds of knowledge to the world of the book. There are surely lessons in the Irish *Lesson Books* that we can learn from today.

ACKNOWLEDGEMENT

I wish to express my thanks to the School of Education Library, University of Leicester, for permission to reproduce the illustrations in this chapter.

NOTES

1 Much of the information in this chapter is taken from my Ph.D., 'Rough-Headed Urchins and Bonnetless Girls: A Study of Irish Childhood in Derby in the Mid-Nineteenth Century', University of Warwick, 1996.
2 T. Barclay, *Memoirs and Medleys: The Autobiography of a Bottle-Washer* (Leicester: Edgar Backus, 1934) pp. 7, 23.
3 C. Connelly, *The Book of the Order of Studies* (1863). This book is held at The Society of the Holy Child Jesus Convent, The Old Palace, Mayfield, Sussex. John Marmion's study of Connelly's work, 'Cornelia Connelly's Work

in Education, 1848–1879', Ph.D. University of Manchester, 1984, presents a detailed account of her educational philosophy.

4 Cited in J. Bastow, 'The Development of Catholic Elementary Education in the Nineteenth Century, in the Five Counties of the Diocese of Nottingham,' M. Phil., University of Nottingham, 1970, pp. 169–71.

5 *The Catholic School*, Vol. 2, No. 7, Catholic Poor School Committee, September 1851, p. 193.

6 Catholic Poor School Committee, General Report, 1851, cited in Convent of Mercy documentation, Convent of Mercy, Derby.

7 Minute Book, Poor Law Records, Derby, May 1840.

8 Ibid., August 1839.

9 Ibid., May 1841.

10 Ibid., November 1855.

11 I. Watts, *A Short View of the Whole Scripture History* (Halifax: Milner & Sowerby, 1863 [first published in 1732]).

12 W.F. Richards, *Manual of Method; For the Use of Teachers in Elementary Schools* (London: National Society's Depository, 1856), p. 4.

13 Minute Book, Poor Law Records, Derby, October 1844.

14 D.H. Akerson, 'The Irish National System of Education in the Nineteenth Century,' Ph.D., Harvard University, 1967, p. 317.

15 J.M. Goldstrom, *The Social Content of Education, 1808–1870: A Study of the Working Class School Reader in England and Ireland* (Shannon: Irish University Press, 1972), pp. 164–5.

16 Akerson, 'Irish National System of Education', p. 317.

17 *Correspondence of Messrs. Longman and Co. and John Murray with the Rt. Hon. Lord John Russell M.P., on the publication of school books by Government at the public expense: the statement of the Commissioners of National Education in Ireland, in reference thereto: and the reply of Lord J. Russell to the Messrs. Longman & Co. and J. Murray* (Dublin: HMSO, 1851).

18 'Editor's Note', *Sequel No. 2 to the Second Book of Lessons* (HMSO, 1844).

19 Cited in Akerson, 'Irish National System of Education', p. 324.

20 S. Brice Heath, *Ways With Words: Language, Life and Work in Communities and Classrooms* (Cambridge: Cambridge University Press, 1983), p. 191.

21 See Goldstrom, *The Social Content of Education*, pp. 71–6.

22 H. Rosen, *Troublesome Boy: Stories and Articles* (London: English and Media Centre, 1993), p. 117.

23 M. Meek, *How Texts Teach What Children Learn* (Stroud: Thimble Press, 1988), p. 16.

24 J. Bruner, *Actual Minds, Possible Worlds* (Massachusetts and London: Cambridge University Press, 1986), p. 49.

25 See, for example, Chapter 1 in P. Coveney, *The Image of Childhood* (Harmondsworth: Penguin, 1967), for a discussion of moralizing literature.

26 J.G. Wood, *The Illustrated Natural History, Vol. III, Reptiles, Fishes, Molluscs, etc,* (London: Routledge), p. 500 [undated, but Preface dated 1863].

27 M.F. Thwaite, *From Primer to Pleasure: An Introduction to the History of Children's Books in England, from the Invention of Printing to 1900* (London: The Library Association, 1963), p. 217.

28 W. MacGillivray, *A History of British Birds, Indigenous and Migratory, Vol. III* (London: Scott, Webster & Geary, 1840), p. 215.

29 T. Bewick, *A History of British Birds, Vol. I* (Newcastle: Longman, 1847), p. 6.

30 See, for example, S. Blackford, *Let's Investigate Birds* (Glasgow and London: Blackie, 1975), p. 12.

31 O. Goldsmith, *A History of the Earth and Animated Nature* (London: Fullarton, 1848), p. 125 [first published in 1774].
32 British Parliamentary Papers, *Report of the Commissioners Appointed to Inquire into The State of Popular Education in England*, Vol. 1 (London: HMSO, 1861), p. 351.
33 Thwaite, *From Primer to Pleasure*, p. 221.

Details of the Irish *Lesson Books* referred to in this chapter are as follows:

First Book of Lessons, compiled by James Carlile (in print from 1831–65).
Second Book of Lessons, compiled by James Carlile (in print from 1831–65).
Sequel No. II to the Second Book of Lessons, compiled by Richard Whately (in print from 1844–65).
Fourth Book of Lessons, compiled by James Carlile (in print from 1835–67).
Fifth Book of Lessons, compiled by James Carlile and Alexander Arthur (in print from 1846–?).

These books were published under the Direction of the Commissioners of National Education in Ireland for Her Majesty's Stationery Office.

13

CRIMINALS, QUADRUPEDS AND STITCHING UP GIRLS OR, CLASSES AND CLASSROOMS IN THE RAGGED SCHOOLS

Julia Swindells

God bless these kind, good-natured folk, 'at sends us
  o this stuff:
We canno' tell 'em o we feel, nor thank 'em hawve
  enuff.
They help to find us meyt an' clooas, an' eddicashun
  too,
An' what creawns o, they gi'en us wage for gooin' to
  th' sewin'-schoo'.

Then, lasses, let's cheer up an' sing; it's no use
  lookin' sad.
We'll mak eawr sewin'-schoo' to ring, and stitch away
  loike mad:
We'll try an' mak' th' best job we con, o'owt we han
  to do,
We read an' write, an' spell and kest, while here at th'
  sewin'-schoo'.

Samuel Laycock, 'Sewin'-Class Song',
in *Ballads and Songs of Lancashire*, 1875[1]

What little debate has been recorded about working-class girls and schooling in Britain has mainly taken place in relation to the later part of the twentieth century. Judith Williamson, Angela McRobbie, Carolyn Steedman and Valerie Walkerdine are amongst those who have intervened powerfully to gender the debate about class and education since the 1970s.[2] Previously, Raymond Williams and Richard Hoggart were amongst those who had been giving attention, itself long overdue, to working-class boys and their encounter with education.[3] But much of their discussion had tended to overlook gender distinctions, rendering working-class girls invisible in the account, or unproblematically conflating them with 'family

199

values'.[4] In terms of nineteenth-century history, parallel absences and oversights have occurred. Much of the work on women's education in the nineteenth century, with notable exceptions such as that of June Purvis's *Hard Lessons*, has tended to focus on the middle classes.[5] Many historians of class in the period have tended to reproduce the emphasis on male experience, again with a few notable exceptions.[6]

This account attempts a small-scale enterprise of building in observations about working-class girls as well as boys to some general speculations about the relationships between class, poverty and education in the earlier part of the nineteenth century. Later, I will turn to specific textual instances, from personal testimony and from fiction, around which I offer some interpretation. But, initially, it is necessary to demonstrate how the period established a particular social and epistemological framework around concepts of grouping and stratification. What follows, therefore, is not intended in any way to produce an exhaustive account of class relations in the period, but pursues this more limited strategy of attempting to illuminate some relationships between class, classroom and classification.

That period of history which sees the making of the English working class is also one which rehearses highly controversial arguments about the education of the poor, and initiates the institutionalization of the state classroom.[7] It was between 1770 and 1840 that 'class' superseded other names for social divisions, and acquired its modern inflection in relation to what has been described as 'the decisive reorganization of society'.[8] The deployment of the terminology of class is part of the growing habit of classification under the Victorians, who constructed entire epistemologies out of the registering and recording of 'classes of quadrupeds, birds, fishes and so forth, which are again subdivided into series or orders and these last into genera'.[9] The extension of this system of classification, this way of articulating 'divisions', to social groups and whole populations significantly implicates the education system, where at least one commentator finds the use of 'class' in the context of 'classroom', denoting 'people banded together for educational purposes', markedly preceding the use of the term in the directly political context.[10]

The social and educational processes which yoked class and classroom together have been explained by historians in a number of different ways. Many have felt the pressure to describe Britain between 1770 and 1840 in terms of a visceral decline, from the 'organic community' of the eighteenth century in which working life brought the worker, 'face to face with the fundamental factors and problems of existence', to widespread alienation and disaffection under the Victorian factory system.[11] In that version, the educational agencies prior to the nineteenth-century factory system were home and occupation, supposedly experienced in an integrated relationship, producing a coherent and meaningful existence.[12] Other accounts, while eschewing any euphoria about the eighteenth century, see both the factory system and schooling for the poor as driven solely by the profit motive, with the state's intervention in schooling being motivated by the need to reduce the expense of 'poor relief'.[13] Then there are those accounts which suggest that, in at least one sense, there was not much to distinguish the two periods of history, both the earlier and the later phases being characterized by 'social control over the subordinate classes' – although this latter type of account tends to imply that 'the shift from ties of tradition, birth and faith' towards 'new conceptions of rationality and knowledge' was a move for the better.[14] The most optimistic scenario is one which sees the birth of the schoolroom for the poor as an attempt at vitiating the worst effects of the factory system by harnessing the consent of the working class to the bourgeois revolution, to new ways of thinking about society and knowledge.

Whatever the differing stresses of these accounts, some implying social decline, others improvement, there is general agreement both in the belief that class and classrooms were in the making and that the models of society and education were strongly interventionist – whether the agents of intervention were the 'kind, good-natured folk' of the sewing-school ballad, or coercive factory owners imposing restrictive and oppressive practices on whole sections of the population, or bourgeois hegemonists seeking to unify the people around commitments to church and state. It is this stress on intervention and on the issue of social control which has politicized the history in very important ways.

Nevertheless, I believe that the focus on theories of decline or improvement between 1770 and 1840 has left something of a gap over questions of gender distinctions and their implications, both for the historical account and, more specifically, for questions of agency and class-consciousness in the making of the English working classroom. I have turned, therefore, to textuality, in an attempt to get some limited access to how working-class children were represented in the period. I include testimonies of working-class boys as well as girls, in order to trace the important gender distinctions in operation in the formation of class, classroom and class-consciousness.

HENRY MAYHEW AND THE RAGGED SCHOOLCHILDREN

In 1850, Mayhew investigated 'the ragged schools', and, in his characteristic manner of reportage, documented some of the responses of children undergoing schooling.[15] His inquiry resulted in a bitter argument with the Secretary of the Ragged School Union about conditions in the schools. Mayhew had claimed that boys who had been educated in ragged schools were 'worse' than boys who had not been educated at all. Later, this account will reference some current work on Mayhew as an interpreter, but the initial task is to acclaim him for having included first-person testimonies of some working-class children in his record, and to offer an interpretation of one example, that of a 12-year-old boy that Mayhew interviewed.

> I am 12, and have been three times in prison once for stealing cigars, once for a piece of calico, and once for some pigs' feet. I have been twice whipped. I was twelve months at the Exeter-buildings Ragged School, Knightsbridge. I learned reading, writing, and Church of England there. I was brought up there to the Church of England. I know I was, because I went to church with the schoolmaster. I know it was a church. A church is bigger than a chapel, and has a steeple. I learned sums, too, and the commandments, and the catechism. I can't read well. [He was tried on an act of Parliament as to his ability to read. It began 'whereas the laws now existing'. 'Whereas' he could not make out anyhow, and 'the laws now' he called 'the Lays no'. He was unable to read any word of two syllables.] At the Ragged School, there were forty or fifty boys. We went at nine, left at twelve, and went back at two. Between twelve and two I was out with the other boys, and we often made up parties to go a thieving. We thieved all sorts of things. We taught one another thieving. We liked to teach very young boys best; they're pluckiest, and the police don't know them at first. I knew good boys at the Ragged school – good when they went there – and we taught them to thieve. If we could get a good boy at the Ragged School, we taught him to thieve, for he's safe some time from the police, and share with him.[16]

Mayhew's account gives every appearance of a scrupulous documentation of first-person testimony, with little intervening judgement and commentary. But every interviewer has an explicit or implicit agenda, and it may be that the boy is responding, in part at least, to what he imagines or interprets Mayhew's concerns to be. For instance, whilst Mayhew might have seen the use of an Act of Parliament as merely functional to the test of reading skills, the choice of that particular text might have set up all manner of presupposition about Mayhew for the boy! Nevertheless, I offer a reading of how the discourses of class and classification play across the testimony in relation to the boy's own agency.

The schoolchildren are there, at the ragged school, to be 'taught', but they 'like to teach themselves'. The overt curriculum is, clearly enough, reading, writing and Church of England. The boy can classify with the best – he can tell a church from a chapel, so he knows that it was Church of England. He has no problems in telling Mayhew what he has learned, but apparently that is not what interests the boy himself. He is more interested in what he, the boy, 'teaches' the young boys, particularly the good boys.[17] The vitality with which he describes what he has learned and what he teaches about crime is in marked distinction to his cryptic and unintentionally (presumably) comic responses to what he has learned about the Church. The intention behind the school's pedagogic strategy is to band children together for educational purposes, in order to establish religious and moral authority (including presumably the prevention of crime). The consequence is one in which the boys band themselves together – 'we taught one another' – in order to organize resistance to poverty, in the process defying moral and religious authority. The school had set out to classify poor children, to group them for one set of purposes. The boys undermine that strategy by classifying and grouping themselves for a counter set of purposes. Definitions of class and class-consciousness are at issue.

A second boy, a 10-year-old interviewed by Mayhew, produces a similar account, but with a little more awareness of morality as an issue.

> I am ten, and have been twice in prison, and once whipped. I was in prison for 'a fork' and 'some lead'. I sold them in rag-shops. I was three months in Pyestreet Ragged School, Westminster. I was a month at the St Margaret's National School (Westminster). At the Ragged School I learned reading, writing, tailoring, shoe-making, and cleaning the place. [He then read a verse in the Bible imperfectly, and by spelling the words, but quite as well as could be expected.] There were forty or fifty boys at the Ragged School; half of them were thieves, and we used to go thieving in gangs of six. When we were away from school we went thieving. We taught any new boy how to thieve, making parties to do it. We would teach any good boy to thieve. I know four or five good boys at the Ragged Schools taught to thieve by me and others. We got them to join us, as we got afraid ourselves, and the police don't so soon 'spect new boys. Thieving is wrong. Some boys where I lived taught me to thieve.[18]

'Thieving is wrong', he says, but that awareness is not enough to prevent him from telling Henry Mayhew about teaching how to thieve, about 'making parties' and getting them 'to join us'. Some may see the schoolboys' use of the language of education, of teaching and learning, to describe their criminal acts as nothing more than a simple irony, and indeed I think it would be looking in the wrong direction to say that they are voicing a commitment to an alternative pedagogy to that of the school. Indeed, the boys appear to accommodate the school's overt pedagogy without hostility. However, I do think that the testimonies of these young boys yield a consciousness of their class in the classroom, and of the need to educate members of their own class in how to take action together, to defend the interests of the group, primarily in attempting, through organized crime, to alleviate that poverty whose existence forms the very basis of why they have been banded together in ragged school classrooms. So, whilst it may be overstating the case to argue that the criminality of the boys in the ragged school is an expression of class-consciousness, it is not an exaggeration to claim that definitions of class are at issue. The classroom, like the factory system, has both brought individuals together in a managerial strategy by the ruling group, and has unintentionally facilitated collective action through a recognition of common interests.

Later in his account, the 10-year-old says that the boys who taught him how to thieve initially did not, to his knowledge, attend ragged schools. In other words, organized thieving amongst children is not peculiar to these schools. Nevertheless, school provides what the prison governor interviewed by Henry Mayhew describes as ripe territory for 'the congregating of criminals', an opportunity for the individual to identify with a group, and for the group to consolidate itself. And as another of Mayhew's interviewees, a superintendent of police, puts it, access to literacy for the working-class boy is in itself by no means the solution to organized crime.

> Mere reading and writing is a harm to a vicious child. It makes him steal more boldly, because with more judgement, for he sees prices marked ... The smartest thieves I have met with, and those having the longest run, could all read and write, and some could defend themselves at trial without a lawyer, just by having studied the newspapers.[19]

If the ragged school classroom shows some of those features of 'combination' which characterize the factory system of the period, it could be for similar reasons. By taking working-class labour out of the home, and into the more public domain of the factory – that apparently integrated model of occupation – home and education, held together by 'tradition, birth and faith', has begun to fracture. Even without a commitment to that model of integration it is possible to see how the factory system has exposed those relationships or, at the very least, rendered them more visible. The unintended consequence of the factory system was that it afforded working people the opportunity for class struggle. The unintended consequence of the ragged school was that it afforded poor boys the opportunity to address the problem of poverty and take action. In the process, the young boy finds his identification with a class, which reinforces his sense of separation from the group which seeks to classify him.

STITCHING UP GIRLS

As the 'working-class' ballad which heads this piece indicates, working-class girls and women were encouraged to *be* in the classroom in the early Victorian period. But for them, the classroom was frequently a reproduction of their own segregated sphere of labour, as in the case of the sewing school where they stitch away like mad (and try not to look sad). In turning to a discussion of working-class girls, it is necessary to register still more versions of the history of that formative seventy years of the class struggle, 1770 to 1840. Women's history has long since exploded the myth that the eighteenth-century model of integrated home and occupation formed an idyllic and coherent identity for working-class women and girls before they were plunged into the (undoubted) horrors of the factory system. (At the same time, there is impressive evidence that, however all-consuming the demands of home as the site of the threefold labour of childcare, housework and occupation, working-class women were involved in political protest against their lot in the early nineteenth century.[20]) Nor, at the other extreme, is there much evidence to suggest that women of any class were allowed significant access to 'new conceptions of rationality and knowledge' in the early nineteenth century.

So, feminist historians have more than begun to give powerful attention to the gender ideologies of the period, and indeed to the writings and interpretations of Henry Mayhew. Mary Poovey and Christina Crosby are each notable, not only for their path-breaking work on Mayhew but also for discovering distinct possibilities in running various arguments about Mayhew alongside a discussion of different aspects of the work of his famous contemporary, Charles Dickens.[21] Dickens shares with Mayhew that combination of being particularly resistant to certain forms of social classification, with a powerful commitment to giving voice to certain conditions of oppression. In this context, Mayhew's record of the ragged schools inevitably brought Dickens's famous novel of education and industry, *Hard Times*, to mind. But first, I make reference to the schoolgirl whose testimony was recorded by Mayhew.

> I learned all I know ... (and I can read any chapter in the Bible), at the Ragged School close by here. But for it I mightn't have known how to read or write. I hope it's a good place but I'm sure I don't know, I've met such bad girls there. I've known them bring songs and notes that they'd written at night, to give to the boys when they met them out of school. I don't know what sort the songs were, or what was in the notes. I never saw either, as it was a secret among them. The schoolmistress knew nothing about it. I don't think I ever heard the girls say anything bad in school; but often when I've left at night I've seen the girls waiting for the boys, or

the boys for the girls as happened. I don't know how many, but a knot of them, and they used to go away together. I don't know where they went, whether thieving or what; but if I've been behind the other girls a minute or so in leaving school, I've had to go through a little knot of them, and might stop a minute or two perhaps and I've heard them swear and curse, and use bad words, such as no modest girl ever would use. I've never done anything a modest girl mightn't, though I've been tempted [she blushed].[22]

It is significant that the only testimony recorded of a schoolgirl is that of a 'good-looking and well-spoken' girl; even so, only taken in the absence of her father, who was to have spoken on her behalf. The girl's account immediately distinguishes itself from those of the boys in that she repeatedly distances herself from her peer group, particularly from the 'bad girls'. In paying tribute to the ragged school – 'I learned all I know' – she is at pains to characterize herself as a 'modest girl' who has been tempted by her peers, but for whom virtue has triumphed.

It is striking that all the accounts I have included here prioritize the issue of relations with peers in speaking of the experience of the ragged school; and the girl is as careful to distance herself from the peer group as the boys are reckless in identifying themselves with it. This is not a simple matter of virtuous girls and vicious boys – there is plenty of evidence of the existence of 'bad' girls – but more an illustration of what Mayhew, at least, takes to be the symptomatic and representative positions of what constitutes the children's experience of the ragged-school classroom. Just as it is no accident that Mayhew chooses to include the testimony of only one girl, so it is appropriate that he should have published only 'a good girl'. For Mayhew is of his time in assuming that it is the boys' experience – male experience – in all its complexity, which will determine whether or not the ragged schools are succeeding or failing. (The 'bad' girls are apparently invisible to him as individuals – they are apparently not proof of anything.)

Like the girls in the sewing school, the working-class girl of the ragged school classroom is meant not only to be grateful for the gift of bourgeois ideology the classroom offers her – to stitch away like mad – but also to articulate that gratitude.[23] The young girl emerges as the classroom conformist – she says later in her testimony, 'if they would only listen to the schoolmistress' – and, appropriately enough, as the class 'informer' to the interviewer Mayhew. Importantly, she is literate (certainly more literate than the boys who Henry Mayhew interviews) but it is a literacy born of her rejection of her peer group, and it is reproduced in her account as the voice of individualism – the one who succeeded against the odds, pleasing the adults by isolating herself from group-consciousness, both in terms of gender and class. It is no little irony that, in certain terms – teaching literacy, developing a moral sense – the ragged schools have been successful with the schoolgirl. But, it seems, this is not the success for which they, nor Henry Mayhew when he attacks the schools, are looking. The literate, working-class girl, rather than producing a testimony which gives Mayhew evidence of the success of the ragged schools, becomes the embarrassment which in part leads him to believe that the schools are not doing their job properly. The evidence of a literate girl only serves to reinforce his anxiety about whether or not the ragged school is 'a good place'.

Later in the encounter with Henry Mayhew, the young girl volunteers to call her brother in from the street where he is playing, so that he can be interviewed. She has given her brother as an example of 'going to the bad' – 'he is a worse boy now than when he went to the school first'. Again, she identifies with the adult listener, with he who strives to believe some 'good' of the ragged schools – 'I hope it's a good place but I'm sure I don't know'. The brother runs away, consolidating both the girl's and the adult investigator's findings, apparently united in their sadness about bad boys.[24]

As it would be romantizing the ragged-school boys to describe their criminality as collective political action, analogous to that of factory workers, so perhaps it would be asking this young girl's testimony to carry too much of a load in suggesting that her position could be seen in analogy with that of a working-class woman, who either allies with her men in class solidarity or becomes alienated from them and her working-class sisters through literacy, at the same time being required to take responsibility, or at least articulate gratitude, for the bourgeois ideology of her employers. It is for some reason of this kind that the lasses in the sewing school are being asked to stitch away like mad. They are perhaps the ones who are being expected to hold the threads for stitching-up the political problems that the introduction of schooling for the poor has entailed; as if it is working-class girls and women, as part of their historic mission of looking after home and family, who are being required to take moral responsibility for the alienation of working-class boys and men, by rulers who fear the consequences of class solidarity and organization. At the same time, some of them are acquiring literacy, which cannot be valued by those for whom the only legitimate form of evidence of success is literate *boys*.

Whilst Dickens's *Hard Times* has been somewhat exhaustively studied by scholars, a comparison of the Mayhew schoolgirl with the infamous Girl no. 20, the working-class Sissy Jupe, proves irresistible. As David Craig argues, 'the stress on schooling is certainly no evasion' in the novel in illuminating the problems of industrialism and class.[25] The novel has been particularly resonant in exposing the mutual oppressions of class, classroom and classified knowledge. Judith Williamson's influential article,

'How Does Girl Number Twenty Understand Ideology?' forcefully captures that continuing resonance.[26] In Gradgrind's classroom in the absent heart of industrial Coketown, it is the boy, Bitzer, who, initially at least, provides Gradgrind and the government inspector, M'Choakumchild, with their educational success story. Bitzer's notorious definition of a horse provides the model answer to their pedagogic and epistemological system:

> Quadruped. Graminivorous. Forty teeth, namely twenty-four grinders, four eye-teeth, and twelve incisive. Sheds coat in the spring; in marshy countries, sheds hoofs, too. Hoofs hard, but requiring to be shod with iron. Age known by marks in mouth.[27]

By contrast, Sissy Jupe (who, as more than one commentator has pointed out, actually works with horses in the circus) is of course a complete failure in the Gradgrind system, retaining barely any classified information of the quadruped kind.

> M'Choakumchild reported that she had a very dense head for figures; that, once possessed with a general idea of the globe, she took the smallest conceivable interest in its exact measurements; that she was extremely slow in the acquisition of dates, unless some pitiful incident happened to be connected therewith; that she would burst into tears on being required (by the mental process) immediately to name the cost of two hundred and forty-seven muslin caps at fourteen pence halfpenny; that she was as low down, in the school, as low could be; that after eight weeks of induction into the elements of Political Economy, she had only yesterday been set right by a prattler three feet high, for returning to the question, 'What is the first principle of this science?' the absurd answer, 'To do unto others as I would that they should do unto me.'[28]

To 'facts, facts, facts', Sissy Jupe responds with sentiment, emotional crisis ('she would burst into tears') and morality ('to do unto others', etc.). In using Sissy Jupe to counterpoint the virtues of sentiment, feeling and morality, alongside the vices of facts and classified knowledge, Dickens constitutes the working-class girl as 'naturally' educated in sentiment and feeling, and in other domains, 'very dense'. It is a typical Dickensian method to deprive the character in whom the novel's true values reside of the consciousness of her own worth. The innocence of the *ingénue* figure is important to his scheme of irony. But in the case of Sissy Jupe he runs a fine line between innocence and stupidity, which poses a threat to the theme of education. By definition, the character is not credited with the consciousness to understand or articulate why it is that the educational regime which she encounters judges her 'very dense', or to be the vehicle by which the alternative values of sentiment and true feeling (and, that old chestnut, personal experience) are upheld in successful classroom practice. She simply suffers the stresses of ignorance and stupidity, until her 'natural' virtues, those of the classic Victorian domestic angel, take her out of the classroom and into home and family to provide the novel's ideological and narrative resolutions (the reward for working-class girls? – 'happy Sissy's happy children' – happy families of course).

Dickens's representational concerns mirror Mayhew's interpretative ones. The boys – Bitzer, and Gradgrind's son, Tom – become criminalized by the Gradgrindian classroom, in analogy with the boys that Mayhew interviews. By contrast, the working-class girl, like the one whose testimony Mayhew records, upholds the values of family morality, characterized by true sentiment and feeling. In these ways, Dickens's powerful indictment of a class system which operates across factory town and classroom, to deprive its people of 'those imaginative graces and delights' without which he believes that both the individual and social fabric will decay, is dependent on requiring working-class girls to take responsibility for individual and social morality, via their supposedly natural family values. Clearly, it is a particular method of education that Dickens is condemning in *Hard Times*, but the representational devices around Sissy Jupe leave just a slight suspicion that the logic is one in which working-class girls, since they are 'naturally' educated in sentiment and true feeling and 'naturally' resistant to the retention of classified data (and 'very dense' with it), might just not be in a position to make use of education at all.

I am arguing that, despite the ideological pressures reflected in fiction and social commentary, the ragged-school classroom itself appears to have offered a set of possibilities, even opportunities, for the schoolboy to find his class, and for the schoolgirl to have access to literacy, even where its acquirement was not thought to be proof of the school's success. The availability of those courses of action, together with the evidence that schoolchildren could exploit various possibilities, even where there was the cost of landing up in prison, or ventriloquizing the voice of the ruler (deploring bad children), gives evidence of the working classroom as an organizing principle of social class. In other words, the English working classroom, between 1770 and 1840, may well have been one of a number of powerful agencies by which class and gender relations organized themselves.

NOTES

1 John Harland (ed.), *Ballads and Songs of Lancashire* (London: Routledge, 1875).
2 For example: Judith Williamson, 'How Does Girl Number Twenty Understand Ideology?', *Screen Education* 40, Autumn/Winter (1981/2), pp. 80–7; Angela

McRobbie, 'Working Class Girls and the Culture of Femininity', *Women Take Issue*, by Women's Studies Group, Centre for Contemporary Cultural Studies (London: Hutchinson, 1978); Carolyn Steedman, Cathy Urwin and Valerie Walkerdine (eds), *Language, Gender and Childhood* (London: Routledge & Kegan Paul, 1985).

3 Raymond Williams, *The Long Revolution* (London: Chatto & Windus, 1961). Richard Hoggart, *The Uses of Literacy* (London: Chatto & Windus, 1957).

4 Lisa Jardine and Julia Swindells, 'Culture in the Working Classroom', Chapter 6 in *What's Left? Women in Culture and the Labour Movement* (London: Routledge, 1990) for more of the discussion about Hoggart, Williams and 'family values'.

5 June Purvis, *Hard Lessons, The Lives and Education of Working-Class Women in Nineteenth-Century England* (Cambridge and Oxford: Polity Press, 1989).

6 See, for example, essays in Martha Vicinus (ed.), *Suffer and Be Still, Women in the Victorian Age* (Indiana: Indiana University Press, 1972), and other North American scholarship, such as the work of Mary Poovey (see note 21).

7 E.P. Thompson *The Making of the English Working Class* (London: Gollancz, 1963), as the obvious marker of this class history.

8 Raymond Williams, *Keywords* (Glasgow: Fontana, 1976).

9 Asa Briggs, 'The Language of "Class" in Early Nineteenth-Century England', in Asa Briggs and John Saville (eds), *Essays in Labour History* (London: Macmillan, 1960), p. 43.

10 Ibid.

11 Frank Smith, *A History of English Elementary Education*, (London: University of London Press, 1931), p. 37.

12 Ibid.

13 Karen Jones and Kevin Williamson, 'The Birth of the Schoolroom', *Ideology and Consciousness* 6, Autumn (1979), pp. 59–63.

14 James Donald, 'Language, Literacy and Schooling,' *Open University Course, U203 Popular Culture* (Milton Keynes: Open University Press, 1982), pp. 51–2 of Unit 29.

15 Henry Mayhew, *The Morning Chronicle Survey of Labour and the Poor: The Metropolitan Districts* (Horsham, Sussex: Caliban Books, 1981 edn [1st edn 1850]), Letter XLIV, March 25th, 1850, pp. 48–63. Further discussion of 'the ragged schools' continues in Letter XLV. Also, E.P. Thompson and Eileen Yeo (eds), *The Unknown Mayhew: Selections from the Morning Chronicle 1849–50* (Harmondsworth: Penguin, 1984 edn).

16 Mayhew, *The Morning Chronicle Survey*, p. 59. It is of significance that both boys whose testimonies are reproduced in my account were in prison when Mayhew interviewed them.

17 Carl F. Kaestle (ed.), *Joseph Lancaster and the Monitorial School Movement* (New York and London: Teachers College Press, Columbia University, 1973), pp. 48–9, contains a useful reminder that the pedagogy of the monitorial schools of the time relied on a system whereby children taught each other – and that 'the regimentation, classification, competition, constant testing, and factory mentality of the monitorial school', however much it was later dismissed in favour of a more individualistic pedagogy, was what 'helped spread common education among the poor'. There may be something of an irony in seeing the ragged schoolboys organizing themselves around the Lancaster method in their criminal activities.

18 Mayhew, *The Morning Chronicle Survey*, p. 59.

19 Ibid., p. 57.

20 Barbara Taylor, *Eve and the New Jerusalem: socialism and feminism in the nineteenth century* (London: Virago, 1983), and Ruth and Edmund Frow (eds), *Political Women 1800–1850* (London: Pluto Press, 1989) are notable in having dispensed with the myth that women were absent from the public sphere and not engaged in political activism.

21 Mary Poovey, *Uneven Developments: The Ideological Work of Gender in Mid-Victorian England* (Chicago: University of Chicago Press, 1988); Christina Crosby, *The Ends of History, Victorians and 'the woman question'* (New York and London: Routledge, 1991).

22 Mayhew, *The Morning Chronicle Survey*, pp. 61–2.

23 It is when the schoolgirl's account is put alongside those of the boys that it is possible to see just how far the schoolboys are relatively free of the pressure to subscribe to another set of class values than those of their own.

24 Mayhew, *The Morning Chronicle Survey*, p. 62.

25 Charles Dickens, *Hard Times* (Harmondsworth: Penguin, 1969 edn with an introduction by David Craig [1st edn 1854]).

26 Williamson, *Screen Education*.

27 Dickens, *Hard Times*, pp. 48–53.

28 Ibid., pp. 95–102.

Part V

'CONFIGURING A WORLD'

14

CONFIGURING A WORLD
Some childhood writings of Charlotte Brontë
Heather Glen

My story begins nearly a hundred years later than that of Jane Johnson's nursery library, and its outline is far better known – so well known, in fact, that I am only going to sketch it here. In June 1826, five years after the death of his wife and a year after the deaths of his two older daughters, the Reverend Patrick Brontë brought his son Branwell a box of wooden soldiers from Leeds. To the four remaining children in that motherless household, those soldiers became the starting-point for an increasingly complex series of fantasies or 'plays' – the original *dramatis personae* of an imaginary world which continued to allure and preoccupy each of the four well into adulthood, and in one case at least, until death. It was a world which quite quickly began to be elaborated in writing – in dozens of microscopically printed poems, stories and journals, produced over a period of nearly twenty years. Many of these juvenile manuscripts – including very nearly all those by Emily and Anne Brontë – have been destroyed. But many of those by Charlotte and by Branwell have, by lucky chance, survived; and those by Charlotte Brontë are now being published in a definitive edition, of which the first two volumes have appeared.[1] These writings are very different from those which Jane Johnson produced for her family. Yet like Jane Johnson's – if in a rather different way – they throw an extraordinary light on those questions about the cultural significance of reading and writing in childhood which it is the purpose of this volume to discuss.

The difference, of course, lies in the fact that this is not a body of material written *for* the child, but one written *by* her; indeed, perhaps the fullest record there is of the literary apprenticeship of one of our major writers. And it is in this light that these writings have usually been seen, as the overheated precursors of the more 'mature' and more 'balanced' achievements of Charlotte Brontë's later years. Christine Alexander, the pioneering editor whose work on these manuscripts has placed Brontë scholars forever in her debt, articulates the contemporary critical consensus thus:

The hypnotic attraction of Angria had stunted her development as a writer of realistic fiction; it was only grudgingly, and over a period of years, that childhood romance gave way to the balanced perception of reality that marks her mature work.[2]

Yet – leaving aside the question of whether, in fact, Charlotte Brontë's published novels are not altogether stranger, less assimilable to criteria of 'maturity' or 'balance' or 'realism' than their defenders have often assumed – it seems to me worth considering these early writings from another point of view. I shall not be attempting to claim great literary merit for them: I shall, indeed, set that question aside. But I shall be suggesting that to read them carefully is to discover within them evidence of an altogether more interesting 'play' than that unrestrained indulgence in uncritical or escapist fantasy that critics concerned to trace Charlotte Brontë's 'development' to maturity have tended to find.[3] Far from ignoring 'the constraints of tradition and convention',[4] this, we shall find, is a play which takes those constraints as its materials. And in this it has a very great deal to tell us about the complexity and sophistication with which the processes of reading and writing may be used, in childhood, to configure a world.

If the archive that remains is that of a child's writings, it also has a good deal to say about her reading. Indeed, it is with the act of reading that the first of the manuscripts I wish to consider opens. This, unlike most of these youthful writings, is a not a work of fiction but a factual 'history': the 12-year-old Charlotte Brontë's account of her own situation in the year 1829. It is here reproduced in its original sparsely punctuated and erratically spelled form:

The History of the year

Once papa lent my Sister Maria A Book it was an old Geography and she wrote on its Blank leaf papa lent me this Book. the Book is an hundred and twenty years old it is at this moment lying Before me while I write this I am in the kitchin of the parsonage house Haworth Taby the servent is washing up after Breakfast and Anne my youngest sister (Maria was my eldest) is kneeling on a chair looking at some cakes which Tabby has been Baking for us. Emily is in the parlour brushing it papa and Branwell are gone to Keighly Aunt is up stairs in her Room and I am sitting by the table writing this in the kitchin. Keighly is a small town four miles from here papa and Branwell are gone for the newspaper the Leeds Intelligencer is a most excellent Tory newspaper edited by Mr Wood the proprieter Mr henneman we take 2 and see three Newspapers a week we take the Leeds Intelligencer party Tory and the Leeds Mercury Whig – Edited by Mr Bain and His Brother Soninlaw and his 2 sons Edward and Talbot. We see the John Bull it is a High Tory very violent Mr

Driver lends us it as Likewise Blackwood's Magazine the most able periodical there is the editor is Mr Christopher North an old man 74 years of age the 1st of April is his Birthday his company are Timothy Tickler Morgan Odoherty Macrabin Mordecai Mullion Warrell and James Hogg a man of most extraordinary genius a Scottish Sheppard. Our plays were established Young Men June 1826 Our fellows July 1827 islanders December 1827. those are our three great plays that are not kept secret Emily's and my Bed plays where Established the 1st December 1827 the other March 1828 Bed plays mean secret plays they are very nice ones all our plays are very strange ones there nature I need not write on paper for I think I shall always remember them. the young men play took its rise from some wooden soldiers Branwell had Our fellows from Esops fables and the Islanders from several events which happened I will skecth out the origin of our plays more explicitly if I can 1 Young mens papa bought Branwell some Soldiers at Leeds when papa came home it was night and we were in Bed. so next morning Branwell came to our door with a Box of Soldiers Emily and me Jumped out of Bed and I snatched up one and exclaimed this is the Duke of Wellington it shall be mine. when I had said this Emily likewise took one and said it should be hers and when Ane came down she said one should be hers Branwell likewise took one to be his Mine was the prettiest of the whole and the tallest and perfect in every part Emilys was a grave looking fellow and we called him Gravey Ane's was a queer little thing much like herself he was called waiting Boy Branwell chose Bonuparte

March 12 1829

This is certainly not a 'History of the year' such as an adult might write. Here, there is no coherent narrative, but an apparently random movement from subject to subject, and – most interestingly for our purposes – between 'the kitchin of the parsonage house Haworth' and the more expansive landscape of the contemporary literary world. To this child, the newspapers she reads and the opinions of those who write for them are as important a part of her world as the activities of the inhabitants of her home. Indeed, her 'history' begins with a book, 'an old Geography... an hundred and twenty years old': like the Bewick's *History of British Birds* which she was later to portray as fascinating the youthful Jane Eyre, at once a solid, material feature of her actual world, and evocative of perspectives of time and space remote from her. If this is not, like the volume which Jane appropriates, used as a weapon against her, it belongs, like that, to the male head of the household: like that, it appears within her narrative as an emblem of patriarchal power.[5] Yet, like the book which fires the soon-to-rebel Jane's dreams, it has, also, a

217

more complex suggestiveness. For what this 'history' records is not the passive reception of a benefit ('papa lent my Sister ... A Book ... she read what it contained'), but an altogether more open-ended activity: 'papa lent my Sister ... A Book ... she wrote on its Blank leaf ...' And the drama that is sketched in miniature here is echoed in the longer description of the children's 'play' at the end, where 'papa lent ... she wrote' becomes 'papa bought Branwell some Soldiers at Leeds ... I snatched up one and exclaimed this is the Duke of Wellington'. This 'history' is less a description of an immutable set of facts than a record of the process whereby the parameters and possibilities of a world were realized. And crucial, central, to that process, it seems, were the activities of reading and writing.

'The History of the year' has a lot to say about the circumstances in which it was written: rather more, I shall be suggesting, than might at first appear. But we might simply, at this point, note one feature of the world of 1829 which it reflects: that which Byron, in a journal entry of 1812, had called 'the mighty stir made about scribbling and scribes, by themselves and others' at this time.[6] The early years of the nineteenth century saw the heyday of the romantic ideology which envisaged and promoted the man of letters as a man of power. This, as 'The History of the year' suggests, was an ideology which periodicals such as *Blackwood's* were tremendously important in establishing and sustaining. And it was one which captivated the young Brontës. The extraordinarily prolific writings in which they elaborated their 'plays' may be seen, indeed, on the simplest level, as an attempt to appropriate something of this culturally valorized power for themselves – and in doing so, to enter a space quite different from that which they occupied in actual life. Their sense of that difference is quite evident in the appearance of the little volumes they produced. For whereas the unselfconsciously factual 'History of the year' is untidily scrawled in a large, childish copperplate on a spare scrap of paper, the fictional writings in which the 'plays' were developed are altogether more carefully presented to the reader. 'I have had a curious packet confided to me, containing an immense amount of manuscript, in an inconceivably small space', wrote Mrs Gaskell, the first person outside the Brontë family to set eyes on this archive, in 1856. (It was to disappear from public view for a further forty years.) '[T]ales, dramas, poems, romances, written principally by Charlotte, in a hand which it is almost impossible to decipher without the aid of a magnifying glass.'[7] The tiny volumes of the Glass Town saga were originally designed to be 'read' by soldiers twelve inches high. They were painstakingly bound and sewn into paper wrappers in imitation of actual published books, and written in a tiny script designed to look as much like print as possible – a script which Charlotte Brontë seems to have continued to use for fictional creation (as distinct from letter-writing) throughout her writing life. Their elaborate tables of contents and title pages ('The Search After Happiness A Tale by Charlotte Brontë Printed By Herself And Sold By Nobody') likewise imitated those with which the children were familiar from the volumes in their father's library. Indeed, their whole presentation bespeaks that deep fascination with the world of books and bookishness which the young author more ingenuously registers in her realistic 'History of the year'.

And so, too, do the different kinds of writing these tiny volumes contain. On 3 August, 1830, the 14-year-old author drew up a 'Catalogue of my Books', 'making in the whole 22 volumes': her list includes several 'Tales' in one or three volumes, poetry, a 'Drama' – and six numbers of a magazine. For prominent amongst the Brontë juvenilia are several series of a periodical (at first named *Blackwood's Young Men's Magazine* and later simply *The Young Men's Magazine*): elaborate childish imitations of the journal whose monthly numbers enthralled the parsonage children in the 1820s, and of which the young Charlotte speaks so eloquently in 'The History of the year'.[8] The tables of contents for this magazine, like those of the actual *Blackwood's*, list stories and articles by various hands, poems, book reviews, and letters to the editor. *Blackwood's* famous imaginary conversations on topical and literary subjects, *Noctes Ambrosianae* (in which all the figures named in 'A History of the year' took part) are imitated in the 'Conversations' which record evenings with the worthies of Glass Town at Bravey's Inn. And there are, in each issue, advertisements for books – either for imaginary books by the inhabitants of this imaginary world ('Adventures in the Glass Town, by a young man, in 3 vols.' is announced, for example, in the August 1829 number) or actual books which had impressed the young Brontës (the same issue advertises *Tales of Captain Lemuel Gulliver in Houynhmhm Land* at '10 shillings 6d.'). For the characters of Glass Town are not merely noblemen, politicians and soldiers, but also authors, artists, poets and critics, who refer often to one another's productions, in the manner of those real men of letters whose discussions and controversies in these years filled the pages of the real *Blackwood's Magazine*.

Most of these youthful writings, then, are not autobiographical jottings like 'A history of the year', but careful imitations of a whole range of contemporary literary forms. And they are filled with the traces of the young author's reading, both in the 'Geography' and the newspapers mentioned in 'The History of the year', and also in imaginative literature. There are echoes of the Bible and of Shakespeare. Walter Scott (whose *Tales of a Grandfather* had been given to the Brontë children for Christmas in 1828) is hailed as a hero: and Charlotte Brontë copies extracts from his *Life of Napoleon* into one of these little books.[9] If there are references to only two specifically children's books, those two seem to be of pivotal importance: *Aesop's Fables* is named as the origin of one of the very early plays,[10] and even more prominent is that favourite of the nineteenth-century nursery, *The Arabian Nights' Entertainments* – to which I shall return. But above all it is the multi-voiced *Blackwood's*, with its literary reviews and controversies, its lively discussion – both serious and satiric – of all the topics of the day, so intimately familiar that even the birthdays of its authors are known, that is a potent presence here. And its influence may be traced not merely in *The Young Men's Magazine* for which it was the model, but in the sense that pervades all these writings, of the literary world as a place in which different roles may be tried out, contemplated, explored and satirized: a place not of monologic utterance but of diverse and self-reflexive play.

For the stories and articles, dialogues and verses which appear in these little volumes are written not in the autobiographical mode of 'A history of the year', but through the voices of the differing personae of this imaginary world. And these personae are themselves the objects of admiring or satiric contemplation;[11] their perspectives are questioned and ironized; their limitations are sharply, often comically seen. Such narrators, it might here be noted, are, in these early juvenilia, always male. Indeed, the use of the masculine voice in these early 'plays' poses a significant challenge to the frequently asserted view that Brontë's choice of a masculine narrator in *The Professor* was an unsophisticated attempt to arrogate male power to herself. For even these earliest of her masculine narrators are very far from straightforward figures of masculine potency: they are objectified, questioned, mocked, in highly critical ways. It is not merely that they are frequently the objects of deflating, sometimes slapstick humour. Right through these early manuscripts (rather different, in this respect, from those of Charlotte Brontë's later teens and twenties) runs the more radically ironic sense that the figures of power and pretension who inhabit the fictional world are in reality mere fictions, created by beings far more powerful than they. For if these highly elaborated, wittily self-reflexive writings may seem, at first, very far from that simple endowment of toys with imaginary life which is one of the most ordinary of early childhood acts, they do not forget their origins: that shared 'play' with her siblings which Charlotte Brontë more than once recorded and memorialized in an autobiographical 'history', a 'play' whose implications are explored within the fictional world in unexpectedly suggestive ways.

There is considerable evidence, in these writings, that the young author pondered the questions raised by her own exercise of fictive power a very great deal. It was an exercise of power for which her childhood reading provided a resonant image – an image which was to recur, indeed, throughout her later writings, to the very last of her published works.[12] Very early in the development of their 'plays', the Brontë children – fired by their reading of *The Arabian Nights' Entertainments* and (probably) Sir Charles Morell's *Tales of the Genii*, assumed for themselves the roles of controlling 'Genii', who wielded absolute power over the imaginary world, and who, like their fictional prototypes, could be depicted as entering that world in decisive and disconcerting ways.[13] But where in the *Arabian Nights* or *Tales of the Genii* this entry of the creator into the fictional world is merely a fantastic device, a way of magically resolving the story, in these early writings by Charlotte Brontë it becomes the vehicle for a more sophisticated play with radically differing points of view. Thus, in 'The History of the year', the young author 'sketches out the origin of our plays':

> papa bought Branwell some Soldiers at Leeds when papa came home it was night and we were in Bed. so next morning Branwell came to our door with a Box of Soldiers Emily and me Jumped out of Bed and I snatched up one and exclaimed this is the Duke of Wellington it shall be mine.[14]

But a story entitled *A Romantic Tale*, written in the same year, presents the same event from a rather different perspective. This, like most of these youthful writings, imitates a familiar contemporary literary form: in this case, that of the narrative of travel and adventure, which tells of a journey to the distant places of the earth. Such narratives of exploration were very popular in the early years of the nineteenth century. Accounts of the voyages of Parry and Ross to the Arctic and of Mungo Park to Africa had appeared in *Blackwood's* in the late 1820s, and the young Brontës were clearly stirred by them. Many of the place-names of their early kingdom of Glass Town come from descriptions of Africa published in *Blackwood's*,[15] and Emily and Anne were eventually to name their two soldier-heroes after the Arctic explorers Parry and Ross. It is just such a story that *A Romantic Tale* recounts, through the voice of one of 'twelve adventurers': of a 'voyage of discovery' to an 'immense continent', whose wonders are minutely described. After battling with the natives and establishing a colony, the intrepid heroes make their way to the middle of a great desert, and come upon 'the palace of the Genii':

> Out of the barren desert arose a palace of diamond, the pillars of which were ruby and emerald illuminated with lamps too bright to look upon. The Genius led us into a hall of sapphire in which were thrones of gold. On the thrones sat the Princes of the Genii. In the midst of the hall hung a lamp like the sun. Around it stood genii and fairies without, whose robes were of beaten gold sparkling with diamonds. As soon as their chiefs saw us they sprang up from their thrones, and one of them seizing Arthur Wellesley exclaimed, 'This is the Duke of Wellington!'[16]

And even in this simple, unintrospective little story the identification with the perspective of the teller is such that it is with a shock that one realizes

221

that this bold adventurer is in the real world but a little wooden soldier, and that the mighty Prince of the Genii of whom he tells is none other than the child Charlotte herself.

Again and again in these early stories the Brontës appear not merely as the all-powerful movers of events but from the point of view of their creations. Thus, throughout the issues of the *Young Men's Magazine*, the Four Chief Genii become the objects of fearful or wondering speculation on the part of the contributors. An advertisement in the August 1829 number announces that

> A magnificent painting of the Chief Genii in Council is now to be seen at Captain Cloven's house. Terms of admittance 3s.[17]

That for September 1829 carries a song in their praise:

> Let our mighty chieftains come,
> Clothed in glory infinite,
> With the sound of harp and drum,
> Loud peeling to their might.[18]

And a letter apparently intended for the editor in July 1829 begins:

> Sir – it is well known that the Genii have declared that unless they [presumably the Young Men] 'perform certain arduous duties every year, of a mysterious nature, all the worlds in the firmament will be burnt up and gathered together in one mighty globe, which will roll in lonely grandeur through the vast wilderness of space, inhabited only by the four high Princes of the Genii, till time shall be succeeded by eternity'.[19]

(This writer, at least, seems unawed by the demands of the Genii: he deplores their 'impudence' and goes on to speak of their 'horrible wickedness'.) Even in these earliest of her surviving juvenilia, Charlotte Brontë seems to be engaging in a 'play' far more complex than simple escapist fantasy: a 'play' which is flexibly and wittily self-reflexive, and which permits an identification with radically opposing points of view. For if the magical plots and sudden denouements of these stories, the sheer variety and exuberance of the fictional Glass Town and its inhabitants, bespeak a felt capacity to make and unmake worlds and the creatures who inhabit them (that fictional power which Charlotte was to wield in 'making alive' the dead after the battles in which her brother loved to engage)[20] the world of these writings is also one in which the perspectives of the powerless are realized and elaborated: in which power is not simply exercised but contemplated – and contemplated in a potentially disturbing way.

Of course, these little books were produced simply for entertainment: the young author's enjoyment of the 'play' is manifest on every page.

But the unexpected sophistication with which they confront the implications of fictional creation brings to mind, also, the double meaning that the word 'entertain' has come to bear in our language. If its primary sense – as in *The Arabian Nights' Entertainments* – seems now to be 'to amuse', and often carries the implication of a less than serious purpose ('mere entertainment'), another, older constellation of meanings, relating to a central notion of 'offering hospitality', points toward a valuation of a rather different kind. For to 'entertain' may mean, also, 'to admit to consideration', 'to harbour', 'to take into the mind' even, it seems, 'to experience'. This is the sense invoked by Coleridge, defending *The Arabian Nights' Entertainments* in 1797 against those who argued that 'rational education' would better equip the child for dealing with the world. In a letter to his friend Thomas Poole he recalls how, when he was 8 years old, his father told him 'the names of the stars – and how Jupiter was a thousand times larger than our world – and that the other twinkling stars were Suns that had other worlds rolling round them...' 'I heard him with a profound delight and admiration', he continues,

> but without the least mixture of wonder or incredulity. For from my early reading of Faery Tales, and Genii etc. etc. – my mind had been habituated *to the Vast* – and I never regarded *my senses* in any way as the criteria of my belief. I regulated all my creeds by my conceptions not by my *sight* – even at that age. Should children be permitted to read Romances, and Relations of Giants and Magicians, and Genii? I know all that has been said against it; but I have formed my faith in the affirmative.[21]

And the writings of this other child, drawing, more than thirty years later, upon the same 'early reading', offer their own potent demonstration of that of which Coleridge speaks. For here one sees most sharply the way in which those 'Romances, and Relations of Giants and Magicians, and Genii' might provide not an escape from but a framework for engaging with the real: how the projection of a fictional world might enable the child not merely to 'entertain', or experience, a power denied to her in actual life (the heady omnipotence of the creator), but also to 'entertain' more disquieting intuitions (of powerlessness, of creaturehood), not with the traumatic force of direct experience, but with the freedom that objectification could give. These childish fictions are indeed 'entertaining' – witty, amusing, often downright comic. But the questions with which they play – questions about the relation between power and reality, about what it means to be an object as well as a subject – are real and disquieting ones. And in one, at least, of the stories of this early period, Charlotte Brontë confronts them in a way which allows some sense of their darker implications to emerge. In doing so, she does not merely give figurative shape to a constellation of feelings which resonates – in ways which there is no space to discuss here – through the novels of her maturity: she also, I shall argue, engages with the issues raised by her own particular 'history' in a way hardly possible to the voice of autobiographical realism.

The story, which appeared in the December 1830 number of *The Young Men's Magazine*, is entitled 'Strange Events'.[22] Like the other contributions to that childish periodical, it is a witty imitation of the kind of thing which might be found in the actual *Blackwood's*: in this case, the quasi-scientific 'anecdote' which offered a rational account of a supernatural experience or dream. Its 'author', Lord Charles Wellesley, is a frequent narrator in Charlotte Brontë's early stories – a Byronically disaffected, 'haughty and sarcastic' young man, who usually surveys the heroic passions of Glass Town with mocking cynicism and is himself presented with considerable authorial irony. He opens his account very much in this vein:

> It is the fashion nowadays to put no faith whatsoever in supernatural appearances or warnings. I am, however, a happy exception to the general rule, and firmly believe in everything of the kind. Instances of the good foundation I have for this obsolete belief often meet my observation, tending to confirm me in it. For the present I shall content myself with mentioning a few.

But as his story unfolds, this comically exaggerated disaffectedness takes on a rather peculiar character:

> One day last June happening to be extremely wet and foggy, I felt, as is usual with Englishmen, very dull. The common remedies – razor, rope and arsenic – presented themselves in series, but as is unusual with Englishmen, I did not relish any of them. At last the expedient of repairing to the Public Library for diversion entered my head. Thither I accordingly went, taking care to avoid crossing the great bridge lest the calm aspect of the liquid world beneath it might induce me to make a summary descent.

The Dickensian absurdity with which the idea of suicide is entertained creates a sense of a world in which the choice between being and non-being is curiously arbitrary. On a humorously literal level, there seems to be something strangely precarious about the speaker who began his tale with such easy grandiloquence. And as he continues, this sense becomes more prominent:

> When I entered the room a bright fire flickering against the polished sienna hearth somewhat cheered my drooping spirits. No one was there, so I shut the door. Taking down Brandart's *Finished Lawyer*, I placed myself on a sofa in the ingle-cheek. Whilst I was listlessly turning over the leaves of that most ponderous volume, I fell into

224

the strangest train of thought that ever visited even my mind, eccentric and unstable as it is said by some insolent puppies to be.

It seemed as if I was a non-existent shadow, that I neither spoke, eat, imagined or lived of myself, but I was the mere idea of some other creature's brain. The Glass Town seemed so likewise. My father, Arthur and everyone with whom I am acquainted, passed into a state of annihilation; but suddenly I thought again that I and my relatives did exist, and yet not us but our minds and our bodies without ourselves. Then this supposition – the oddest of any – followed the former quickly, namely, that WE without US were shadows; also, but at the end of a long vista, as it were, appeared dimly and indistinctly, beings that really lived in a tangible shape, that were called by our names and were US from whom WE had been copied by something – I could not tell what.

'It seemed as if I was a non-existent shadow'. On one level, this is a childish joke – a sophisticated elaboration of that play with the implications of fictional creation which runs right through these little volumes. To himself, this speaker is Lord Charles Wellesley, a world-weary Byronic hero; but in fact he is nothing but a little wooden soldier, whose fictional identity has been 'copied' from that of the Duke of Wellington's son. And as he begins to intuit this, his confidence in his own existence, and in that of those close to him – indeed, in his whole familiar world – falters and fails. His sense of his own, and others', coherence disappears, and is replaced by a disconcerting awareness of a split between self as subject – 'WE' – and self as object – 'US'. And as the paragraph ends, there is a dim intuition of the powerful 'something – I could not tell what' to which these 'shadows' owe such being as they have.

As in a dream, he catches only a hazy glimpse of this. And in the next paragraph the dreamlike quality takes over, as features of the real England of 1830 (Wellington as Prime Minister, his sons living at his home at Stratfield Saye, George IV as king) are distorted and displaced into the imagined landscape of Glass Town. The controlling 'I' disappears, and the prose almost disintegrates, as the self becomes part of a fantastic panorama, in which the familiar is recombined and inverted and curiously estranged:

Another world formed part of this reverie in which was no Glass Town or British Realm in Africa except Hindoustan, India, Calcutta. England was there but totally different in manners, laws, customs and inhabitants – governed by a sailor – my father Prime Minister – I and Arthur young noblemen living at Strathaye, or something with a name like that – visionary fairies, elves, brownies, the East Wind, and wild Arab-broken horses – shooting in moors with a fat man who was a great book. But I am lost, I cannot get on.

225

'I am lost, I cannot get on': for his tale can only be told by the grammatical assumption of that stable, substantive identity which has begun to be thrown into question. And when the remembering 'I' reappears in control, it has an odder and odder story to tell:

> For hours I continued in this state, striving to fathom a bottomless ocean of Mystery, till at length I was aroused by a loud noise above my head. I looked up and thick obscurity was before my eyes. Voices, one like my own but larger and dimmer (if sound may be characterized by such epithets) and another which sounded familiar, yet I had never, that I could remember, heard it before, murmuring unceasingly in my ears.
>
> I saw books removing from the top shelves and returning, apparently of their own accord. By degrees the mistiness cleared off. I felt myself raised suddenly to the ceiling, and ere I was aware, behold two immense, sparkling, bright blue globes within a few yards of me. I was in [a] hand wide enough almost to grasp the Tower of All Nations, and when it lowered me to the floor I saw a huge personification of myself – hundreds of feet high – standing against the great Oriel.

The dimly intuited 'other creature' of whose brain 'I was the mere idea' here comes gradually into focus: first as a sound, at once familiar and unfamiliar; then as a force, magically animating a world grown strange, lifting the now puppet-like speaker; and finally as a visual apparition – a pair of eyes, a mighty form. This is not a god, but something far stranger – a being whose actions have prodigious results, whose motives are unknowable, one who seems to occupy an order of existence quite different from that of the hapless narrator. There are echoes here of *Gulliver's Travels*, which the Brontë children appear to have read at this time, and which Charlotte Brontë was later to present as fascinating the child Jane Eyre: this figure has clear affinities with the giant farmer who lifts a suddenly dwarfed Gulliver in Brobdignag. But it is not, like that farmer, an other with whom it seems possible to interact. It may only be regarded with 'astonishment'. And in face of its unchallengeable potency that sense of the unreality of the self which appeared earlier in the passage is absolutely confirmed:

> This filled me with a weight of astonishment greater than the mind of man ever before had to endure, and I was now perfectly convinced of my non-existence except in another corporeal frame which dwelt in the real world, for ours, I thought, was nothing but idea.

'Strange Events' in one way, of course, merely elaborates those speculations on the nature of the Genii which had appeared in earlier issues of *The Young Men's Magazine*. The figure that appears before the amazed eyes of Lord Charles Wellesley is none other than the 'Chief Genius Tallii' – his all-powerful creator, Charlotte Brontë herself. But that recognition comes with a shock, and does not dissolve the disquiet the story has raised, because it is with the first-person speaking voice – its existential destabilizing, its vertigo, its 'astonishment' – that the reader identifies. That 'huge personification of myself' remains a mere shape, silhouetted 'against the great Oriel', imperfectly seen and not at all understood. 'I am left', the narrator concludes, 'in dismal uncertainty as to whether I am or am not for the remnant of my doubting days.' And the reader familiar with the 'plays' is made comically aware that this 'strange' intuition, so at odds with anything 'fashion' or common sense would accept, in fact points toward the actual ontological status of this creature in his world.

'While her description of any real occurrence is . . . homely, graphic and forcible, when she gives way to her powers of creation, her fancy and her language alike run riot, sometimes to the very borders of apparent delirium.' Such was Mrs Gaskell's verdict on the packet of childhood writings which she was the first outside the Brontë family to see. Lord Charles Wellesley's peculiar 'anecdote', with its central 'strange event' and its descent into surrealism, might seem at first to confirm this view. Yet to the reader familiar with its young author's autobiographical 'History' it presents, I think, a rather different face. For each of these two childish documents illuminates the other in an extraordinarily suggestive way. Most obviously, that 'History', 'homely, graphic, forcible', tells of the 'real occurrence' which underwrites Sir Charles Wellesley's predicament: he is 'really' but a wooden soldier, dependent for such life he has on 'some other creature's brain'. But the story he tells points back also to that 'History', and to significances within it which might otherwise go unremarked.

Nothing could be further from Sir Charles Wellesley's world-weary disaffection than the lively interest, the confident creative enthusiasm, with which the child Charlotte Brontë speaks directly of her world. There is certainly nothing, in her own account of herself, like that 'strange' intuition of provisionality and precariousness at which her hero arrives. Yet the one is not quite as remote from the other as might at first appear. For even as this child 'sketches out' her sense of a world in which she is central, her 'History' registers another, and rather different, awareness. If the first object she mentions is a book, the first person is not herself, but 'papa'. It is he, it seems, who determines events: he who provides the book, the newspapers, the soldiers. Indeed, the child Maria's one reported act might be seen simply as an acknowledgement of his power: she simply records his benevolence. The other children's actions at first appear very different. They do not complete a closed circle, but open out into possibility. From the starting-point provided by 'papa''s gift, they have literally seized power for themselves ('I snatched one up and exclaimed this is the Duke of Wellington'): the whole second half of the manuscript is charged with the excitement of their still developing 'plays'. But if the passage ends with a heady act of creation, it traces, very exactly, the limits within which that act is framed. For, as the unobtrusive but pivotal presence of 'papa' suggests, the world it describes is one in which the writing child has, in fact, almost no effective power. The figures which compel her imagination – the editors of newspapers, those involved in literary and political controversy, the military heroes of the day – move in spheres quite remote from her own situation in this isolated parsonage. If they provide the inspiration for the heroes of the plays, in actuality those heroes are simply little wooden soldiers, whose distinctive physiognomies suggest their different roles. And if in relation to these, their creatures, the children are powerful, the actual givers of life, in larger terms they are utterly powerless, less agents than objects of forces beyond their control. This fact is not stressed, but it is there from the beginning. For if the first figure in this 'History' is 'papa', the second is 'Maria' – the vanished sister, whose death is acknowledged only obliquely, in the past tense of a parenthesis. And it is in the light of an awareness of that death – a death which even 'papa' could not prevent – that the whole of that which follows unfolds.

Unsystematic and unsophisticated as it is, this 'History' is not simply a random series of facts. It presents a particular child's quite distinctive sense of the significant features of her world. In essentials, the dilemma it evokes is one which is perhaps common to all human childhoods: the attraction to powers which one does not possess; the need to carve out a sphere within which agency is possible, yet the awareness of self as powerless and others as powerful; the apprehension that one inhabits a world that one does not control. Here, these universal problems can be seen in a particular inflection: that of a specific childhood, in a specific time and place – and one in which, we may infer, they might have been felt with unusual sharpness. For this was a childhood peculiarly nourished by fantasies of power, a childhood spent in a time and place in which the cultural celebration of power – whether of literary 'genius' or military heroism or romantic conquest – was extraordinarily compelling. ('In all senses we worship and follow after Power', says Carlyle, in his *Signs of the Times*, published in the same year.) Yet this was also a childhood in which actual powerlessness might have been more than usually evident. For it was one in which the authority of others appeared in peculiarly unsoftened form: the childhood of a girl within an early nineteenth-century patriarchal family (in this 'History', the girls attend to household duties while the boy goes abroad, adventurously, with papa), in which the emotionally distant yet dominating father was also a priest of a religion which made its own uncompromising claims. And this was a childhood more shadowed than most by that ultimate proof of human impotence, the fact of death: a childhood spent in a house surrounded by graves, in a place in which more than 40 per cent of the population died before reaching the age of 6,[23] and in a family which had lost three of its eight members – mother and two older sisters – by the time the young writer reached the age of 9.

Nothing like this analysis appears, of course, here. This young historian scarcely reflects upon the material she presents at all. One sees the things which engage her interest, the order in which they present themselves to her, but she makes little attempt to record her response to them. The surrounding fact of her powerlessness is only obliquely acknowledged. But the parenthetical reference to Maria's death at the beginning, the delighted creation of 'the Duke of Wellington' at the end, both seem to map out a more elemental drama than might at first be apparent: a drama in which an assertion of absolute power, the power to determine existence itself, is made in face of an apprehension of absolute powerlessness, potential non-existence. At the end, creative confidence seems to triumph over awareness of creaturehood. But the 'I' which creates is, it seems, premised on a repression of that annihilating awareness.

And to turn from this to 'Strange Events' is, I think, to see with a shock that it is in this apparently quite fantastic little story that the essential dynamics of the 'History' are objectified and explored. Of course, on one level, 'Strange Events' speaks only of power. Nicely presented, accomplished as it is, it is, after all, the product of that childish creative fiat with which that 'History' ends. In creating her own journal, her own *dramatis personae*, her own imaginary world, Charlotte Brontë has appropriated the glamorous potency of that distant literary sphere: within this space, she is one of the all-powerful, controlling Genii. Yet the imaginative activity her story evinces is rather more complex than the mere fantasy-realization of wishes which reality denied. For what one sees here is not, most prominently, identification with power, but, far more centrally and intimately, the imagination of powerlessness. Here, what had started as a childish 'play' – the contemplation of the Genii by their creatures – seems to have enabled the young author to objectify and explore that which is inscribed but not confronted in her 'History': a sense of self not as autonomous and free, but as dependent and determined, not as omnipotent, but as potentially non-existent. The ironic joke that is the mainspring of the fiction permits the entertainment of feelings which the 'realistic' mode of the history could not accommodate, feelings which indeed question and problematize its most fundamental assumption, the sense of reality itself.

Such feelings are more amenable, it might seem, to psychoanalytic than to historicist analysis. And of course it would be possible to interpret 'Strange Events' psychobiographically, as Charlotte Brontë's later novels have often been interpreted. Thus, Lord Charles Wellesley's dilemma might be read as expressive of the insecurity of a child whose sense of self was (we might conjecture) inadequately recognized or confirmed, whose parent remained a mysteriously, though perhaps unreliably, powerful and distanced figure: or of a more primitive terror of the parent's power to decide between being and non-being. But to read it simply thus is, I think, hardly to begin to account for the nature of the expression such feelings here receive. For what we see in this little story is very far from unmediated psychic fantasy. It is not a work of terror, but of ironic humour: within it, the disturbing is objectified, contemplated, contained. And it seems to be the product not of a kind of private 'delirium', but of a highly sophisticated play with cultural configurations which its author could be confident others would recognize and share. Lord Charles Wellesley, the flippantly cynical Byronic hero, is, after all, a familiar figure of early nineteenth-century self-posturing masculinity: his studied world-weariedness, his raffish appeal to the reader's sympathy, are – as the young author's shorthand way with them suggests – virtually clichés of the contemporary literary scene. The sardonic humour with which, in this 'anecdote', his predicament is contemplated is that of the *Blackwood's* of the 1820s – that enticing literary world of which her 'History' so eloquently speaks. And that shadowy, controlling figure whose incomprehensible otherness so radically confirms this hero's uncertainties comes from an older, yet more deeply familiar, world: that of *The Arabian Nights' Entertainments*, with their more elemental, direct confrontation of issues of power and powerlessness – indeed, of life and death.[24] Within the short space of this little anecdote, all these components of the contemporary culture are orchestrated and entertained. This is a mode of writing very different from that 'trance-like' confessional outpouring often attributed even to the mature Charlotte Brontë:[25] flexible, witty, assured. Yet in its 'strange power of subjective representation'[26] it is, I would argue, one which, far more closely than that of that autobiographical 'History', prefigures the extraordinary, and far from conventionally realistic, achievement of her later work.

For it is a mode of writing which allows the articulation of intuitions which the realistic mode of the 'History' must, it seems, suppress. Indeed, to read that 'History' is to see, quite sharply, why the feelings objectified in 'Strange Events' might by this child be expressed so clearly only in fictional form: why she called the imaginary realm in which she allowed them play 'the infernal world'. In most Western cultures, perhaps, human beings to a large extent repress the awareness that they are contingent beings, who do not control the world they inhabit: a very great deal of human enterprise and endeavour is built upon such repression.[27] And the public culture of early nineteenth-century England – the largely masculine culture of individual genius, romantic assertion, military heroism, which fuelled this child's imagination, which her 'History' so artlessly evokes –

was certainly one in which such awareness was rarely entertained. 'The language of poetry naturally falls in with the language of power', Hazlitt had written twelve years earlier, in an attempt to characterize the spirit of the time.[28] Yet, as that 'History' also registers, the experiences which led to such awareness, though they might be denied, could scarcely be escaped. For some (the emotionally or socially or economically or sexually disadvantaged) such experiences might be more various, more mutually reinforcing, less softened, than they were for the more fortunate: but none could avoid the powerlessness and vulnerability of childhood, or the fact of mortality. The impotence, the marginalization, the disconfirmation imaged in 'Strange Events' were as central to life in early nineteenth-century England as were the confidence, the success, the heroic achievement described in 'The History of the year' and promoted as the self-image of the age. And here, in this childish story, through the unlikely figure of a cynical Byronic hero, this denied sense of creaturehood is confronted and explored.

And here, very clearly, one catches a glimpse of the complex and creative way in which a child may use the processes of reading and writing to configure a sense of her world. For to say that such awareness could be confronted 'only in fiction' is not to reduce the fictional to the level of mere disguise, a device for the indirect expression of inadmissible feelings: it is to make a rather larger claim for it, as a distinctive space within which experiences inassimilable to 'official' versions of reality might be realized, contemplated, understood. This child, as her 'History' so disarmingly reveals, was in one way quite uncritically compelled by that which her culture valorized and her childhood reading offered: the glamour of military heroism, of literary fame and achievement, the power of the written word. Yet what we see, in the fictions which grew out of that fascination, is not slavish imitation, but a peculiarly creative play: a play which offers its own distinctive and unexpected comment on that public 'language of power' which she herself found so enticing, and which Hazlitt saw as the inevitable voice of the age. Even at the age of 14 it seems, Charlotte Brontë was beginning to explore the intuition that 'reality' might be less simply that which is than that which is constructed by the powerful: even at the age of 14 – as her extraordinary rendition of Lord Charles Wellesley's predicament suggests – she seems to have been quite centrally concerned with what it might mean to conceive of self as a powerless creature, of effective power as residing elsewhere. And her concern emerges, it seems, not out of an introspective or autobiographical impulse on the young author's part (a point worth bearing in mind when one considers the later novels, so often, patronizingly, read in this way), and not – certainly not – from any analytic questioning of the presuppositions of her culture, but from this witty imaginative

231

'entertainment' of differing possibilities and perspectives which may be traced even in the earliest of her surviving works.

NOTES

1 Christine Alexander (ed.), *An Edition of the Early Writings of Charlotte Brontë* 2 vols (Oxford: Basil Blackwell, 1987–91). For a detailed account of the development of the 'plays' see Christine Alexander, *The Early Writings of Charlotte Brontë* (Oxford: Basil Blackwell, 1983).

2 Alexander, *Early Writings*, p. 246.

3 Thus, for example, Karen Chase, *Eros and Psyche: The Representation of Personality in Charlotte Brontë, Charles Dickens and George Eliot* (Methuen: London, 1984): 'Precisely because of their youth, the Brontës deepened and extended the romantic inclination, acknowledging no constraints to their imaginative fantasies, making no concessions (since none were demanded) to editor, publisher, reader, or critic, and indulging therefore in Byronic romance uncorrected by Byronic irony' (p. 7). But as we shall see, editor, publisher, reader and critic did enter into this world – if only in the shapes of the differing personae the Brontë children adopted – and this fact enabled the entertainment of quite sophisticated ironies.

4 Ibid. p. 81. Chase describes these juvenile writings as 'a body of imaginative labor which has not yet surrendered to the constraints of tradition or convention'.

5 In chapter 1 of the novel, Jane's cousin John Reed demands that she 'show the book' she was reading, and berates her: 'You have no business to take our books; you are a dependent, mamma says; you have no money; your father left you none ... Now, I'll teach you to rummage my book-shelves: for they *are* mine; all the house belongs to me, or will do in a few years ...' He concludes this tirade by flinging the volume at her and causing her head to be cut open.

6 Thomas Moore, *Works of Lord Byron, with his Letters and Journals, and his Life* (London: John Murray, 1833), Vol. II, p. 277.

7 Elizabeth Gaskell, *Life of Charlotte Brontë*, ed. Alan Shelston (London: Penguin, 1975), p. 112.

8 Years later, Branwell Brontë was to write to its editor: 'I cannot express the heavenliness of associations Connected with such articles as Professor Wilson's, read and re-read while a little child, with all their poetry of language and divine flight into that visionary realm of imagination which one very young would believe reality ... I speak so, Sir, because while a child Blackwood's formed my chief delight' (Branwell Brontë to John Wilson, 8 December 1835, in T.J. Wise and J.A. Symington, *The Lives, Friendships and Correspondence of the Brontë Family* (Oxford: Basil Blackwell, 1933), Vol. I, pp. 133–4).

9 Alexander, *Edition*, Vol. I, p. 90.

10 'The Origin of the O Dears', 12 March 1829. For a discussion of this 'play', see Juliet Barker, *The Brontës* (London: Weidenfeld & Nicolson, 1994), p. 159 and p. 865 n. 74.

11 See, for example, *Characters of the Celebrated Men of the Present Time*, December 1829; Alexander, *Edition*, Vol. I, pp. 123–30.

12 Thus *Villette*, ch. 16:

> I thought of Bedriddin Hassan, transported in his sleep from Cairo to the gates of Damascus. Had a Genius stooped his dark wing down the

storm to whose stress I had succumbed, and gathering me from the church-steps, and 'rising high into the air', as the eastern tale said, had he borne me over land and ocean, and laid me down quietly beside a hearth of Old England?

13 The Genii appear for the last time in *The Foundling*, written in May–June 1833, when Charlotte Brontë was 17. Here, the magician Manfred speaks of 'those high and unseen spirits to whom even I, potent as I am among men, must yield', and tells how they 'smote my presumption with a curse'. As Christine Alexander observes, they appear in *The Green Dwarf*, written in the same year, 'simply as part of the "olden days" of the Glass Town and gradually degenerate into the expletive "By the Genii!" in subsequent stories' (Alexander, *Edition*, Vol. II.1, p. 105).

14 Branwell's account of the origin of the Young Men's Play is suggestively different from this:

> When I first saw them in the morning after they were bought I carried them to Emily Charlotte and Anne they each took up a soldier gave them names which I consented to and I gave Charlotte Twemy [i.e. Wellington] to Emily Parre [Parry] to Anne Trott [Ross] to take care of them though they were to be mine and I to have the disposal of them as I would – shortly after this I gave them to them as their own – P.B. Brontë.
>
> (Patrick Branwell Brontë, *The History of the Young Men*, 15 December 1830–7 May 1831: MS Ashley 2468, p. 9, British Library. I am grateful to Juliet Barker for supplying me with this transcript.)

15 See Barker, *The Brontës*, p. 155 and notes.
16 *A Romantic Tale* (15 April 1829), Alexander, *Edition*, Vol. I, p. 14.
17 Ibid., p. 60.
18 Ibid., p. 63.
19 Ibid., p. 39.
20 Alexander, *Early Writings*, p. 34.
21 Coleridge to Thomas Poole, *Collected Letters of Samuel Taylor Coleridge*, ed. Earl Leslie Griggs, 2 vols (Oxford: Oxford University Press, 1956), letter 210.
22 The manuscript, which was transcribed and described by Davidson Cook in 1925, is a hand-sewn booklet of twenty pages, 5 × 3.5 cm, in a brown paper cover: its present whereabouts are unknown. Davidson Cook's transcription is reprinted in Alexander, *Edition*, Vol. I, pp. 256–60: in my discussion, I deal only with the first of the two 'strange events' the story records.
23 See Benjamin Herschel Babbage, *Report to the General Board of Health of a Preliminary Inquiry into the Sewerage, Drainage and Supply of Water and Sanitary Condition of Haworth* (London, 1850).
24 In *The Arabian Nights*, suggestively, the telling of stories is a means of preserving life itself. This is most obviously true of Scherezade, who remains alive only if she can continue to tell stories: but, as Todorov points out, this situation is repeated within the individual tales themselves. Again and again, 'for the characters to be able to live, they must narrate'. Tzvetan Todorov, *The Poetics of Prose*, trans. Richard Howard, (Oxford: Oxford University Press, 1977), pp. 73–6.
25 See, for example, Winifred Gérin, in her Introduction to Charlotte Brontë, *Five Novelettes* (London: Folio Press, 1971), p. 16: 'There was, as Charlotte's school journals reveal, a trance-like quality in her method of writing which excluded all possibility of self-criticism and almost, one is tempted to think, suspended consciousness.' See also Sandra Gilbert and Susan Gubar, *The*

Madwoman in the Attic: the Woman Writer and the Nineteenth-Century Literary Imagination (New Haven and London: Yale University Press, 1979), p. 311: 'Charlotte Brontë was essentially a trance-writer.'

26 The phrase is used by G.H. Lewes in an unsigned review of *Jane Eyre* ('Recent Novels: English and French', *Fraser's Magazine*, XXXVI, December 1847, pp. 686–95); reprinted in Miriam Allott (ed.), *The Brontës: The Critical Heritage* (London: Macmillan, 1974), p. 86.

27 See Ernest Becker, *The Denial of Death* (New York: Macmillan, 1973).

28 William Hazlitt, *The Complete Works of William Hazlitt in Twenty-One Volumes: Centenary Edition*, ed. P.P. Howe, 21 vols (London: Secker, 1930–4), Vol. IV, p. 24.

INDEX

Printed in the United Kingdom
by Lightning Source UK Ltd.
126102UK00003B/109/A